SPO[RT]

BEST

BOOK & DVD SERIES

Inshore Books:
Sportsman's Best: Inshore Fishing
Sportsman's Best: Surf Fishing
Sportsman's Best: Snook
Sportsman's Best: Redfish
Sportsman's Best: Trout

Offshore Books:
Sportsman's Best: Offshore Fishing
Sportsman's Best: Snapper & Grouper
Sportsman's Best: Sailfish
Sportsman's Best: Dolphin

Other Sportsman's Best Books:
Sportsman's Best: Baits, Rigs & Tackle
Sportsman's Best: Boats
Sportsman's Best: Kayak Fishing
Sportsman's Best: Sight Fishing

Sport Fish Books:
Sport Fish of Florida
Sport Fish of the Gulf of Mexico
Sport Fish of the Atlantic
Sport Fish of Fresh Water
Sport Fish of the Pacific

Other Books & Publications:
Annual Fishing Planner
The Angler's Cookbook

Florida Sportsman Magazine
Florida Sportsman Best Boat

Florida Sportsman Fishing Charts
Lawsticks
Law Boatstickers
Field Guide ID Lawsticks

All available at www.floridasportsman.com/store

Written by Vic Dunaway and Rick Ryals
Photo credits: Florida Sportsman, Mark Naumovitz, Drew Wickstrom, David Conway
Edited by Florida Sportsman Editors
Design by Mark Naumovitz, Drew Wickstrom
Illustrations by Jeff Macharyas

Fifth Edition, Second Printing
Copyright ©2015 by Florida Sportsman
2700 S. Kanner Hwy., Stuart, FL 34994
All Rights Reserved
Printed in the United States of America

ISBN-13: 978-1-934622-25-4
ISBN-10: 1-934622-25-7

www.floridasportsman.com
 Find us on Facebook
 twitter

BAITS, RIGS & TACKLE

Over 100 Knots & Rigs ■ Tips From the Pros ■ Live and Natural Baits

NATIONAL ALL-TIME BEST SELLER ON FISHING KNOW-HOW

By Vic Dunaway and Rick Ryals

CONTENTS

SPORTSMAN'S BEST
BAITS, RIGS & TACKLE

10

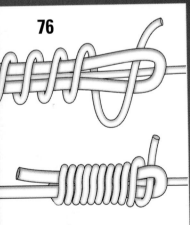

76

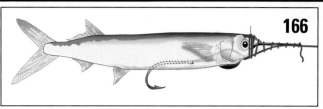

Foreword

Here's Your Updated and Expanded Best-Selling How-To Fishing Book

The national all-time most popular how-to fishing book just got bigger and better, like your next catch may well be.

This is legendary author-angler Vic Dunaway's Complete Book of *Baits, Rigs & Tackle*, now revised and enlarged by veteran expert Rick Ryals. Rick's skills and knowledge, developed over four decades, provide the perfect complement to Vic's classic.

Here you'll find all-new photos and info on the latest gear and tackle, in a clean and easy-to-read design and layout. Whether you're fishing for the first time or hundredth time, for bream or billfish, you'll find no better source for all things rigging.

Plus, you get a new instructional 60-minute DVD featuring Rick and other experts covering the basics of knot tying and rigging for all kinds of fishing at its best.

And we're including full-color illustrations of popular gamefish species as well as tips on how to catch them.

All you need now is to get a hook in the water. We wish you every success.

Karl Wickstrom

Karl Wickstrom
Editor in Chief, Florida Sportsman Magazine

Oftentimes the thrill of
catching a great fish can
be matched by watching it
swim away to fight again.

Introduction
A Classic Updated

Welcome to the world of *Baits, Rigs & Tackle*. Whether this is the first time you've been bitten by the bug that is sport fishing, or you're a lifelong addict, we think you'll find plenty to learn here in the new *Baits, Rigs & Tackle*.

So much has changed since the legendary Vic Dunaway first penned the highest selling, most comprehensive reference book in fishing history, the original BRT. Having fished with Vic, I know just how much he would love today's innovations. Drags so smooth you have to look down to see if you're losing line. Hooks so sharp they're ready to fish right out of the box, and lures so lifelike you'll want to try and clean them for dinner all would amaze the fishermen of Vic's day.

In fact, looking at today's world of fishing, I don't yearn at all for the "good old days." We sometimes overlook just how great our sport is. Our motors almost always work to perfection, our new gear is so often perfect and so many of our fisheries are protected and monitored to ensure great fishing for generations to come. In fact today may be the best time in history to join the family of folks listing fishing as their number one hobby.

Whether you're trying to "grunt" enough worms to help you catch tonight's dinner, or about to build a wind-on leader for a giant tuna, we think you'll find the answers in these pages.

You know as much as things have changed in the 42 years since Vic penned the original BRT, some things he taught us are truer today than ever. He would want me to tell you to, "Fish every day like it was your last trip, tie every knot like the fish of your dreams is about to bite, and treat every bite like it'll be the last one you'll ever get."

Welcome to the family,

Rick Ryals, Author

A trip filled with the promise of adventure, fish and good company.

cial Thanks:

pt. Dent Magee who took me out between the Mayport jetties 50 years ago, and set the course for the rest of my life.

pt. Fred Morrow who taught me what being a captain means.

bbie, who is the best angler ever, and has always been standing on the dock with a cold iced tea, waiting for me to get home.

eight grandkids who I hope will someday find the time to take their grandpa fishing.

CHAPTER 1

Rods and Reels

Rods and reels are the tools of the trade for a fisherman, much like a set of wrenches enable a mechanic to get his job done. There are some outfits that serve as "crescent wrenches," letting an angler use them for many different applications. A medium-size spinning outfit, for example, can throw several different size baits, appealing to everything from bream to Spanish mackerel.

There are also rods and reels that are far more specialized. A five-weight fly rod is great for catching panfish, or maybe brook trout, but if you're going to hunt a big redfish or a salmon, you'll need a rod that can withstand much more pressure and strain.

Selecting the right rod and reel for the job is a balancing act of matching the rod to the reel, to the line size, to the bait, to the hook, to the fish you're after.

A trip to a quality tackle shop is the fisherman's version of a kid visiting a candy store.

Spend some time planning your trip the night before. Make sure you have a rod rigged for every opportunity.

Spinning Tackle

Having multiple spinning rods at the ready enabled these guys to triple up on fish.

Open-face spinning outfits are generally accepted as the most versatile form of rod and reel combos. These rigs are available in every size from two-pound test panfish rigs, to extra-heavy-duty jigging outfits capable of taming everything from giant grouper to tuna weighing hundreds of pounds.

The difference in spinning tackle and conventional tackle is in how the reel operates. A spinning reel has a fixed spool which never revolves during the cast or retrieve. Line is retrieved by a pickup mechanism (bail) which revolves around the spool when you turn the reel handle, which stacks the line onto the spool. When you cast, you simply move the bail out of the way, and the line literally falls off the spool.

By contrast a conventional, or revolving-spool reel is designed so the spool turns to release the

Spinning outfits are available in every size, from 2-pound panfish rigs to those capable of taming giant grouper and tuna.

line on a cast, and retrieve line as you turn the handle.

Both styles of reels have their place. Conventional reels are traditionally considered to be more powerful. On a spinning reel the spool is largely supported on the bottom only. The line is run through the bail instead of being connected directly to the spool. On a conventional reel the spool is supported on both sides, and the connection between line and reel is direct.

The biggest obstacle for beginning fishermen using conventional reels is the dreaded "backlash." Backlashes occur when the spool starts turning faster than the line comes off the reel. The result is several loops of line weaving in and out of each other until the inevitable bird's nest causes a deterioration of the caster's vocabulary. Conventional reels are decidedly more difficult to perfect than spinners. However, once they are mastered

► ReelTip:

You can move most spinning reel handles to whichever side is easier to turn the handle with. Straddle the reel foot, with two fingers in front of the reel seat, and two behind. Unlike a conventional reel, the rod never switches from one hand to the other.

they are often preferred by serious anglers when a precise cast is necessary, and are usually capable of applying more pressure on a big fish.

The ease of operation of spinning tackle results in a much shorter learning time before an aspiring angler of any age is ready for their first solo fishing trip. Simply opening the bail, holding the line, and letting go as the rod comes forward will propel a bait into the water, and basically get you out fishing. It won't be pretty, and it will require loads more practice before you perfect distance or accuracy, but at least you'll be fishing.

Let it be plainly said that spinning gear is not free from tangles, especially when using braided line. The use of braid has always been made more difficult by what is commonly referred to as "wind knots." Wind knots actually start at the spool on a spinner. When the line is retrieved too loosely, it often fails to pack properly on the spool. Wind knots can be avoided two ways. If you're willing to deal with a little less line on your spool, it will tangle less frequently. Better yet, if you close your bail manually, instead of just turning the handle, you'll invariably notice any loops of line crossing the spool instead of going around it. Eliminate loops of line cutting across the top of the spool, and you'll deal with far fewer wind knots.

Other characteristics of open-faced spinning tackle set it apart from conventional gear. The reel is mounted on the underside of the rod. Naturally, the guides are also on the bottom, and extend farther out from the shaft than on a conventional rod. Spinning guides are also larger. Conventional logic says bigger guides at the base of the rod, tapering to a small tip would increase the caster's distance and con-trol. Innovators experiment with new designs for rod guides. The "microwave guide" that actually has a tiny eye just inside the big first guide is one such design.

The beginning angler looking for his first fishing outfit needs to ask himself not only what size fish he's after, but is it prevalent in fresh or salt water. More importantly, what weight bait or lure will he use most often. Generally speaking, if you are planning on casting a bait or lure ¼ ounce or less, a spinner will be easier to master. For lures ½ ounce or bigger, I strongly recommend you calm yourself by whatever means necessary, and learn to master conventional baitcasters.

The ease of casting a spinning reel makes it a great inshore choice for many anglers.

Spinning Rods

This angler prefers a big spinner for targeting tarpon at night.

Unfortunately there is no industry standard to define rod action. Most manufacturers will list a line class the rods are best suited for. If you see a rod is stamped "12-20 lb. test" you can generally assume that means that the rod is best suited for that size monofilament. Generally speaking, if you are throwing lightweight baits after fish of modest size, lean toward the smaller pound test. If there's a choice between a rod for "8-15 lb. test" and "12-20 lb. test," you could fish 12-pound test on either. Smaller line class rod equals longer casts, and more fun battles. Bigger line class rod equals putting the brakes on a big snook or largemouth.

Spinning rods shorter than 6 feet are generally designed for a very specific fishery. Having been used for everything from ice fishing to jigging speckled perch out of the Florida lily pads, shorter rods are best suited for fishing vertically, instead of a traditional cast-and-retrieve method. Some deepwater jigging methods, primarily in salt water, work best with short, stout spinning rods. Vertical speed jigging for grouper and tuna is one such case.

The next category is called intermediate. Rods range in length from 7 to 9 feet, but vary a great deal in action. East Coast saltwater anglers often prefer a stout tip with plenty of beef throughout since they use their intermediate rods for tough inshore fish like stripers, reds, snook, and even tarpon. On the other hand, West Coast and Great Lakes fishermen are

S pinning rods range in length from as short as 3 feet (extremely powerful deep jigging rods) to as long as 13 feet for surfcasting. The most popular lengths for most applications are between 6 and 8 feet. For many years tubular fiberglass was the standard for spinning rods, but today's market features everything from superlight rods made out of graphite to composites made from combinations of graphite and glass that can outperform anything our dads ever thought of. Generally speaking fiberglass is more forgiving than graphite, and graphite is more sensitive. I need a graphite rod to help me feel the wobble of my crankbaits, that can magically transform to fiberglass to keep me from pulling the hooks out when fighting a fish.

more apt to reach for a rod with a softer tip and still plenty of beef in the butt section.

Aside from deep jigging, many offshore anglers prefer big spinners for sailfish and other sight fishing pursuits. These rods generally fall in the same 7 to 9 foot range as intermediate rods, but are much beefer, and are matched with reels capable of holding enough line to sustain the long runs of many blue water species.

A similar category is surf spinning tackle with rods running 9 to 13 feet in length. The obvious advantage of such length is to power out long casts in the surf. The rods can also be used in other applications where distance is important, such as getting a lightweight live bait far from shore.

Note that the categories defined are general classifications, and that there is much overlap of usefulness.

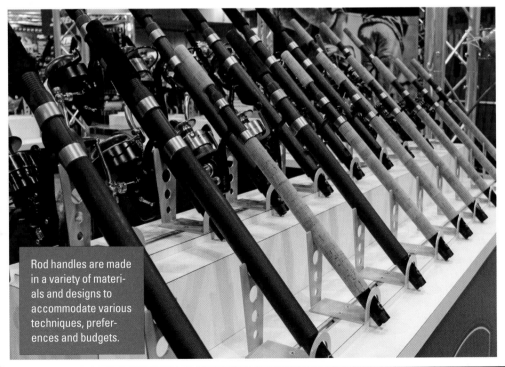

Large-spool spinning outfits are capable of handling bottom species like this black grouper.

Rod handles are made in a variety of materials and designs to accommodate various techniques, preferences and budgets.

Types of Spinning Rods

LIGHT SPINNING ROD Can deliver tiny baits farther and heighten the fun of catching smaller fish.

TWO-HAND SPINNING ROD Casting with two hands can add accuracy and distance to the cast.

SURF SPINNING Specialized rods made for delivering baits great distances from shore.

You will hear the terms "fast taper" and "regular taper" often used in describing spinning rods (fly and plug rods, too).

One, Two, Three or Four-Piece?

By and large, a two-piece rod or even a three- or four-piece travel rod is not significantly weaker, for most practical fishing purposes, than a one-piece. And the takedown feature, obviously, is appealing for ease of transportation. Butt and tip sections of nearly all rods today fit together without a ferrule, glass-over-glass or graphite-

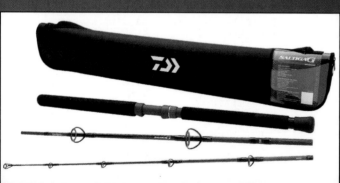

over-graphite. Some fishermen, mostly saltwater veterans, still prefer one-piece spinning rods, and with reasonable cause. While it's true that two-piece rods are not apt to fail at the joint in most fishing, it could happen in a prolonged fight with a rugged fish, especially if the rod is in the hands of an experienced light-tackle angler who's in the habit of putting, and keeping, maximum strain on the rod. Under such conditions, a one-piece rod definitely is stronger, and fishermen who need such strength are more than willing to put up with the inconvenience of a stick that can't be taken down.

One more word about rod action. You will hear the terms "fast taper" and "regular taper" often used in describing spinning rods (fly and plug rods, too). A fast taper rod is one in which the diameter of the blank at the butt end is quite large. The whole blank tapers with obvious abruptness from the broad butt section to the slender tip. In rods of regular taper (also called slow action or parabolic), the variation in diameter of the blank is more gradual from the butt to tip.

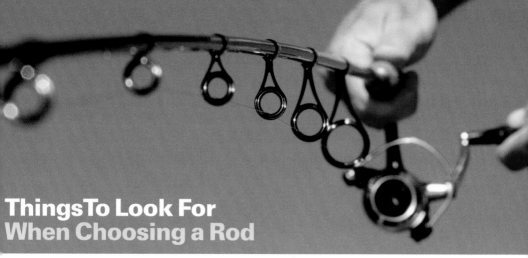

ThingsTo Look For
When Choosing a Rod

REEL SEATS These should be of screw-locking design and corrosion-resistant material. Graphite is widely used, even in relatively low-price rods and certainly is the most corrosion-free and trouble-free.

GUIDES Those with interior rings of aluminum oxide and other high-tech ceramic materials are extremely smooth and hard, thus virtually eliminating severe line fray. Stainless steel rings are also very good, and proven in years of use. Guides should be checked frequently for signs of wear or damage.

WRAPS The double-wrap is traditionally the most solid method of fixing guides to the rod blank. Under each guide there is a wrap of thread. The feet of the guide are placed on the under-wrap, and another wrap is made, usually with thread of contrasting color. Single wraps — winding the guide feet directly on the rod shaft — are found these days on many top-quality rods and are reliable because of the strength provided by epoxy finishes. Intricate decorative wraps, such as the diamond or variations, have no functional purpose, but add to the rod's appearance.

FINISH Some low-priced rods are simply dipped in varnish. This provides a suitable finish but not a long-lasting one. Epoxy finishes, or finishes of other tough modern coatings, are widely used by the top tackle manufacturers, even on many of their lower-priced models. All quality rods will show you a gleaming coat of tough, modern material; and on the most carefully made ones, the finish is so thick and glass-smooth that the wraps underneath cannot be felt by your fingers.

Epoxy finishes, or finishes of other tough coatings, are widely used by top tackle makers, even on their lower-priced models.

A quality reel seat will keep the reel firmly in place on the rod.

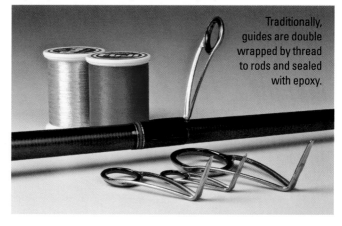

Traditionally, guides are double wrapped by thread to rods and sealed with epoxy.

Spinning Reels

The advent of low diameter braids has changed the formula for selecting a spinning reel.

Spinning reels are functionally the same, regardless of size. The basic reason there are so many sizes is so the angler can match the reel to the size line he plans on using. The advent of low diameter braids has changed the formula on selecting a spinning reel, considerably. Although line capacity is less important for most fresh water applications, it's everything when deciding which reel to select to catch a fish that can outrun an Olympic athlete for a quarter mile. A basic rule of thumb is to use a spinning reel that handles at least 250 yards of the line you plan to use. Obviously

Reels with knobby handles give a good grip to battle big fish.

fishing with braid has enabled more and more anglers to tame bigger fish on lighter gear.

Spin Drags

FRONT DRAG Adjusted simply by turning the front cap. The discs (washers) are alternately hard and soft. The hard ones being of stainless steel and the soft ones of composite synthetic material, leather, Teflon, felt, or combination of those. The soft washers, with the exception of Teflon, should be kept lightly oiled. Also, drags will work far more smoothly if all pressure is backed off after a day of fishing.

REAR DRAG Many spinning reels have "rear drags" which are adjusted by means of a dial at the back of the gear housing. This type of drag is far less efficient because it is more difficult to service and maintain and because heat cannot dissipate very easily from the washers, which are inside the gear housing. Rear drags are fine on light reels, but should be avoided for heavy-duty applications.

"FREE SPIN" REELS Some spinning reels have what we'll call a "free-spin" feature, which is something of a counterpart to the "free-spool" setting on a conventional reel and is activated by means of a lever or button at the rear of the housing. In free-spin mode, the reel allows a striking fish to take line freely without feeling pressure, even though the bail remains closed. Turn the crank handle (or flip the lever in some models) to re-engage the gears.

Reel by Size

MINI SYSTEMS Here are the tiniest of spinning reels. They're little jewels that sit on wispy rods. Obviously, mini-systems turn baby fish into brawny ones, thus increasing the fun. But mini-outfits also can be used on bass and larger fish in open water.

ULTRALIGHT These are the smallest reels in popular use. They can be used with the same line sizes as the minis and although a bit heavier, their larger spools provide more capacity and faster line pickup.

STANDARD These are light reels in the most commonly used size range. This size is ideal for lines of anywhere from 6 to 12 pounds.

INTERMEDIATE A popular size for coastal fishing and in fresh water. Frequently used with 10- or 12-pound test when extra capacity is needed.

HEAVY There are now a lot of big spinning reels and you should be able to find the size you need to handle a healthy amount of any line from 12- to 30-pound test.

Makes a Reel Difference...

BALLBEARING ACTION Not essential, but very desirable for greater ease in cranking and for dependability and reduced wear at critical mechanical points.

CONSTRUCTION & FINISH Housings should be of graphite or anodized aluminum. Reels with anodized aluminum spools are the best choice for large reels and reels used heavily in salt water.

BAIL Should be of heavy stainless steel wire and should click solidly into the open position and snap back sharply. In skirted spool reels, you will find a choice between internal trip mechanisms for closing the bail and a setup that simply knocks the bail closed when it hits an external projection on the reel mount. Both systems allow you to close the bail either by cranking or manipulating the bail wire by hand. The external trip is good because a bail using this device seldom goes out of whack, requiring repair.

LINE ROLLER This should revolve easily to minimize line wear and should be of hardened, corrosion-resistant material. Those with internal bushings are less likely to freeze, but keep all rollers well maintained and lightly oiled.

DRAG A positive, smooth-working drag is a necessity for spinning reels because of the light and easily-broken lines that are used.

Baitcasting Tackle

The term "Baitcasting," refers to a system that makes use of small revolving spool reels, most of which are equipped with a levelwind mechanism. This system is sometimes referred to as "plug casting." As small diameter braid has increased spool capacity, the sizes of baitcasters has continued to shrink, making the little reels easier to cast and more popular than ever. I often wonder what yesterday's catches would have looked like, if anglers would have been able to cast a lure even half as far as today's baitcasters can.

During the early days of spinning reel's popularity boom, it was predicted that baitcasting would fade entirely from the angler's arsenal, and for a while it seemed everybody was fishing with spinning tackle. Modern technology has made baitcasters so much better that their numbers have not only rebounded, but baitcasters have clearly become the workhorse of inshore angling, for both fresh and salt water.

This rejuvenation has been due to the development of modern reels that offer a combination of freespool casting, and dependable, adjustable drags. Anti-backlash aids, multiple ball bearings, and variable gearing have all been part of making today's bait caster the weapon of choice for most serious inshore fishermen.

Different profiles of baitcasting reels are preferred by anglers, depending on their purposes and famililarity.

Baitcasting Reels

The principal disadvantages of the "round reels" are their weight and balance. This is what led to a new family of baitcasters—those identified by their generally smaller size, elliptical side plates, and the use of graphite material, wherever practical to reduce weight. Another characteristic of these reels is that their spools are considerably smaller. Today's braids make it possible for smaller, more efficient spools to cast with pinpoint accuracy, while still holding enough line to be practical in most inshore applications.

Years ago, baitcasting reels were sometimes called "quadruple multipliers" in reference to the fact that their spools turned four times for every revolution of the handle. Today, it's almost unheard of for a reel to not have 5-to-1 or 6-to-1, and some are even faster. In theory, a higher ratio allows you to move a lure and retrieve your line faster. Spool size also has a great deal to do with line retrieve. The larger diameter spools pick up with about a 4.5-to-1 speed. That allows them to pick up line and lures quickly, without sacrificing the "horsing" power of a lower ratio.

Baitcasting Rods

The traditional baitcasting rod featured an offset reel seat with a short, one-hand grip and an even shorter foregrip. Once, nearly every baitcasting rod of this design had a removable handle—the blank being fitted to a separate grip assembly. Good modern rods, however, feature through-blank construction, meaning that the shaft extends the full length of the grip. Not only did this bring a huge improvement in strength but also in sensitivity. By far, the most popular lengths for one-hand baitcasting rods are 5, 5.5 and 6 feet.

Another major "family" of baitcasting rods now seems to have taken over from the shortgrip style in overall popularity. These feature extra-long butts for two-handed casting with better control. They also are of through-blank construction and usually have substantial foregrips that are of great help in tussling big fish. This style of butt got its start in coastal waters, where it was used on sticks known as "popping rods," but has long since been embraced by many freshwater fishermen, especially bass anglers and pursuers of steelhead and salmon.

Two-handed rods are offered in a huge variety of lengths and actions, from as short as 4.5 and 5 feet to 7 or 7.5 feet. Saltwater fishermen in general lean toward heavy-action baitcasting rods, but bassers like stout rods as well. Flipping rods are a common example of this design.

As in spinning, Great Lakes and West Coast salmon and trout anglers lean toward lighter actions and greater length. Flipping rods are long too—7 or 7.5 feet, usually—and many have telescoping butts that reduce the length by a foot or more for easier storing and transporting.

Freshwater Rods

Choosing baitcasting rods is not as simple as deciding between freshwater and saltwater. There's a reason why today's freshwater bass boats have far more rod storage than you would think necessary for two fishermen.

The decision on which freshwater baitcaster

This angler knows that his rod can handle the task at hand: flipping this bass aboard.

you need must include deciding on how far you need to cast, how big a bait you want to throw, and what kind of cover you're fishing in.

Generally speaking, casting soft plastics, which require a stout hookset, or big baits relatively short distances is best done with a shorter, stouter rod. Throwing a lighter, smaller bait a long way is generally done with a longer rod with a soft tip, while throwing a big live bait, such as a shiner, requires a long, stiff rod, which can double as a "flipping rod."

Most freshwater anglers will never fish with a rod longer than 7'6". The exception to this is in the Great Lakes or other areas where salmon and lake trout are the targets.

Closed-Face Spinning Tackle

Closed-face spinning tackle (also called push-button or spincast) is a marriage of the spinning reel and baitcasting rod. This tackle is extremely popular in all freshwater areas, but not well suited to saltwater fishing, although it is sometimes used.

The spinning reel, in this case, is of modified design and looks entirely different from an open-face reel—but a spinning reel it is, nevertheless. The spool is fixed and does not revolve during cast and retrieve.

A closed-face spinning reel is identified by the cone which covers the spool. There is a narrow aperture at

Where a lifetime of angling often begins: sitting on a dock with a closed-face spinner.

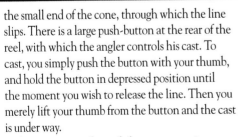

the small end of the cone, through which the line slips. There is a large push-button at the rear of the reel, with which the angler controls his cast. To cast, you simply push the button with your thumb, and hold the button in depressed position until the moment you wish to release the line. Then you merely lift your thumb from the button and the cast is under way.

As you can see, the push-button system is even easier for a beginner to use than open-face spinning. In addition, the closed-face has been welcomed with open arms by many folks who were accustomed to revolving-spool outfits, and who were reluctant to try open-face spinning because the operational mechanics of casting were somewhat different.

All closed-face reels are sold with spools pre-filled, usually with 6- or 8-pound line, although some of the larger models are loaded with line as heavy as 15- or 20-pound. Naturally, you should use a stouter rod with the larger reels and heavier lines.

Counterparts of the tiny mini-systems described in the spinning section are available in spin-cast tackle, and just as pleasant to use.

Closed-face spinning tackle is entirely adequate for every phase of freshwater fishing. One disadvantage, compared to open-face spinning, is that line problems are hidden and more difficult to clear. Another is that the line cannot be so easily controlled (feathered) after the cast is underway. Therefore, accuracy suffers. But with enough practice you can become pretty darned accurate with the closed-face reel nevertheless.

Saltwater fishing is another story. Here, even the large closed-face reels are at a definite disadvantage because of limited line capacity. And closed-face reels also require an extra measure of cleaning and preventative maintenance to keep them operative in a salty environment. All closed-face reels have adjustable drags and many are very good, but none are likely to be as silky smooth and reliable as the front drags on top-quality open-face reels.

As for overall quality in spincast reels, price is a good guide. Many very inexpensive reels with plastic housings are on the market and these are quite adequate for beginners seeking small fish. But just a little more money will change plastic into metal and also provide a higher measure of dependability from gears and other working parts.

Flyfishing Tackle

Almost every angler who has made a reasonable try at fly casting considers this system the ultimate in sportfishing satisfaction and enjoyment. Even more than that, it is often the best way to put meat on the table—especially when that meat is a mess of panfish, small bass or stream trout.

In a few situations, and for certain fish, fly tackle produces more strikes in salt water, too. However, saltwater fly rodders seldom look upon their chosen sport as a better way to catch fish, but as a more challenging and satisfying way.

Flycasting basics are almost as easy to learn as spinning, and with only a couple of short practice sessions virtually anyone can begin using the fly

Fly fishing is almost as easy to learn as spinning. A couple practice sessions, and most people will be ready to fish.

with effect for bass and panfish. On the other hand, it does leave more room for improvement, refinement and development of special abilities than any other system. If you wish, you can progress from panfish and bass fishing (after developing a variety of flyfishing skills in both) to going after trout, steelhead, salmon and all sorts of specialized saltwater targets.

If you are unfamiliar with even the broad concept of how fly casting works, here is a brief explanation: In other forms of casting, the weight of the lure carries out your line. In fly fishing, all the casting weight is distributed over the working length of the fly line itself; flies and flyrod lures are, for practical purposes, weightless.

As you can now guess, fly casting requires completely different timing from spinning or baitcasting; you have to make your backcast with 20 or 30 feet of line protruding from the end of the rod. That's why spin and plug fishermen may have a hard time learning to cast a fly. The problem doesn't really lie in learning how to fly cast, but in unlearning the techniques and timing they use with spinning and baitcasting tackle.

A beginner who has never used any kind of gear usually masters his flycasting basics without the least bit of trouble.

A freshwater fly reel designed to be palmed to add drag.

Many kinds of saltwater fish, like this false albacore, take flies in nearshore waters and in blue water, too.

Flyfishing Rods

Most fly rods today are made of graphite of one sort or another, although many glass rods and graphite glass composites are available too. Split bamboo remains in favor among a few traditionalists. Regardless of materials, the common range of lengths in this country is from 7 feet to 9.5 feet. Specialized, two-handed Spey rods of 12 to 14 feet are popular with some fly fishermen, primarily those casting streamer patterns on large rivers for steelhead or salmon.

Graphite rods are sold at several different price levels. Some very good ones of 100% graphite

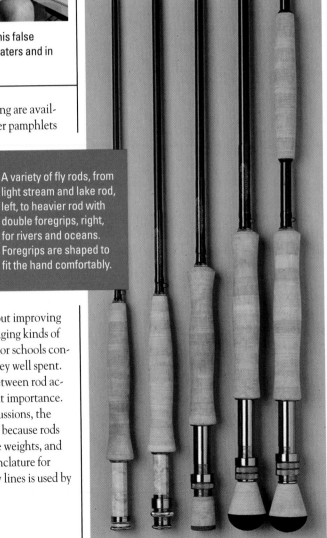

A variety of fly rods, from light stream and lake rod, left, to heavier rod with double foregrips, right, for rivers and oceans. Foregrips are shaped to fit the hand comfortably.

Numerous good books on fly casting are available, and the line manufacturers offer pamphlets of instruction. It is indeed possible to learn from the printed word. But it is many times easier to learn through personal teaching. If you have friends who are proficient in fly casting they can be of great help, but they may not be able to spot flaws in timing or stroke that are holding back your progress. If you are serious about learning to fly cast, or about improving enough to take on the more challenging kinds of fishing, then the expense of lessons or schools conducted by professionals will be money well spent.

In selecting fly tackle, balance between rod action and line weight is of paramount importance. As we will see in the following discussions, the task is not overly difficult anymore, because rods are marked with recommended line weights, and because a standard system of nomenclature for designating weight and design of fly lines is used by all major manufacturers.

The numbers on the rod indicate the model, line weight class, the length and the actual weight of the rod.

SAGE METHOD 790-4 #7 LINE 9'0" 3 9/16 OZ.

Graphite's advantage over fiberglass in the eyes of most fly casters is its exceptional weight-to-power ratio.

(or close) are offered at reasonable prices by most full-line rod manufacturers, as well as by specialty fly houses. The latter, however, can also show you rods costing several times as much, the difference being in advanced graphite formulas, combined with superior finish and cosmetics. Needless to say, beginners should stick to the low end of the graphite scale. Only after considerable experience are you likely to gain much benefit from the latest advances in graphite materials.

Graphite's main advantage over fiberglass, in the eyes of most fly casters, is its exceptional weight-to-power ratio. Fly rodders like it for other reasons too, among them outstanding recovery. This means that, at the end of your casting strokes, the graphite rod straightens and becomes still much more quickly. To the eye, recovery looks virtually instantaneous with most graphite rods. Glass and bamboo tend to "wobble" considerably longer, and so transmit waves to the line that reduce casting efficiency.

In general, fly rods become heavier—in action, strength and balancing line size—as their lengths increase. The variations to this rule of thumb are relatively small until you reach 9 feet. American fly

fishermen seem to shun rods longer than about 9.5 feet, no matter how heavy the fishing. Therefore, you will find quite a large spread of actions in rods 9 to 9.5 feet long. Avid fly casters often own several rods of different actions in that size range—not only heavy ones for bass, salmon, salt water and offshore, but also light ones for fishing lakes or wide streams.

Another rule of thumb in fly fishing is that when two rods use the same weight of line, the longer one will be easier to cast with, and capable of casting farther.

The beginning fly fisherman will find a slow-action rod desirable because it is more forgiving of minor errors in timing.

A good fly outfit feels balanced in the hand at every point in the cast.

A stripping basket gathers line as it is pulled off the reel, avoiding having it on the ground or underfoot.

Fly Reels

Most single-action reels are inexpensive. They are called single-action because they contain no gears; the spool revolves one turn for every turn of the crank.

Some people find automatic fly reels desirable for light freshwater fishing. These have no crank handle at all. You wind up a spring mechanism and then retrieve line as needed by pressing a trigger with your finger. Automatic reels are not suitable when backing line must be used.

For saltwater fly fishing, as well as for a few large freshwater fish such as pike, salmon and steelhead, you'll be after fish that can make runs, sometimes long runs—much longer than the length of your fly line, which is only around 90 feet. Now your reel becomes important because it has a part to play—like any other fishing reel—in fighting and bringing in the fish. The reel now must have a larger capacity in order to hold not only your flyline, but

Backing Line

First, choose a reel that will hold the fly line you intend to use, along with the amount of backing you prefer. For big steelhead and salmon, a minimum of 100 yards of backing is desirable. For salt water, the minimum should be 200 yards inshore and 300 or more offshore. The biggest machined reels, designed for billfish and tuna, hold 500 to 600 yards of backing, depending on the diameter of the backing line chosen.

There are no rules regarding the test of backing line, but you should always use backing that is considerably stronger than the lightest section of your leader (see Chapter 6 for information on flyfishing leaders) in order to reduce the possibility of having the backing break first, causing you to lose the expensive fly line. There is much leeway but 20-pound test is a common backing size for salmon and inshore salt water; 30-pound test for tarpon and offshore fishing.

Fly Line
Backing Line

an attached quantity of backing line, which usually is of braided Dacron. It is also desirable to use a reel with an adjustable drag—and downright necessary if you go after real ocean toughies, such as tarpon and offshore fish. Unlike the basic single-action reels, heavy-duty machined models with good drags wear hefty price tags.

Reels are distinguished by their materials, their arbor size and their drag systems.

> **The weight of the line should be balanced to your rod's action for good casting performance.**

Tenkara fly rod (inset) requires no reel and is made for close-quarter fishing, like rivers.

Fly Lines

Fly lines come in a wide variety of tapers and weights, the designated weight referring to the primary working portion of the line. For a beginner, it is of the utmost importance that the weight of the line be balanced to your rod's action for good casting performance. Fortunately, standardization in line labeling, plus the fact that all factory fly rods are labeled with recommended line sizes, makes this job pretty easy.

Standardized line labeling means that you don't have to remember actual line weight, in grams, but only relative weight, as defined by a standard numbering system. Although both smaller and larger line sizes are available, the common range of line weights runs from No. 4 (for light rods used for small trout or panfish) to No. 12 (balancing heavy rods used for tarpon or billfish).

In the standard labeling system, letters are used both before and after the weight number, and these denote the particular line's characteristics. Letters in front of the number refer to the *taper* of the line—L stands for level; DT for double taper; WF for weight-forward taper. Letters behind the number refer to the *buoyancy* of the particular line: F for floating; S for sinking; I for intermediate or slow-sinking; FS for floating-sinking (only the tip sinks). There are also specialty lines, such as shooting heads, that wear additional prefixes or suffixes.

We have seen that fly lines come in different weights and different tapers. In addition, there are lines that float and lines that sink. The great majority of fly lines have always been designed to float, but with today's emphasis on using fly tackle in virtually every angling situation imaginable, from shallow streams and flats to mighty rivers and deep channels, sinking lines are very popular. Even in waters where floating lines are the standard, sinking lines can often salvage

Lines come in a variety of weights, to match with rods, and with a variety of performance characteristics.

some action on a day when the fish aren't rising.

Only the number (not the letters) is important to rod balance. If a rod, for example, is suited to a No. 8 line, it can be used with any line that bears that number, regardless of taper and regardless of whether the line floats or sinks. Practiced casters can, by adjusting the amount of line they work with during the cast, do very well with line weights somewhat lower or higher than the basic weight for which the particular rod is designed. But beginners should stick to the recommendations.

Flyline Tapers

LEVEL LINE as the name denotes, has no taper at all.

DOUBLE TAPER LINE features identical thin tapers at both ends of a thick middle section. Designed for utmost delicacy in presenting small flies to trout, the double taper is seldom chosen for other kinds of fishing. Anglers who find the double taper suitable for their fishing needs also save money, because this line can be reversed—in effect giving them a brand-new line when their old one becomes tired and frazzled at the tip.

WEIGHT-FORWARD LINE (sometimes called TORPEDO TAPER) has a short, thin tip section which swells abruptly to a thick portion, behind the tip. This thick portion averages about 20 feet long. Behind it, the rest of the line is very thin and is referred to as the "running line." Weight-forward tapers are designed for long casting, particularly with heavy or bulky flies. Within the Weight-Forward family are such designations as "Bug taper," "Saltwater taper" and "Rocket taper." All are true weight-forwards, differing mainly in the length of the "torpedo" portion. Those with shorter heads can be put into action with a minimum of false casting, especially useful for bass fishing and in salt water. They are the "bug" and "saltwater" tapers.

SHOOTING TAPER in effect, is nothing more than the forward portion of a weight-forward line. The angler attaches this head to a very thin running line of his own choice. The running line may be of limp monofilament, braid, or simply a very, very thin fly line that is marketed as running line. Only after a fly fisherman becomes proficient with standard weight-forward lines is he likely to start looking at shooting tapers.

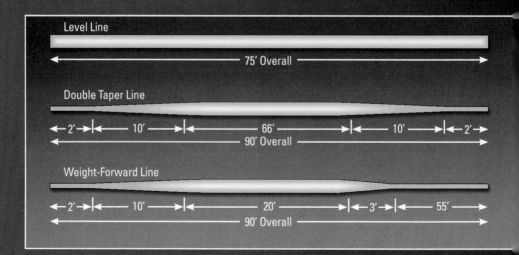

Level Line
75' Overall

Double Taper Line
2' | 10' | 66' | 10' | 2'
90' Overall

Weight-Forward Line
2' | 10' | 20' | 3' | 55'
90' Overall

Conventional Offshore Tackle

Offshore tackle is evolving so fast, in so many different directions, it's enough to make you dizzy. In years gone by, the theory was pretty simple. Most offshore hooks came out of the box so dull it took a broom stick rod to penetrate the bony mouth of most offshore species. If that weren't enough of a problem, sticky drags, and big diameter Dacron line required reels too heavy for most people to fish with comfortably. In short, many a 10-pound

The sight of a rocket launcher filled with rods rigged and ready thrills the heart of every big game angler.

Today's offshore fishermen have learned the importance of balance when it comes to tackle.

kingfish was deemed to be a poor fighting fish while trying to pull drag from a 6/0 reel loaded with 80-pound Dacron.

Today's accomplished offshore fishermen have learned the importance of balance when it comes to their tackle. In many cases anglers find themselves working from the inside out when choosing today's outfits. New age hooks are often so small and so sharp, they take hold in the fish's jaw on the strike. Now, instead of trying to sink a dull hook, the trick has become more a game of not pulling a small hook out, instead of driving a big hook home. That trick requires a smoother drag and lighter rod.

Offshore Reels

The reels used in making up matched sets for line-class fishing are divided into two broad categories:

1. Star-Drag Reels with a free-spool lever and a separate star-drag mechanism. These reels generally are inexpensive but quite sturdy and dependable.

2. Leverdrag Reels that incorporate the freespool and drag-setting lever into a single unit. You have your choice of any drag in between the extremes at any time. In full forward position, the lever gives maximum preset drag. When the lever is in full rearward position, the reel is in freespool. The presetting of the drag range is handled by a separate adjusting device.

Some fish are fast, some jump higher, but nothing beats a great catch of bottom fish on the dinner table.

pressure at the wrong time and breaking the line.

All single-lever reels (also called dual-drag reels because of the presetting feature) are expensive, but some brands cost considerably more than others. At the high end, spools are machined from solid bars of special-alloy aluminum, and more hand machine work may go into other parts as well. But the lower-priced leverdrag reels are generally quite strong and dependable, using modern alloys and mass manufacturing techniques to replace costly labor.

Most reels today are labeled according to the size of line they best handle—for instance, 20, 50, 130. Some labels suggest a range of appropriate sizes, such as 50-80. In any case, those labels are easily understood; however, some currently marketed ocean reels—both star-drag and single-lever—date back to the days when lines were classified by the number of threads they contained, rather than actual breaking strength. Those reels use a strange size-designation system made up of numbers and slashes and maybe fractions too. Examples: 2/0, 3/0, 4/0, 9/0 and 12/0.

The larger the number, the larger the reel. The

Star-drag

Leverdrag

Obviously, the single-lever reels offer a dramatic advantage over star-drag models, which do not allow instant and positive drag changes during the heat of battle—an advantage that is especially welcome when using heavier tests of line for big ocean fish, such as marlin and giant tuna. Different drag pressures are called for at different stages of a battle with a monster fish. With the single-lever, the angler can change drag settings at will, without risk of applying too much

D.I.Y. Deep Fishing

Tackle makes it possible to drop baits deeper than we thought possible a few decades ago. Sometimes the fish are thousands of feet down, making "hand cranking" almost impossible. Some anglers will use electric reels where pushing a button is the angler's only job. Others will use a simple hand drill with an attachment to the reel to be able to quickly retrieve the rig at those depths.

number also gives at least a broad clue as to the appropriate size of line, although there is considerable latitude. For instance, you might use 20-pound line on a 2/0 or 3/0. You might use 30-pound line on either a 3/0 or 4/0. To continue, 50-pound line on a 6/0, 7.5/0 or 9/0; 80-pound on a 9/0 or 10/0; 130-pound on a 10/0, 12/0 or 14/0. Your final choice, of course, would depend on how much capacity you desire. It isn't a bad idea at all to spool up with considerably more line than you would normally think necessary. This is especially true when big-game fishing with heavier classes of line, but valid, too, in the lighter classes. You will be able to cut back line (for re-rigging, abrasion, etc.), and still be sure of having a usable amount for a long time.

In any case, offshore experts consider 400 yards as a minimum amount for the 12-, 20- and 30-pound classes; 600 yards for heavier lines. In practice, most choose reels that will hold considerably more line than those suggested minimums.

Two-Speed Reels

Two speeds work exactly as the name suggests. With the push of a button (usually on the side plate inside the base of the reel handle) you can switch gears, slowing the retrieve and increasing the torque.

Modern offshore reels retrieve line at a rate of approximately 4 to 1. That means every time you turn the handle, the spool turns four times. If you go to low gear it cuts it to 2 to 1, but that affords much more torque, making it much easier to turn the handle. If a big tuna, or a fat grouper is determined to stay deep, it's much easier to lift him in low gear. However, trying to keep up with a screaming wahoo in low gear is like leaving your truck in low gear on the highway after you use it to pull your boat up the ramp.

Two-speed offshore reels are roughly 20 percent more expensive than single speeds. Like so many other things in fishing tackle, it's a lot better to have it, and not need it, than to need it and not have it.

Two-Speed Reel

Big Game Rods

Rods designed for fishing in the various IGFA classes are offered by many manufacturers and custom builders, and are plainly labeled as to class, so there is little confusion in picking out a rod of the right specifications. You can indeed shop by price, however.

IGFA class rods are frequently fitted with an entire set of roller guides and a roller top, although a few have a roller first guide, roller top and ring guides in between. Obviously, those with all rollers cost more—and are worth more. IGFA rods also are characterized by a hard butt with a gimbal slot in the end. The slot, of course, is for fitting to the gimbal of a fishing chair or a gimbal belt.

Reel seats often are of strong and dependable chrome-on-brass construction. In light classes,

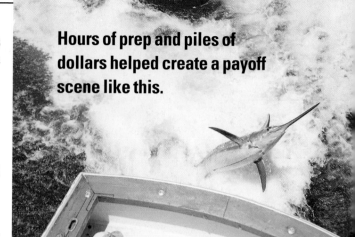

Hours of prep and piles of dollars helped create a payoff scene like this.

Safety lines clipped on big game reels keep them from going overboard.

graphite seats may be used. In the heaviest classes and most expensive rods, the seats are sometimes machined from solid bar stock of special alloys.

The butts must be of strong material to resist scarring and gouging in metallic rod holders. Wood is the most common on less expensive rods. Solid fiberglass and fiberglass-graphite composites are used too, as are butts of heavy anodized aluminum tubing.

Roller guides make for a smooth line release when well lubed.

Most of the shafts (blanks) are of tubular fiberglass or graphite-glass composite material. Solid glass is often used too. It provides great strength and resistance to maltreatment, and weight is no big drawback for tackle to be used with belts and harnesses.

Reel seats often are of strong and dependable chrome-on-brass construction.

Electric Reels

The development of lighter, smaller, and more powerful electric reels designed to take the labor out of fishing deep waters with automatic, motorized spools has opened a whole new world for fishermen.

The primary use of electric reels is for fishing deep water, up to a couple thousand feet deep. There are a variety of kinds of electric reels. Some run on either rechargeable lithium ion batteries or

Deep drop jiggers can even activate a jigging feature to jig their bait halfway up and then drop it back down.

a power source, and most commonly swordfish and deep-dropping anglers use reels that plug into the boat's power supply, either 12- or 24-volt system. Some reels are independent, self-standing machines, and others are motors that attach to a modified conventional reel to power it—the motors are built to connect to the shaft normally holding the reel handle. Either of these styles of reels can be put to use to fight swordfish, sharks and other large fish, and some anglers use electric reels while trolling to hasten retrieve of lures and lessen labor.

Line counters are standard on most electrics. Many come with a memory, which is programmable. This works great for boats using them to pull teasers. Not only can the captain reset them to drop back to the same spot in his wake, he can push retrieve, and have it programmed to stop in the perfect place to be out of the way, when a big fish is close. Deep drop jiggers can even activate a jigging feature to jig their bait halfway up, then drop back to the bottom.

Whether electric reels are sporting or not is up to each angler, but they should have a place on your bluewater boat if maximizing your catch is the goal.

Many species, such as this barrel fish, are only available by fishing in very deep waters.

Standup Tackle

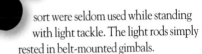

Not too long ago, the idea of fishing with heavy tackle for big-game species—without the aid of a fighting chair—would have been considered nonsensical.

Many offshore anglers did (and still do) prefer to stand while waging battles with billfish and other bluewater foes—but only when fishing the lighter IGFA line classes with their correspondingly lightweight outfits. Most considered 30-pound as the heaviest tackle that was practical for "hand-holding," although a few he-men would occasionally stand and heave with 50-pound gear. Harnesses of any

Basic PVC gimbal belt stabilizes the rod butt while angler pumps to recover line.

sort were seldom used while standing with light tackle. The light rods simply rested in belt-mounted gimbals.

As for the 80- and 130-pound classes—forget it. The common view was that it would take a wrestling champ just to hold the weight of such outfits while remaining erect, and at least a Superman to wage battle for prolonged periods while applying drag pressures ranging up to 40 pounds and sometimes even higher.

Actually that view was quite correct. It would indeed have required superhuman strength to perform such a task—with standard big-game tackle and gimbal belts.

But that was before partyboats on the southern California coast (and later on the North Atlantic shore too) began taking anglers on long-range, multi-day trips in search of huge tuna weighing upwards of 100 pounds; occasionally several hundred pounds. The rails of partyboats are not lined with fighting chairs, and so specialized tackle had to be developed that would allow those adventurous anglers to use heavy lines and apply heavy drag while standing—and not suffer broken bones or hernias in the process.

The kind of gear we currently refer to as "standup tackle" evolved from that challenge, and it covers more than just rods and reels. Entirely new types of harnesses and belts had to be engineered to complete the system. Today a wide variety of all standup components is available. The harnesses and belts will be covered in Chapter 10.

Standup Rods

Standup-style rods are now being marketed for not only the 50-, 80- and 130-pound IGFA classes but also in the light-tackle classes as well. Light-class standup rods simply give the offshore angler an alternative to the traditional rods already discussed. However, in the heavy classes they are not merely an option but a downright necessity for all who want to stand on their own two feet and catch a true big-game trophy.

Superficially similar to traditional tournament rods, the standup design can be immediately identified by two prominent features—a shorter butt and much longer foregrip. The overall length is also shorter and the blank is of the fast-taper design—as opposed to slow, or parabolic, action of most traditional offshore blanks. The standup rod is usually 5.5 feet long, with 6 feet about the longest you'll see. By contrast, the usual lengths of traditional offshore rods are 6.5 or 7 feet.

The short butt of a standup rod will rest in the low-slung gimbal that's used with a special standup harness, enabling the angler to crank with his right arm in a comfortably low position—far less tiring than if he had to lift his arm to reach the crank handle. At the same time, the long foregrip allows him to hang onto the rod with his left arm extended straight in front of him.

Proper use of gear, like a fighting belt and harness, right, can help anglers battle the strength of fish like yellowfin tuna, below.

The combination of harness and belt is so situated as to allow the angler's lower back and legs to do most of the work in keeping up the pressure on a big fish. The rugged part of a struggle with a giant tuna or billfish is the effort to bring the fish close enough to gaff or tag. Often as not, particularly with tuna, there is also the task of heaving up a great weight from far below the surface, and this is where the standup system shines.

Other than sheer strength, there are no special requirements for reels used in standup fishing. They can be evaluated as already described for offshore reels.

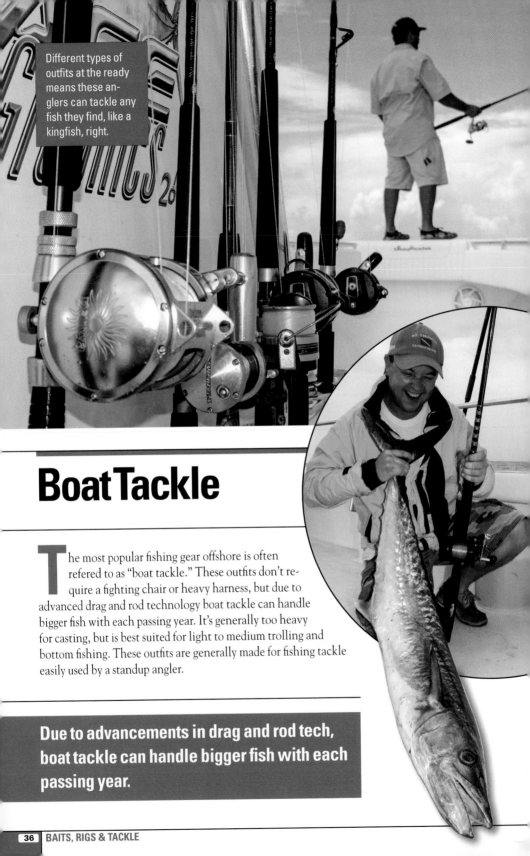

Different types of outfits at the ready means these anglers can tackle any fish they find, like a kingfish, right.

Boat Tackle

The most popular fishing gear offshore is often refered to as "boat tackle." These outfits don't require a fighting chair or heavy harness, but due to advanced drag and rod technology boat tackle can handle bigger fish with each passing year. It's generally too heavy for casting, but is best suited for light to medium trolling and bottom fishing. These outfits are generally made for fishing tackle easily used by a standup angler.

Due to advancements in drag and rod tech, boat tackle can handle bigger fish with each passing year.

Boat Rods

Boat rods can be built out of solid and tubular glass as well as graphite composites. Many of the first quality boat rods were built on solid glass blanks. These are still popular today, but both tubular glass and graphite composites are grabbing bigger market share every year because of their sensitivity and light weight. Superior guides, wraps, and reel seats can drive the price up on any of the rods.

Boat rods can be found in lengths from 5 feet up, but for most purposes 6 to 7 feet prove the most versatile in salt water. As to line-class or power ratings, will you be trying to lift a 100-pound tarpon off the bottom of the bay, or trying to keep that tiny treble hook from pulling out of a kingfish's mouth? Will you troll with downriggers? If you plan on downrigger fishing, a soft tip rod not only lessens the pressure on the release clip, but seeing it suddenly pop up straight will signify a strike the instant it happens.

Generally speaking, boat rods will have the line class best suited for them stamped above the foregrip. Twelve- to 20-pound rods are perfect for slow trolling for kings while a 50- to 80-pound rod may be necessary to stop a big grouper from rocking you up. Modern guide technology has greatly reduced the friction caused by line running through guides. Whereas the lack of a roller tip used to signify a poor quality rod, today's lighter tackle offshore rods rarely have any rollers.

Light tackle rods rarely have roller guides. Modern rings greatly reduce friction on the line.

Aptly named "trident" style rod-holding device converts a single rod holder into one which holds three rods.

Boat Reels

A key decision on which offshore reel to use again revolves around star drag vs. leverdrag. Leverdrags make it easier to adjust your drag during a fight. If a fish is foul hooked, or gets too much line off the reel, you may wish to increase or decrease some drag pressure in small increments within the preset range. For bottom fishing, where you may need to put maximum pressure on a big grouper or halibut, a star drag is easier to slam on the brakes. Many savvy live baiters fish with a leverdrag barely engaged. The goal is for a fish to feel no resistance when it picks up the bait. A barely engaged drag—just enough to keep the reel from backlashing, lets a fish take the bait without feeling unnatural resistance.

Boat reels are just right to handle one of the favorite catches in the Gulf of Mexico, the red snapper.

Boat gear is designed to be of manageable size and heft for most fishing, and most anglers, encountered.

Whereas experienced offshore fishermen rarely use levelwinds anymore, they still have their place for nearshore fishing. Charter boats targeting striped bass, snook, or salmon love the ease of not having to teach their customers how to stack line evenly on the reel as it comes in.

Both star and leverdrags have their place on the offshore scene.

There's almost nothing these medium-size trolling outfits won't handle.

For bottom fishing, where you may need to put maximum pressure on a big grouper or halibut, a star drag is easier to slam on the brakes.

You can count on plenty of advice from your buddies while fighting a big fish.

Surf Tackle

Surf comes in all degrees of wave action, from none to booming breakers. Depending on conditions, and on how far you have to heave your chosen baits or lures, you can use virtually any kind of light tackle, including fly rods and small spinning outfits.

The term "surf tackle," however, is applied to rather stout, long-distance casting equipment—gear designed to toss lures or sinkers weighing several ounces far out over the breakers to reach distant holes or schools of fish.

Conventional surf rods for revolving reels are characterized by stout tips and long butts. Overall length may range from as little as 8 feet to as much as 14, sometimes even longer. (Spinning gear for surf fishing is discussed in the section on spinning tackle.)

The stoutest of all surf outfits are those used for tossing out bottom rigs with heavy pyramid sinkers—mainly in quest of striped bass and red or black drum on the Atlantic Coast. It takes a lot of rod to handle five or six ounces of sinker, and so the tips of these heavy-duty sticks are as big around as your thumb.

Though longer rods are available, many surf specialists agree that 10 or 11 feet is the best all-around length range.

Surf fishing specialists will own at least two outfits and, like all other anglers, probably will have more than that. The first would be one of the "broomstick" rods described earlier, used with 30-pound line for heaving out heavy bottom rigs or his biggest metal squids. The other would be lighter—a more flexible and perhaps longer rod, which he uses with lighter line to throw bass plugs and other popular lures, or bottom rigs with sinkers weighing only two or three ounces.

That second outfit might be a conventional surf rig with 20- to 50-pound braid, or it might be a surf-spinning outfit with 15- or 25-pound monofilament.

Surf Reels

Surf reels are similar in design to other free-spool, star drag saltwater reels, but they generally

One rod is almost never enough for an experienced surf angler.

have wider spools, and other features designed to improve casting efficiency. Long distance casting has become a sport unto itself. No serious distance caster would allow a levelwind on his reel, as it reduces the distance of a long cast. Among the best reels for everyday surf casting are larger versions of inshore bait casters.

Nowhere does the braid vs. mono debate rage hotter than among surfcasters. There's no doubt smaller surf reels can hold more braid. There's also little doubt you can cast braid farther than mono. All these advantages disappear the very first time the braid backlashes and your beautiful day off is spent trying to pick it out of your reel.

Ice Fishing

An angler drills through the ice with a hand auger to make a spot to drop lines.

Enterprising anglers won't let a little cold weather ruin their plans. Many, in fact, actually welcome the cold, and plan for it. In northern U.S. states and Canada, ice fishing season is eagerly anticipated.

Take advantage of what nature gives you. Let the ice get at least 3 inches thick, and you'll see guys cutting holes with a hand auger to drop anything from jigs with minnow heads on them for walleye or pike, to worms or insects to warm up the skillet with some panfish.

Let the ice get thicker and the shanties start to appear. They can range from four bare walls pulled out on sleds to block the wind to condos with microwaves, bunks, heaters and, yes, a television to watch what's happening on Lambeau Field.

Modern electronics have even provided ice anglers the ability to go "ice trolling." Ice trolling simply means going across the ice, stopping on occasion to check the sonar to see if there's fish below. When fish are spotted, drill a few holes (with a gas auger) and drop in on them. Be careful to set your baits at the depths you've spotted fish. Remember fish are a lot like us in the way they don't move around as much when it's cold. You'll want your bait right in the middle of a school you've spotted to ensure a bite.

Unlike sportfish boats, ice anglers can leave their condos on the lake for as long as fishing is good. Just crank up the snow mobile, run to your condo, and turn on the game. Hopefully the fish will only bite during time outs.

Ice fishing rods are made for dropping baits vertically at short range.

CHAPTER 2

Poles & Specialty Gear

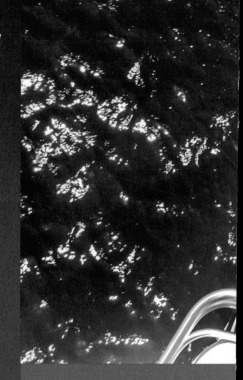

When it comes to fishing there really aren't as many secret weapons as most beginners think.

Chances are the boat that regularly out-fishes you doesn't have a magic bait. They just work a little bit harder at the details. Anybody can throw a lure or troll a bait, but having the specialty gear at the ready that enables you to improve your presentation just the smallest amount makes all the dif-ference. Sure a sailfish will eat a single live blue runner drifted off a rodtip, but the boat that is fishing six baits off two kites is going to show their baits to more fish.

The devil is in the details, and the learn-ing never stops. From bream to marlin, get the gear that will help you make a better presentation, and your success will rise.

> **Sure a sailfish will eat a single live blue runner, but the boat that is fishing six baits off two kites is going to show their baits to more fish and up their chances.**

Right: "Spreader" reinforces outrigger pole to accommodate the drag of large lures. Above: Fishing kite is retrieved.

Kite Fishing Setup

Angler on bow is hooked up and angler in stern sets a bait.

A fishing kite is used to present live baits well away from an anchored or drifting boat—or even from shore, provided the wind is in a favorable direction. The kite can also be used in the manner of an outrigger to troll artificial or rigged baits.

Don't try to build your own kite; buy a manufactured one.

The large illustration shows the arrangement of kite, kite line and fishing lines in a typical deployment from a small boat. The kite can be flown either from a large fishing reel with a specifically manufactured kite rod, or from an electric reel designed for deep dropping, and kite or teaser retrieving. In either case, the kite line should test at least 80 pounds. When using either an electric or converted manual reel, braided line should be used. More experienced captains can handle flying multiple kites from even a small boat. Placing a small splitshot to the outer edge of one corner of a kite can cause it to fly in a specific direction, keeping the kites from tangling.

More experienced anglers can handle flying multiple kites, even from a small boat.

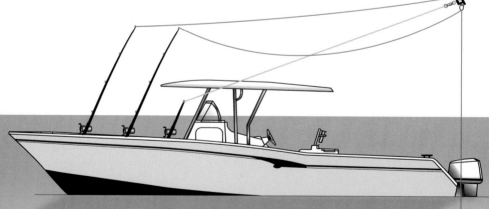

Two-line Kite Rig

1. Tie an offshore snapswivel to the end of the kite line. This will be your attachment for the kite.
2. About 50 feet back from that snapswivel, cut the line and slide on the release pin that has the smaller holes, making sure that the release arm of the pin will open downward. Next, tie on the smaller swivel. Stopped by the swivel, your first pin will slide no farther down the line, but is free (upon retrieving the line) to travel upward.
3. About 40 or 50 feet from the first swivel, cut the line again. Now slide the release pin with the larger hole onto the line and tie the larger swivel below it. Last, tie the kite line to the other eye of the

Kites excel in different fisheries, but nowhere more than in sailfishing. Sails often drive their prey topside.

Two line-release pins are attached to the kite line. Complete kite reels, ready to fish with line and pins in place, are available.

If you rig your own kite reel, note that the release pins run freely on the kite line, and that one pin must have larger line holes than the other. These pins are sometimes sold in pairs, each with holes of a different size, but if you have two pins with the same size holes, you must enlarge the holes on one of them with an electric drill. You will also need two barrel swivels of different sizes. One swivel, perhaps a No. 7, must be large enough to stop the pin that has the smaller holes, yet small enough to allow the pin with the larger holes to run past it. The other swivel, say a No. 5 or 3, must be large enough to stop the pin with the larger holes.

When you crank in the kite line to replace baits or end the trip, the lower release pin will run up the line, "jump" the small swivel and finally come to rest beside the upper pin at the kite-connecting snap-swivel. This makes for easy handling and storing.

One mate on kite duty can keep baits dancing on the surface to attract bites.

larger swivel and your rigging is complete.

4. As your kite goes up, the first release pin will stop at the small swivel. Lock or hold the kite reel and place one fishing line in that pin.

5. Slowly let out more kite line, while the angler lets out his fishing line. When the second release pin stops at the larger swivel, lock the kite reel once more and attach the second fishing line to the second pin.

6. Finally, by simultaneously letting out kite line and fishing lines—and by alertly handling the fishing reels to adjust the position of the baits up or down as necessary—you get both baits the desired distance from the boat. Now lock the kite reel and you are in business. You must continually monitor the baits, however, to take up or let out line as the need arises.

Angler watches the kite bait on the water, ready for a strike from a pelagic.

A double hooked goggle-eye, top, with kite pins at the ready spells hookups on the horizon.

If the target species is some-where between bream and blue marlin, the less tackle you put in the water the better. What could be better than having only the bait in the water?

Steering Your Kite
Kites can be steered to keep multiples apart in the air. Adding a splitshot to one side or the other can send the kite where you want it to go.

Keep Those Baits on Top

No matter the species, the less tackle you put in the water the better. How could you accomplish that better than having everything except the bait hanging suspended in midair? Therein lies the magic of kite fishing. Only the bait is under the surface of the water. The hooks and leader are above the bait, and out of the fish's sight. This is accomplished by constantly watching the kite bait to make sure it is on the surface while the tackle stays above it.

Kites are also excellent at dramatically increasing your spread. While drifting or slow trolling downsea, you can double your presentation by flying a kite out the leeward side.

Give Your Kite a Lift

Most days, having too little wind is not a problem offshore, but on the rare dead-air day, helium balloons can lift the kites. Prepared crews will often carry a portable helium

tank. With the balloon carrying the kite up, lines can be fished from the kite line, same as if wind lifted the kite. Left, crew member fills helium balloon. Waxed rigging thread and sturdy tape will be used to position balloon on the kite.

It's a great feeling to see a billfish swim away healthy with a tag in its shoulder.

Outriggers

It's just this simple: The more baits in the water, the more fish you will raise to take them.

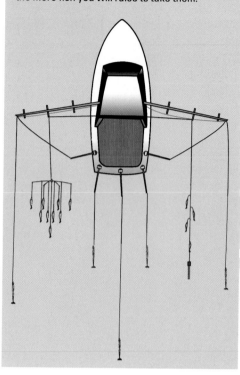

For trolling rigged baits at, or just under, the surface, outriggers are a tremendous aid. They are long poles that angle outward from each side of the boat, thus allowing the fisherman to troll more lines. They also provide a small amount of "dropback," or slack, after a striking fish snaps the line from the outrigger pin. Consider the fact that fish without the cutting teeth of a kingfish or wahoo have to swallow their prey headfirst. "Dropbacks" are so effective because they enable such species as dolphin or billfish the time to turn a bait headfirst. Outriggers are standard equipment on offshore sportfishing boats, and can easily be mounted on smaller boats as well, using components available at marine stores in coastal areas—a gunnel mount that holds a long pole. Ordinarily, the mount is a two-position one that allows the pole to stand upright when running. Or the poles can be removed from the mounts and placed on the deck (or left ashore

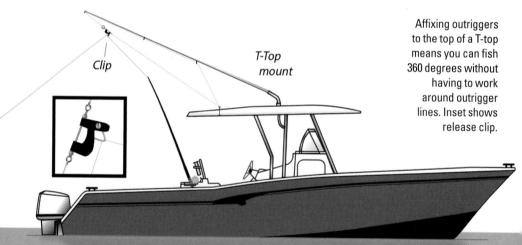

Clip

T-Top mount

Affixing outriggers to the top of a T-top means you can fish 360 degrees without having to work around outrigger lines. Inset shows release clip.

Small Boat Setup

Take your fishing line at the rodtip and clip it to the outrigger pin. Then simultaneously feed line from the fishing reel while hoisting the outrigger line. With a little practice, and a reel that has a clicker mechanism to prevent backlashing, one person can easily do the job.

The clip shown in the diagram is the Black's Clip, identical to that commonly used with a fishing kite.

Outrigger Tech

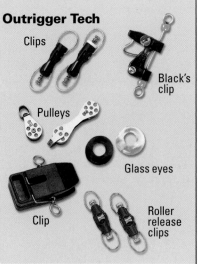

Clips

Black's clip

Pulleys

Glass eyes

Clip

Roller release clips

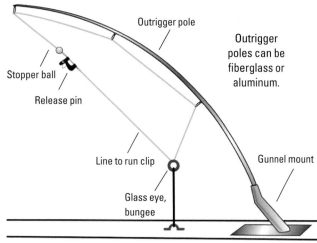

Outrigger pole

Outrigger poles can be fiberglass or aluminum.

Stopper ball

Release pin

Line to run clip

Glass eye, bungee

Gunnel mount

Dropbacks are effective because they enable pelagics to turn the bait in their mouths headfirst.

when they won't be needed). Most modern T-tops come with bases for outriggers included. The advantage to having your outriggers run from the T-top is being able to move around the boat with a fish on, without having to clear the outrigger lines.

The outrigger line is usually of very heavy monofilament, 200-pound test or more. Connected at the ends by means of crimped sleeves, the circle of line runs through guides on the pole, and through a large glass eye, or pulley, that is connected via a shock cord to a cleat behind the mount, as illustrated. Thus rigged, the line remains taut and can be lowered and raised by hand and left in any position desired. One or more release clips—various kinds are available—are incorporated into the outrigger line, also by using crimped sleeves. More than one clip may be used on each outrigger.

An advanced outrigger setup with multiple pins and ring eyes such as this allows crews to handle teasers via outriggers.

Downriggers

By far, the most efficient tool ever designed for deep trolling is the downrigger. It is the only deep-fishing device that allows the angler to present his baits or lures at selected and variable depths, and to keep them there.

Homemade versions of the downrigger were in scattered use for many years, but not until after the introduction of salmon into the Great Lakes in the 1960s did downrigger fishing become a standard angling system. Now, manufactured downriggers and accessories have reached a high level of dependability, portability and sophistication.

Beginning with Great Lakes anglers, downriggers are now standard equipment on many boats fishing offshore in saltwater. Kingfish, wahoo, and even snapper and grouper are now being taken with downriggers. Even sailfish fishermen are using them to take their teasers or dredges deep to try and raise sailfish to their spread.

Coho and chinook salmon can be caught near the surface in spring and fall but throughout the summer can only be taken deep. Coho prefer a temperature of about 53 degrees Fahrenheit; and this may at times be 200 feet down.

But even at much shallower levels, whether for salmon or saltwater battlers, the downrigger still excels as a fishing tool, simply because it will work at any level you desire.

Downriggers are large reels spooled with wire, heavy mono or heavy braid. To the end of the cable or heavy monofilament is fitted a heavy weight, which is lowered via an arm-and-pulley arrangement. On or near the weight is a release device to which the fishing line is clipped.

The weight carries the line and lure to the

Two downriggers, one on each corner of the transom, is the most common installation.

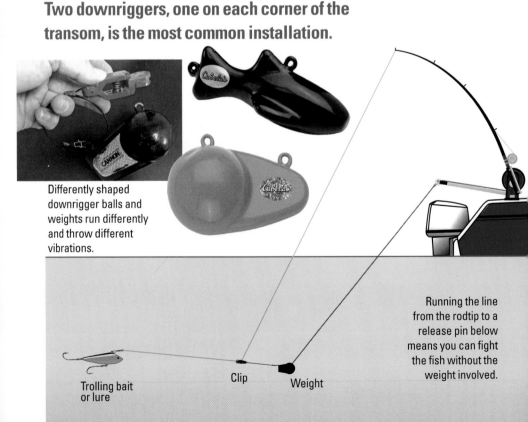

Differently shaped downrigger balls and weights run differently and throw different vibrations.

Trolling bait or lure

Clip

Weight

Running the line from the rodtip to a release pin below means you can fight the fish without the weight involved.

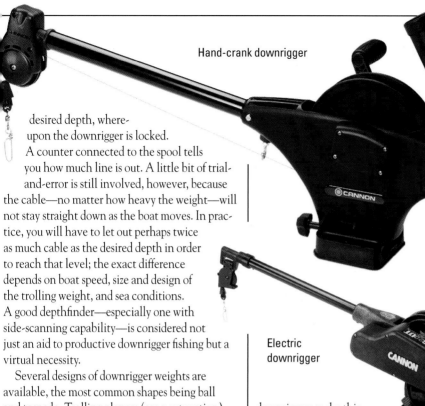

Hand-crank downrigger

desired depth, whereupon the downrigger is locked.

A counter connected to the spool tells you how much line is out. A little bit of trial-and-error is still involved, however, because the cable—no matter how heavy the weight—will not stay straight down as the boat moves. In practice, you will have to let out perhaps twice as much cable as the desired depth in order to reach that level; the exact difference depends on boat speed, size and design of the trolling weight, and sea conditions. A good depthfinder—especially one with side-scanning capability—is considered not just an aid to productive downrigger fishing but a virtual necessity.

Several designs of downrigger weights are available, the most common shapes being ball and torpedo. Trolling planers (see next section) are used by some anglers on their downriggers to replace the traditional heavy weights. Their users think they are more efficient at attaining—and maintaining—selected depths with less bellying of the cable.

Once a fish is hooked, the downrigger weight should be cranked up out of the way. Motorized

Electric downrigger

downriggers make this job easier, but hand-cranking is not too exhausting a task—thanks to the wide diameter of the reel—and many saltwater anglers prefer manual downriggers because of their dependability under corrosive conditions.

Two downriggers, one on each corner of the transom, is a common installation. Great Lakes charter skippers and other routine users of downriggers often mount several on their boats. They may place additional units on the gunnels, with arms positioned outward, or modify the transom to accept downrigger mounts at several positions.

Once a mounting bracket is installed, its downrigger can be set up and removed at will.

Downriggers are key gear in fishing for salmon in lakes and rivers.

Diving Planers

These devices—traditionally rigged directly to the fishing line—are much less expensive than downriggers but they do a good job of allowing anglers to troll baits at depths that are difficult, if not impossible, to obtain just with heavy sinkers, or even wire lines.

Planers are weighted, but the lead has little to do with depth potential. It serves only to keep the planer in the proper attitude, which is such that water pressure on the sloped face of the planer forces the device downward. It's the same principle that causes big-lipped artificial lures to dig deep when they are trolled or retrieved rapidly.

Several sizes of planer are offered. Planer size, combined with trolling speed, how much line is out, line diameter and weight of lure and terminal tackle, all affect the running depth of the lure. Even

Grouper can be taken by trolling with planers and downriggers.

Note, however, that considerable strain is exerted on the rod while the planer is being trolled, so fairly stout rods are necessary.

Rigging is easy. Tie your main fishing line to the front eye of the planer (the one nearest the lead

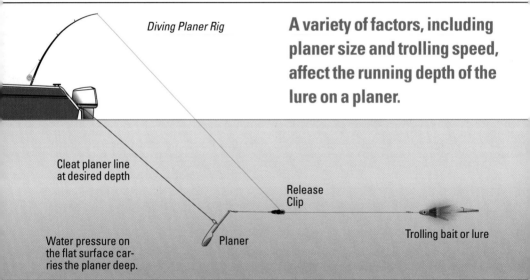

Diving Planer Rig

A variety of factors, including planer size and trolling speed, affect the running depth of the lure on a planer.

Cleat planer line at desired depth

Release Clip

Trolling bait or lure

Water pressure on the flat surface carries the planer deep.

Planer

more than with downriggers, much experimenting will be needed to determine individual needs and desires. Again, a depthsounder is a great help.

The design of manufactured planers allows them to "trip" after a fish is hooked. The running attitude is thereby changed, eliminating the water pressure so that the angler can fight the fish, even on fairly light tackle, without much extra strain.

sinker), and your leader to the back ring. Twenty- to 30 feet of leader is recommended for best results, but requires care when handling and catching a fast striking fish. Your lure, of course, will go at the end of that shorter line. Remember, once the planer reaches the rod, the battle switches to hand to hand combat with no rod or drag. A heavy leader, a strong hook, a good pair of gloves, and enough sense to let go and start over again are mandatory.

Some diving planers can be adjusted to carry the fishing line not only deep but also off to one side or the other, thus permitting additional lines to be trolled.

Various types of clips and at bottom, Z Wing planers.

High Speed Downrigger

A large planer can be made into a high speed downrigger by crimping a separate heavy line to its front eye, and throwing it overboard tied securely to a stern cleat. (Boat owners proud of their gelcoat may wish to place a rubber mat or just a towel to keep the planer line from rubbing the wax off the transom.) Once the planer is set, simply clip one end of a double-ended snapswivel to the planer line. Holding the snapswivel in place, open the other end and slide on a rubber band. After setting your bait as far back as you want it (at least

30 feet) wrap the rubber band around the fishing line four times and hook it on the swivel again. Close the swivel, and let it go. The forward motion of the boat will force the snap swivel to slide down very close to the planer.

This rig seems to work well with about 50 feet of 250-pound mono for the planer line. The bigger diameter line not only makes a secure connection to the planer, but it makes it easier to pull up the planer. You may need to experiment with rubber band sizes. For 30- to 50-pound test trolling line, a No. 32 rubber band breaks when you get a solid strike. When you get a strike simply rig another double-ended snapswivel, and send another bait down.

Large diving planer and cord, wound on hand-line spool for convenient deployment. Illustration below shows system in use.

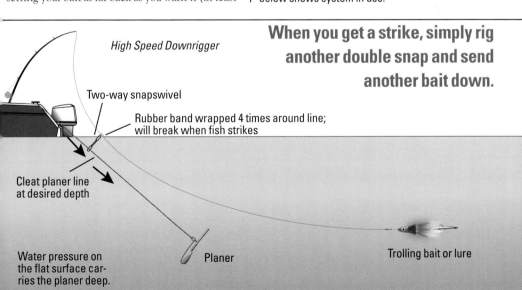

High Speed Downrigger

When you get a strike, simply rig another double snap and send another bait down.

Two-way snapswivel

Rubber band wrapped 4 times around line; will break when fish strikes

Cleat planer line at desired depth

Water pressure on the flat surface carries the planer deep.

Planer

Trolling bait or lure

Side Planers

For freshwater trolling in open lakes or wide rivers, side planers (also called planing boards) perform much the same function as outriggers. They are also popular on the Pacific Coast and, in fact, over much of

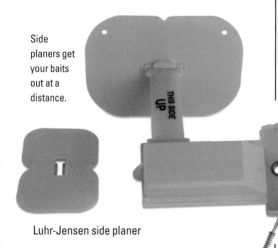

A diving planer

the country wherever lake trolling is a common fishing method, not only for salmon and trout but for various other species, particularly walleye. Where a good current is present, a side planer can also serve to carry a shore fisherman's lure out into the middle portions of a stream.

Planers are designed so that water pressure carries them away from the boat and off to the side when under way. Many large fishing vessels on the Great Lakes are fitted with masts, from which planers are sent out on both sides of the boat. Reels are mounted to the mast and hold the planer lines. In this elabo-

rate kind of setup, dual boards generally are used; that is, planers built of two connected boards, much like a little outrigger canoe. The planer lines carry release clips to which the fishing lines are attached. One or two release clips also may be incorporated into the planer itself. By using planners, large craft can troll lines directly behind the boat and several planer lines off to either side, all at the same time.

A style more easily used on small, open boats is the in-line planer. It is a single board that rides directly on the fishing line, which runs through a slit or hole in the board. Once the line is let out to the chosen trolling distance, it is clipped to a release device mounted on the board. After being pulled free by a strike, the line runs freely through the aforementioned opening in the board, putting but little additional pressure on the rod while a fish is being fought.

Rigging particulars are not given here because the actual setups differ slightly among various brands of boards; however, all come with detailed instructions.

Drift Socks and Sea Anchors

The devices that mariners call sea anchors are large fabric structures, shaped like a parachute or a cone, which help to stabilize the boat in rough seas or loss of power scenarios by catching the current and acting like an anchor.

Smaller sea anchors are generally referred to as drift socks by small-boat fishermen and are used to stabilize the boat in the current to aid in fishing. Many tackle dealers carry them in various sizes, for boats ranging from as small as 14 feet in length to as large as 30 feet or so.

The socks are often worth their weight in gold when drift fishing or slow trolling live baits in open water. What they do is slow the boat's speed dramatically, so that it doesn't move too fast out of the productive area. The slower speed also allows anglers to get their baits deep more quickly and keep them down longer.

In the Great Lakes and other large bodies of fresh

Side planers get your baits out at a distance.

THIS SIDE UP

Luhr-Jensen side planer

The drift sock can be deployed even in shallow water in windy conditions to slow the boat's drift.

water, drift socks are particularly well appreciated by walleye fishermen, who make excellent use of them to work relatively small patches of sunken structure. In coastal areas, drift socks help reef and bottom fishermen work sunken wrecks or ledges in depths too deep for comfortable anchoring by small boats. They are also standard equipment on many large open boats and charter craft that specialize in kite fishing, which often is practiced under conditions of strong wind and current.

Angling drift socks are generally made of nylon, with design features that allow them to open quickly and remain fully open just under the surface. They can be deployed amidships to achieve a broadside drift, which is a common approach when waves are not too rambunctious. Putting one small sea anchor deployed amidships on both sides of a slow trolling boat can be very effective. While drifting, the broadside attitude can be risky when waves grow high enough to pose any danger of swamping.

Kite fishermen generally run their drift socks off the bow, which is fine for that type of angling and also safe, even in high seas.

A correctly deployed parachute sea anchor keeps your boat's bow into the wind, allowing a controlled and slower downwind drift. Anglers often position a flatline bait close to the chute.

Rigging the Canepole

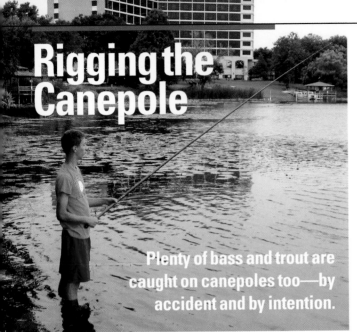

Plenty of bass and trout are caught on canepoles too—by accident and by intention.

Canepoles can pick fish out of lily pad-strewn and weedy waters.

Canepoles are not only maintaining their popularity, but are actually increasing in use as the years go by. Kids use them, of course, but so do countless grownups. Nobody can dispute the effectiveness of a pole for producing good strings of bream, perch, catfish and many other species.

Plenty of bass and trout are caught on canepoles too—sometimes by chance, but often by design.

Advances in poles have managed to keep pretty well abreast of advances in rods and reels. You can still buy the traditional bamboo pole just about everywhere, and in a great variety of lengths and actions. You can also buy jointed bamboo poles in two, three or four pieces.

And heading the array of poles are the modern, telescoping fiberglass sticks, which cost a few bucks but which stow and transport more easily and generally outlast their equivalent cost in canepoles.

As a rule of thumb, you should use as long a pole as you can comfortably handle—although, of course, shorter poles better fit certain requirements, such as fishing small, bush-lined creeks. Most fishermen in open water use 12- or 14- footers; a few prefer 16, or even 18, feet of pole in their hands.

For panfishing—where the pole really shines—the line should be of monofilament averaging 10 to 15 pounds in test. Some prefer lighter line, but panfish are not too selective, and the extra test will save a lot of re-rigging.

First, tie the line snugly around the pole about two feet down from the tip—just under the third or fourth "knuckle" of the bamboo. Then spiral the line upward and tie it around the tip. A good way to do this is to half-hitch it several times and then tape the end. Should the tip break, you're protected by the second tie and may not lose your fish or rig. Glass poles generally feature an eye at the end to make tying easy.

Your line should be about the same length as the pole—not much longer or it will become difficult to handle; not much shorter or it will limit your reach and/or fishing depth. By taping a small cleat near the butt of the pole, you can keep extra line on hand to be paid out when needed. Conversely, if your line happens to be too long, you can wrap the excess around the cleat. A rubber band or tape is used to keep line snug on the cleat. Small and inexpensive canepole reels serve the same purpose.

Although the great majority of pole fishermen use floats to signal a bite, some of the very best ones use no cork at all. They can better explore various depths, and are always sure of getting their bait to bottom when they want to, without having to test and adjust corks. It is surprisingly easy to feel a bite—even a nibble—with a pole. The movement of line through the water also signals a bite.

Cork

Hook

The Trotline

Used mostly for catfish, the trotline is merely a long, stout line that has dropper lines coming off it at regularly spaced intervals. Each dropper line is fitted with a hook and, usually, a sinker. To avoid the costs of sinkers, a trotliner may weight his droppers with old nuts or other scrap metal.

Many different baits can be used. Cutbait is a popular one. The bait doesn't necessarily have to rest on bottom, since trotlines are left out overnight, or longer, and catfish roam and feed throughout the water column after dark.

Ready-made trotlines are available, usually with up to about 30 dropper lines and hooks. Commercial fishermen use much longer lines with many more droppers.

In areas where boat traffic is little problem, trotlines are often rigged as in the illustration—with buoys and heavy weights at either end. Sometimes the trotline is tied between two trees or snags. One end of the line can be tied to a tree on shore, and the other end anchored out in the water.

Be sure to check for legal restrictions on trotlines in your state, or in the local waters you plan to fish. They are sometimes prohibited, and sometimes limited as to length or number of hooks. Live bait is not allowed on trotlines in most jurisdictions.

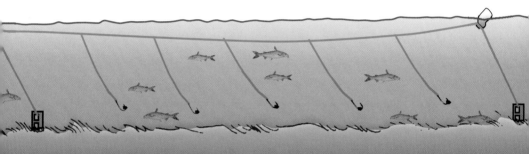

Recreational trotlines have comparatively few hooks and can be bought ready-made.

The Bush Line

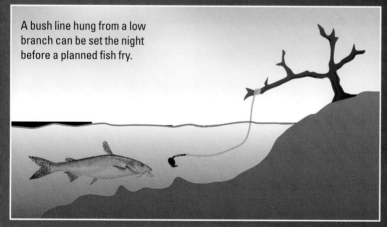

A bush line hung from a low branch can be set the night before a planned fish fry.

A favorite of catfishermen is the bush line. These lines are normally tied individually to springy branches along the bank of a river or creek before dark, then checked once or twice during the night, or next morning. The individual sets are short lengths of braided line with hooks tied to the end, baited with live or cutbait, liver, or the fisherman's secret potion. The line need only reach a foot or less under the surface. At night, catfish forage boldly and readily come to the top. When a fish is hooked, the springy limb "plays" it and keeps the line from breaking or the hook from pulling out. As with trotlines, be sure to check the legality of bush lines in particular areas. Also be sure to remove all lines, along with any markers you might put out, the next day.

CHAPTER 3

Fishing Lines & Terminal Tackle

Many an angler has suffered the despair of having the perfect size rod and reel, brand-new line, perfect leaders and the right lure for his target. Finally his magic moment comes, but he ends up broken hearted as his "fish of a lifetime" swims free because he had put it together with the wrong size swivel.

Choosing the right line and terminal tackle for the job is about keeping your entire outfit in balance. You want a natural presentation (think minimal tackle) with enough horsepower to maximize not only the size and number of fish you catch, but also how much you enjoy it.

For most of us, it's just about having a good time and catching a few fish. Let's look at what tools you'll need to close the deal.

You want a natural presentation with enough horsepower to maximize the size and number of fish you catch, but also how much you enjoy it.

A double hookup indicates that anglers are using the right size tackle for the quarry.

Fishing Lines

Modern lines are a quantum improvement over materials used in past generations.

Modern fishing lines are made of synthetic materials, either multiple small fibers (polyethylene braided line) or an extruded single strand (monofilament). They all represent a quantum improvement over natural materials used in past generations, such as cotton, silk and linen. The synthetics don't rot, they need not be dried after use, and they are more uniform in strength and diameter. The various types of modern fishing lines can be summarized as follows:

MONOFILAMENT Mono is ideal for all spinning reels, regardless of reel size, because the "springiness" inherent in even the limpest monofilaments helps increase casting performance with fixed-spool tackle. Mono is also widely used for baitcasting, for ocean trolling and for saltwater fishing in general. Moreover, it is the least expensive of all, and is used for leader material as well as for line.

ULTRA-THIN BRAIDS Introduced in the early 1990s, ultra-thin braids comprise the newest family of braided lines. They are characterized by their narrow diameter and incredible strength when compared to monofilament. The original versions had zero stretch, but some of the newest additions to the market have included a fiber that provides up to 10% stretch compared to any other lines.

The newer lines are far more supple than the first versions, and thus easier to tie and less likely to knot. On average, these lines test as strong as monofilament lines three to four times thicker. They are built of many tiny strands of modern synthetic fibers, primarily Kevlar and polyethylene.

FLUOROCARBON Fluoro is another high-tech product that's lately been tossed into competition for the modern angler's favor. Composed of polyvinylidene fluoride (PVDF), it technically is a monofilament but is seldom referred to as such, so as to avoid confusion with nylon monofilament. Because it is tougher and has better abrasion resistance than nylon, and because it is less visible in the water, fluorocarbon quickly gained wide and enthusiastic endorsement as leader material, but its high cost and stiff handling qualities held back its early acceptance as fishing line. Now, however, there are several different formulations available, some of them soft for use as fishing line, others retaining the traditional hardness that is superior for leaders. Lines made by "blending" fluorocarbon with other synthetic substances have greatly improved both the handling qualities and price attractiveness.

Another distinctive characteristic of fluorocarbon line is that it sinks more readily than monofilament or braided polyethylene. Anglers casting diving crankbaits or certain kinds of worm rigs often favor the fluorocarbon for that reason.

Nylon monofilament is practical and affordable. It's also recyclable, for bird-safe disposal.

FISHING WITH FLUOROCARBON Competitive bass fishing has taught us that success and failure is hidden in a thousand little details. For a dedicated bass fisherman it is not enough to have the greatest new lure. Each situation can call for a completely different presentation of that lure.

A bass fisherman flipping into heavy cover is going to have to use braid, because of its incredible strength to diameter ratio and its superior abrasion resistance. It has essentially no stretch, and is impervious to weeds and logs that would shred any mono. It also floats. That means that instead of sinking down and around the logs, it floats over the top of them. Braid's tiny diameter also means that it casts farther than mono of the same pound test. Braid also has its own set of drawbacks. It's much more apt to get wind knots that can amount to the worst backlash you've ever seen. It's also far more visible in the water than mono of any kind.

When our bass fisherman moves to fishing clear water, he will probably throw his favorite lure on fluorocarbon. Fluorocarbon reflects far less light than regular mono which makes it much harder for fish to see. Many bass fishermen pack their entire reels with it. Fluorocarbon sinks faster than regular nylon monofilament. That makes it perfect for fishing worms and other baits you need to crawl across the bottom of a clear lake, even when you'll be dealing with logs or other bottom structure.

MODERN ARGUMENTS FOR MONO Traditional nylon monofilament has stretch, forgiveness, and is easier to tie securely than braid or fluorocarbon. Because it is softer and more flexible, you can throw it farther than fluorocarbon of the same diameter. Forgiveness can be crucial when throwing a topwater bait. The most common reason all fishermen miss a topwater bite is because they strike too soon. It's impossible to see a big fish rush your topwater lure after hours of fruitless casting and yet resist the urge to strike too soon. The fraction of a second that mono will take to tighten up and react to your hookset may well mean the difference in a trophy or just another fish story.

Modern Braids vs. Monofilament

Line abrasion on structure such as these mangrove roots can lead to a lost fish—and speculation about which type of line is best for the application.

Whether he fishes in salt water or fresh, today's angler is pretty sure to be faced with a common dilemma: Should he use monofilament line or one of the "super" braids that in recent years have taken the fishing world by storm? There are no quick or easy answers. Although the new braids can boast vast numbers of converts in every watery arena, the over-all sales of monofilament haven't suffered much and so, obviously, there remains much room for debate. In the end, each fisherman will have to determine his personal preference.

No doubt the biggest appeal of the modern braided lines is their strength-to-diameter ratio. These lines average three or four times the breaking test of most monofilaments of comparable diameter. The advantages of thinner line include increased casting distance, more reel capacity, and less drag in the water—which can aid a line's ability to get deep. The latter is of immense value in certain types of fishing, including deep jigging with lures and baits and with deep dropping for deep-living bottom species. And of course, greater strength in a line of easily castable size means that fewer fish will be lost to breakoffs and snags.

The absence of stretch benefits the fisherman by making it easier to "feel" a softly biting fish. The hook can also be set more easily and, during the fight, all of the angler's pressure is felt by the fish; none is absorbed by the stretchiness of monofilament. However, for some applications, like trolling, that stretchiness of monofilament becomes very valuable when it absorbs the shock of a strike by a fish and lets the fish take the bait. That "shock absorber" quality of monofilament is still highly prized by many anglers.

One big disadvantage of the braids is higher price. Although the cost continues to decline, manufacturing differences will always keep monofilament considerably cheaper. Another bad rap is that the braids tend to "dig in" on a reel spool. For this and other reasons, it's a good idea to use some softer backing line, or filler, on the reel before spooling the braid. This will also soften the cost, since less line need be used.

Mono is less visible and is usually needed for leader, even with braided line. Also, mono will win most arguments for fishing true-test in the lightest line classes. The finest braids are just too thin for easy handling and knot-tying. And when the line becomes accidentally knotted it can be nearly impossible to clear.

When using heavy tests of braided line, the angler must realize that the absence of stretch can impart serious jolts to both tackle and fishermen when a big fish strikes or lunges suddenly. Pain, and even injury, to wrist or shoulder have occurred in such instances, so if your aim is to administer heavy punishment to a big fish, you should wear a good harness. Otherwise, the fish may be the one who does the punishing. Another danger inherent in the braids is that they can cut your hand severely if you don't take care when drawing knots tight. Many big game anglers are now using a combination of mono and hollow core braid as a great two-part system. They use the relatively thin, hollow braid as a backing for the "topshot" of monofilament. This increases the effective line capacity of the reel while offering some of the benefits of braid—such as reduced friction—without sacrificing the shock-absorption of monofilament.

Choosing Monofilament

There are many different brands of monofilament line, and they vary widely in handling qualities. There is really no "best" brand, or type, for all kinds of fishing. And price is not always a reliable guide to the best choice for your own fishing. As a rule, the highest-priced lines are those which have been highly processed for limpness, and for the smallest ratio of breaking test to line diameter. The limpest lines, of course, are a joy to handle because they lie on the spool beautifully and do not tend to bulge or spring off in unwanted fashion (it bears repeating, however, that even the limpest monofilaments are not nearly so relaxed as braided lines, and that some spring is beneficial to spincasters. For most freshwater fishing, limp monos are often preferred.)

The saltwater angler, however, often finds that the ultra-soft monofilaments are not his cup of tea. They may "fatigue" or weaken faster under the pressures of big fish, big lures and various other

Lines are sold in a variety of sizes to fit your needs— spooling one reel or ten.

rigors of salty fishing. Also, the knot strength of some is below acceptable standards for ocean heavyweights. Therefore, the saltwater veteran is quite willing to sacrifice some limpness for lines which better resist abrasion and "fatigue," and which—because they probably also have a slightly harder finish—provide greater knot strength. Most of the major manufacturers now offer several different kinds (not grades) of monofilament lines, so that anglers can pick out those that best fit the needs of various angling specialties.

Here's an important word about line-test: In most cases, the line you buy will actually test heavier than is stated on the label. This is the way most anglers like it. But if you go in for competitive fishing in clubs and public tournaments, or if you have your aim set on possible world records, you want to make sure that your line does not test heavier than the allowable limit. If you plan on fishing tournaments based on line test, or fishing for world record line class fish, make sure you buy line stamped "IGFA class."

No matter what you may think of the metric system, the first impact of metric conversion on the world of sportfishing was a definite boon to American anglers, for it had the effect of giving their lines a safety margin of about 10 percent in the light-tackle classes when tested for world-record catches. The International Game Fish

IGFA line classes for world records, and the maximum test in each class

Pound Class	Kilogram Class	Max. IGFA Test (in pounds)
2	1	2.20
4	2	4.40
6	3	6.61
8	4	8.81
12	6	13.22
16	8	17.63
20	10	22.04
30	15	33.06
50	24	52.91
80	37	82.57
130	60	132.27

Filling an offshore reel takes an experienced hand. It requires just the right amount of pressure on the spool to pack it evenly.

Association, keeper of world records, adopted the metric system for its line-test classes in 1976—not because it was trying to hasten American exposure to the metric system, but simply because the kilogram is the standard measurement of weight in most other countries. The IGFA, after all, keeps records world-wide.

Since line classes now are listed for both pounds and kilograms, and since the maximum allowable line strength is based on the kilogram class, it amounts to a liberalization of about 10 percent for lines that are labeled in pounds. Before we bog down in decimal points, let's just say that many premium brands of line you buy nowadays may well test in their labeled class for IGFA purposes, whereas, before liberalization, record-size catches made on standard-labeled lines often were thrown out because the line overtested. To play it safe, anglers had to pre-test their lines, or else buy special tournament-grade line. Of course, if record-chasing is your game, that's still a good idea.

That kind of fiddling with line-test always has been a headache for the record-seeking angler. And even though most fishermen don't actively seek records, they have frequently run afoul of line-test problems when they happened to catch a potential record.

Avid light-tackle anglers were quick to recognize and welcome the liberalized maximum tests, but many failed to take into account the fact that, in all cases, the tests listed are WET tests. The IGFA always soaks lines before testing—and wet lines lose about 15 percent of strength. Therefore, anglers who continue to use "tournament" lines may be short-changing themselves. As a comparative example, let's look in the table to get a comparison of "tournament" 12-pound line, as opposed to "regular" 12-pound line. Often, 12-pound tournament line will dry-test around 10 pounds. Take away 15 percent for wet-test, and the actual strength of the line is 8.5—nearly 5 pounds lighter than the 13.22 pounds allowed by the IGFA in the 12-pound class! Since you pay a premium price for "tournament" line, you might be dishing out extra money to buy yourself a handicap. If you go chasing records, it's always a good idea to pre-test your line.

The increased use of braided lines led the IGFA to recently introduce length-category records for species, which do not require pound-test breaking strength tests, so that all anglers, no matter their choice of lines, can participate in the quest for IGFA records.

Table of Wet and Dry Tests

Standard Label (Pounds)	If Dry Test Is	Wet Test Would Be	Allowable Wet Test Is
2	2.5	2.13	2.2
4	5	4.25	4.4
8	10	8.5	8.8
12	15	12.75	13.22
16	20	17	17.6
20	25	21.3	22
30	38	32.3	33

Spooling Line
REVOLVING SPOOL REEL

Mount the reel firmly on the rod butt. Place the supply spool on a firm spindle of some sort, or have someone hold the supply spool on a pencil or similar object to serve as an axle. Grasp the foregrip of the rod with your left hand, and with the same hand extend your thumb and one or two fingers upward so that you can grasp the line simultaneously. As you crank the reel with your right hand, apply pressure to the line with the fingers of your left hand. You will have to judge the proper amount of pressure; very little is needed for light lines, but with lines of 50-pound or up, you will have to bear down hard and perhaps even wear a glove.

On a levelwind reel you can crank on line nearly to the rim of the spool, but if your reel has no level-wind you should leave a margin of about a quarter of an inch to provide at least a small margin for uneven winding.

In the excitement of trying to bring in a big fish it's easy for an inexperienced angler not to notice when line starts to pile up on one side of the spool until it binds and "freezes" the reel. Doing a little level-winding with your thumb will prevent this but it doesn't hurt, either, to avoid filling the spool too high to begin with.

In the excitement of bringing in a big fish, it's easy not to notice when line starts to pile up on one side of the spool.

SPINNING REELS

Mount the reel firmly on the rod butt. Grasp the rod ahead of the foregrip with your non-cranking hand, and take the line in the same grasp, so that it runs between thumb and one or two fingers. Place your spool of line on the floor. Do not allow the supply spool to surrender line by revolving, but merely let the line slip off the end of the spool. Turn the reel crank as you apply light pressure with thumb and finger to the oncoming line. Use just enough pressure to assure a snug wrap. Do not fill quite to the edge of the spool's lip. Too much line will cause several wraps to jump off at the same time and tangle. If this should happen, cut off the excess line

Having a portable line winder at home makes it possible to make last-minute line changes.

and your spool will be filled just right!

Before spooling line in the manner described above, you must check the bail of your reel to see in which direction it travels around your reel spool. Bails on most spinning reels travel in a clockwise direction, therefore the line must slip off the supply spool in a counter-clockwise direction or else severe twist will be imparted to the line as you wind it on.

Anglers who re-spool often might consider buying a line-winding machine. Since a typical machine of this sort turns both the reel spool and the supply spool as line goes on, it can be used to fill both revolving and spinning reel spools. As a less costly approach, many larger tackle shops will spool your line for you, by machine, if you buy it from them.

Most spinning reel bails rotate clock-wise. So line must come off the spool counterclockwise.

Removing Line   When the old line has to go

Motorized tools that use flashlight batteries are available for removing old line from reels. Or you can buy an attachment—or make your own—that converts any electric drill into a line de-spooler. Lacking any such gadget, you must pull the line off manually, a long and tiresome chore.

Monofilament may be disposed of in containers labeled for recycling, available at many tackle shops and marinas. It's critically important not to leave mono or braided lines of any length on the waterways where they pose a risk of entanglement and death to birds and other creatures.

Left, a drill and plastic bottle has been fashioned into a line remover. Left lower, a de-spooling tool run on battery power.

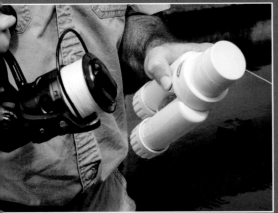

No matter how you gather old line off of reels, make sure to dispose of it properly. Recycle it where that option is available.

Fish Hooks

Set hook on foot of guide, not to scratch guide's inner ring.

The first step in selecting an appropriate hook is to rid yourself of the notion that an exact size of an exact pattern is necessary for fishing success. Certain patterns are desirable for different specialties, and you have to be somewhere in the neighborhood when it comes to size. But there is a great deal of leeway, as evidenced by the fact that even professional guides may have vastly different ideas as to what makes the best hook for a specific task.

Before trying to select a pattern and size, it will help to understand how hook sizes are designated. Small hooks are scaled by a system of straight numbers—the larger the number, the smaller the hook. The biggest hook labeled by this system is a No. 1. Some very tiny hooks, used mostly for certain demanding types of trout fishing, might wear numbers as high as 20 or 22.

For some strange reason, hooks larger than No. 1 (as almost all saltwater and many freshwater hooks are) wear numbers that begin with No. 1/0, and go up as the hook size goes up. The largest sizes you're ever apt to see in sportfishing run from 14/0 to 20/0. Usually, the effective range for a specific application spans several sizes. But there are general considerations that must be always taken into account.

First, the size of the hook is often determined more by the size of the bait than by the size of the fish you're after. You need a hook that will leave ample point and barb exposure after your bait is fixed to it but, on the other hand, you don't want a hook so large that the live bait you're using is unable to swim naturally while carrying it, or so large that it throws a rigged bait out of balance and deprives it of attractive action.

Second, your hook must be strong enough to prevent its straightening out under the drag pressure you plan on using. Hook strength is increased slightly as size of the hook is increased—but only slightly. In marginal cases you can increase the size of your hook by a couple of numbers and feel safer. But to obtain any drastic change in strength, while keeping the size range within reasonable limits, you'll have to go to a different hook altogether—one of similar size but heavier, sturdier construction. Take note, though, that as the strength of your line decreases and the whippiness of your rod increases, you will have to use hooks of thinner wire to insure a positive hookset, because of the light striking force you will be able to apply.

When in doubt about choosing from among several available hooks in a range of no more than three size numbers, pick the smallest size. It is a much more common mistake to use a hook too large than one too small.

Following are some other hook characteristics that can help you make a common-sense choice.

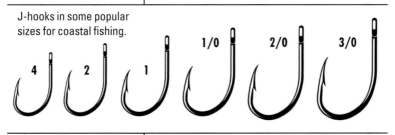

J-hooks in some popular sizes for coastal fishing.

4 2 1 1/0 2/0 3/0

Fish hook numeration decreases as hook size increases—until you reach the largest models, the "ought" sizes, whereupon the numeration begins to increase. The livebait J-hooks above, and the hook illustrations on the following pages, are of VMC brand hooks.

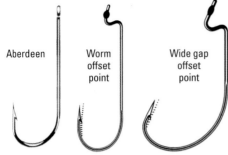

Aberdeen | Worm offset point | Wide gap offset point

Many styles of "worm" hooks are available for rigging natural and artificial baits. Note that the term "offset" commonly refers to the point of the hook (described below), but may also be applied to hooks wherein the eye is offset from the shank. Offset eye hooks are often used for rigging soft-plastic baits.

Freshwater Hooks

Hooks used in fresh water are generally made of lighter wire than hooks designed principally for use in the salt. The usual finishes are bronze and blue. Most fishermen feel a subdued tone is less likely to alert a potential biter, especially when using insect baits or bottom baits. Some live baiters, however, do prefer a nickel-plated or gold-plated hook, figuring that a little extra flash can only add to the appeal of the swimming bait.

There are numerous style variations, which you can find on hooks of either of the two basic designs—long shanks and short shanks, turned-up eyes and turned-down eyes, straight points and curved points.

Hooks with turned-up eyes are used mainly in making certain artificial lures (flies and jigs, mostly). They are of little concern to the bait fisherman, except in a few specialties, such as fishing salmon eggs for trout. Hooks with turned-down eyes are used to make snells.

A long-shank hook is more easily removed from a fish after you catch him, and is often chosen by anglers for just that advantage. But hooks of normal and short-shank design are less likely to be noticed by fish, and so you may have to abandon

The short shank and extra strength make the octopus-style hook (non-circle) perfect for hauling big bass out of heavy cover on the bass fisherman's "Wacky Worm."

the long-shank if it seems to be cutting down on your number of bites.

Some freshwater panfishermen like to use hooks made of very light wire that bends easily. When you get snagged on bottom, extra pressure straightens the hook and allows it to come free. You simply bend the light wire back into proper position and go on fishing. Naturally, you don't want the hook so light that it might bend when you have a fish on. And if you think you might hook a bass or big catfish while fishing for perch, then you definitely should use a hook of stouter wire.

Straight or Offset?

Wading past the numerous patterns of freshwater hooks, we will consider only two basic designs. (1) The straight design, where the shank, the bend and the point are in a single plane: that is, if you lay the straight hook flat on a table, the point does not protrude, but lies as flat as the shank. (2) The offset hook, in which the point is bent to one side or other of the shank.

The offset point hook is the choice of many fishermen, because it is less likely to be pulled from a fish's mouth without digging in.

On the other hand, the straight design will usually hook a striking fish, although occasionally it might miss one that an offset would have hooked. The difference in hooking percentage is slight, at best, but enough to swing many folks on the side of the offset. Offset hooks, however, are not often used on artificial lures because they can affect lure balance and action.

3° OFFSET POINT
Hook point is offset from line of bend.

Weedless Hooks

A word must be said about weedless hooks, as these are important to many freshwater fishermen, and are also commonly used in salt water.

The usual weedless hook is nothing more than a familiar style of hook to which has been added an extension of light wire that protects the point, and helps keep it from snagging on weeds or obstructions.

Some artificial lures—usually spoons and spinners, but often flies, jigs and plugs—come equipped with weedguards. When an angler buys separate weedless hooks, he normally intends to use them for rigging artificial worms and other plastic baits, but they can be handy, as well, for fishing minnows and other live baits. Usually, you should hook a minnow or other baitfish through the lips when using a weedless hook. Sizes of weedless hooks are denoted by the standard "0" system given earlier.

RIGGING WEEDLESS

Another family of weedless hooks is made weedless by design, rather than by adding a wire weedguard. In most of these, the shank is bent near the eye, so that the point is on the same level as the eye. Therefore, the eye and extreme forward portion of the shank serve as a weedguard. Further snag-proofing is provided by the way in which plastic baits are rigged to these hooks— with the point buried in the body of the soft bait. These hooks are commonly referred to as "worm hooks," although plastic worms can be rigged in weedless fashion— that is, with the point buried—to long-shank hooks of standard patterns as well.

It should also be noted that circle hooks are fairly weedless and so would make good choices for use on many lures used among snags and weeds.

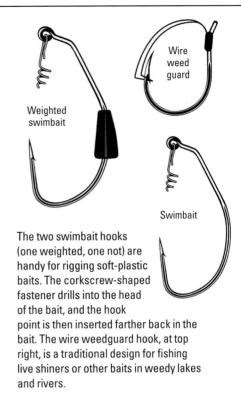

The two swimbait hooks (one weighted, one not) are handy for rigging soft-plastic baits. The corkscrew-shaped fastener drills into the head of the bait, and the hook point is then inserted farther back in the bait. The wire weedguard hook, at top right, is a traditional design for fishing live shiners or other baits in weedy lakes and rivers.

Offset shank hook with jerkbait. Start by piercing the center point of the head and almost immediately bringing the point out the bottom of the bait, and insert it back into the slit mid-way in the bait. Many anglers will bring the point all the way through the bait and then reinsert it lightly into the top of the bait.

Saltwater Hooks

If you haven't already done so, read the discussion of freshwater hooks for a comparison of the straight design and offset design, and for notes on point and eye variations.

In general, offset hooks make excellent choices for stillfishing in salt water with any sort of natural bait, whether live or cut. Snelling an offset eye means you will always have a direct pull opposite the bend of the hook. Straight-design hooks may be freely substituted for offset hooks in any kind of still-fishing. However, the offset hooks probably have a slightly higher percentage of solid hookups. A hook tied by the eye has the same potential problem regardless of the knot used. You may cast it out or drop it down with the knot at the top of the eye, but nibblers and potential bait stealers may soon tug on the bait until your knot is off center. A snelled hook is attached directly to the shank, and can't be knocked off center.

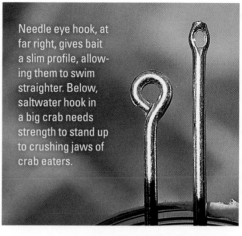

Needle eye hook, at far right, gives bait a slim profile, allowing them to swim straighter. Below, saltwater hook in a big crab needs strength to stand up to crushing jaws of crab eaters.

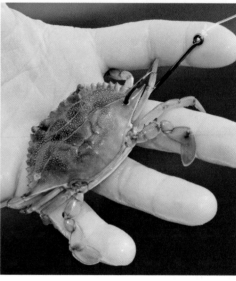

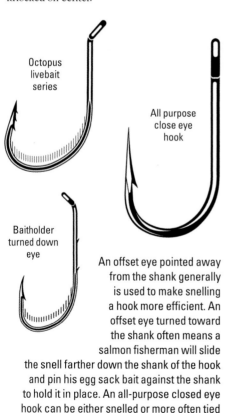

Octopus livebait series

All purpose close eye hook

Baitholder turned down eye

An offset eye pointed away from the shank generally is used to make snelling a hook more efficient. An offset eye turned toward the shank often means a salmon fisherman will slide the snell farther down the shank of the hook and pin his egg sack bait against the shank to hold it in place. An all-purpose closed eye hook can be either snelled or more often tied with an improved clinch or uni knot.

Kahle or "wide gap" hooks are commonly used in surf fishing rigs. They hook fish even without a hookset by the angler.

Kahle hook

Straight-design hooks should be used with all rigged saltwater baits (strip, ballyhoo, mullet, etc.), because offset hooks often cause the bait to spin, impairing a trolled presentation.

Hooks with ringed eyes are used for most inshore fishing, and much offshore fishing as well (with fairly light tackle and reasonably low drag).

Hooks with needle eyes (that is, with the eye drilled through the shank, rather than formed by bending the shank into a circle) are chosen by many offshore fishermen for bluewater trolling. Baits such as ballyhoo or mullet are more natural looking when rigged without the eye of the hook causing the gills to flare.

For the really heavy offshore specialties—marlin, shark, giant bluefin tuna, monster bottom fish—you must use a big-game hook, forged of extra-thick metal as added protection against straightening. These can be identified at a glance by their flattened appearance, as well as by size. Naturally, the eyes of big-game hooks are also of the heavy-duty type—either a needle-eye or else a ring-eye that has been braised in closed position for strength. "Monster hooks" of this sort may also be used inshore for shark fishing.

Very short-shanked hooks—almost a perfect "U" in shape—are commonly referred to as livebait hooks. They are usually chosen in small sizes so that live baits don't have much weight to tote around, yet they are built strong because they are often used to target large fish. A rule of thumb is to select the smallest live-bait hook that will afford complete clearance of the point and barb after the bait is hooked up.

Keep in mind that in some waters, hook types may be specified by law, such as the stipulation that when targeting reef fish with natural baits in Gulf of Mexico waters, non-offset circle hooks must be used.

When choosing livebait hooks, extra emphasis should be given to the diameter of the shank, which should be thin enough not to kill the bait.

Livebait hook

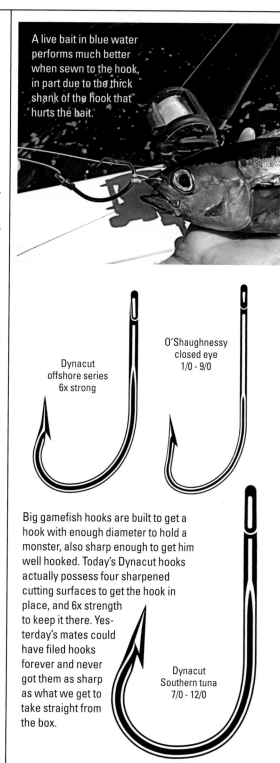

A live bait in blue water performs much better when sewn to the hook, in part due to the thick shank of the hook that hurts the bait.

Dynacut offshore series 6x strong

O'Shaughnessy closed eye 1/0 - 9/0

Big gamefish hooks are built to get a hook with enough diameter to hold a monster, also sharp enough to get him well hooked. Today's Dynacut hooks actually possess four sharpened cutting surfaces to get the hook in place, and 6x strength to keep it there. Yesterday's mates could have filed hooks forever and never got them as sharp as what we get to take straight from the box.

Dynacut Southern tuna 7/0 - 12/0

Circle hook works on hooking the mouth.

Circle Hooks

For fishing with natural bait, circle hooks have been surging in popularity in recent years, and are now seeing wide use on artificial lures as well. Circle hooks aren't really new, having been the mainstay of commercial longliners and a few recreational bottom-fishing captains for many years, but the masses of sportfishermen have been slow in taking them to heart—the main reason being that they simply do not look as if their points could ever grab hold of a fish. Not only do they provide a more positive hookup with less hook-setting effort, but they almost always take hold in the corner of a fish's mouth. Therefore, circle hooks are as valuable to the meat fisherman as to the angler who wishes to release his catch without harm! In many areas of the country, circle hooks are now required when using natural baits. Also, the use of circle hooks when fishing for sailfish is widely credited with helping rebuild stocks off the Eastern U.S. due to decreased mortality.

As the name indicates, the hook is shaped in nearly a circle, with the point curved inward toward the shank, and downward. The gap between point and shank is often quite narrow. All in all, as already mentioned, the circle hook is a most unlikely apparatus—until you put it into use. To oversimplify the explanation of how it works, most fish take the hook and bait in a single gulp, but when pressure is applied by the tightened line and the fish turns away, the hook nearly always slips easily from the throat and lodges in the corner of the mouth.

New users of circle hooks must learn quickly that they must not strike in the traditional hard-yanking way, but must instead simply crank the reel until the line comes tight, and then apply strong, steady pressure with the rod.

Circle hooks have been used mainly for heavier saltwater applications and with natural bait. More recently, though, they have made huge gains in shallow salt water and also in fresh water for both natural bait and for artificial lures—due not only to growing awareness on the part of anglers, but also to the fact that manufacturers are now turning out a full array of circle hooks in all sizes, from tiny ones suitable for use with dry flies, to mammoth ones that hook and hold the biggest gamefish. Moreover, circle hooks are available in many styles, covering all the same options as traditional hooks, such as flat or offset, turned-up or turned-down eye, and light or heavy wire. You'll also find circle hooks with various slight differences in the shape of the "circle"—some being more elliptical than round. All, however, retain the same relative position of hook point to shank.

If using circle hooks for the first time, be sure to affix the bait so that the point and barb are left fully exposed, and the small clearance between point and shank is entirely unobstructed. Good point clearance is advisable with any type of hook, but is absolutely critical to success with the circles.

Sureset circle hook

Nemesis circle hook 3x strong

Tournament circle hook 1x strong

Tournament circle hook 6x strong

Circle hooks have been gaining popularity for several decades now. Still mostly used in salt water, they have spread from the longline commercial fishery into almost everywhere natural bait is used. They are also spreading among lure makers. Circle hooks are designed to twist into the corner of the mouth of a fish and prevent mortally wounding the fish by snagging in his gills or stomach. Long a staple in the billfish fishery, circle hooks are now mandated by law in many bottom fishing areas.

Swivels and Snapswivels

Swivels perform two major functions for fishermen: They reduce or prevent line twist, and they serve as handy connectors between line and leader.

All swivels are basically the same in that they have two (or more) eyes that revolve on either end of a central unit. The major divisions within the basic design are the barrel or crane swivels on the one hand, and ballbearing swivels on the other. All types become snapswivels when they are combined with snaps of any sort that open and close to afford a quick connection to leader or rig. Three-eyed swivels are used in making specialized rigs, some of which are shown in Chapter 6.

Make sure that your selected swivel is stronger than your line but not big enough to spook the fish.

Premium barrel swivel with stainless steel eyes is much stronger than all-brass model.

As with all terminal tackle the age-old principle still applies. The less tackle you put in the water the better. Whether it's down-sizing to 4-pound test to fool the wariest bluegill or dropping to a 40-pound fluorocarbon leader for a picky white marlin, oftentimes less is more. The less tackle you show a fish, the more natural your bait appears. Today's fishermen needing swivels have the choice, for example, of using a conventional 50-pound swivel or the option of using a similar strength, but smaller (and more expensive) stainless swivel the size of an ant.

Non-stainless barrel and crane swivels are sized

Yellowfin tuna are sure to test your tackle and connections.

Barrel Swivels

Non stainless barrel swivels, because they are inexpensive, get the call for most duties. They can be used for any sort of connection where the potential for line twist is minimal or nonexistent.

Two factors should influence your decision as to what size barrel swivel to buy. You only have to make sure the swivel is strong enough to withstand the drag pressures to which they will be subjected, and large enough to accommodate the diameter of the lines or leaders with which they will be used.

Today's fishermen have the choice of using a conventional 50-pound swivel or a similar-strength swivel that's ant-size.

by exactly the same weird numerical system as are hooks: that is, large numbers mean small swivels. As the numbers get smaller the swivel gets larger—up to a No. 1. At that point, the "0" system kicks

To really solve the problem of line twist with lures or rigs that spin, you'll have to move up to a ballbearing swivel.

in, and the number designations start to rise—the range being from 1/0 to a huge 12/0.

Most casting and light-line applications, whether with spinning or revolving-spool tackle, can be covered with No. 12, 10 or 8 swivels. General angling with light tackle (lines up to 30-pound test) calls for No. 8 up to about No. 1 or 1/0. The heaviest applications, with rods and reels, will require swivels no bigger than 1/0 to 3/0. The really big swivels are designed for use with heavy handlines, outrigger lines and such. Another choice you'll be faced with is in color or finish—and that matters but little unless you fish in situations where toothy fish might possibly mistake your bright swivel for the flash of a small baitfish and cut your line. If that's a consideration—and it usually is in salt water—choose swivels with a dull black finish. Non stainless barrel swivels can reduce line twist to some extent, but their ability to do so vanishes rapidly as load, or pressure, increases. To really solve the problem of line twist when you use lures or rigs that spin a great deal, you have to move up to a higher class of swivel—the ballbearing swivel.

Snapswivels

Several types of snaps are attached to either barrel or ballbearing swivels to turn them into snapswivels. Snapswivels serve definite purposes—one of which is NOT to be tied routinely to the end of every fishing line, as beginners often seem to think.

Casters can make fine use of small snapswivels when they fling twisting lures, such as most spoons and many

spinners. Those lures are metallic themselves, so the dab of extra metal that a snapswivel puts at their noses is not likely to detract from their appeal. However, with natural bait rigs that pose a spinning problem, it's best to position a swivel somewhere farther up the line rather than to stick a snapswivel

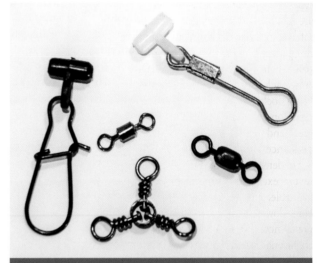

Above, from left to right, sinker slide, ballbearing swivel, three-way swivel, conventional swivel, sinker slide with plastic sleeve. Below, from top, tactical clip, ballbearing locking snaps (2), and conventional barrel locking snaps (2).

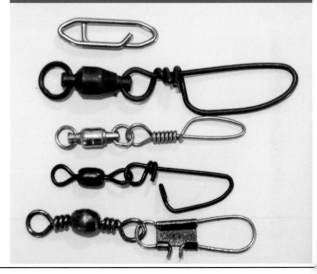

to your plain hook. For casters the choice of where to put any swivel is pretty easy. Determine the proper distance you want your lure to hang below your rodtip, and use either a small snapswivel or a swivel to join your line and leader. Bottom fishermen and trollers have the option of moving the swivel farther from the bait, if they prefer.

As mentioned, there are several types of snaps, and not all of them are reliable—least of all the common safety-pin type, which too often opens at inopportune moments—meaning when you're fighting a tougher-than-usual fish. A better bet for freshwater anglers would be the lock snap, similar in design to the common safety snap, but with a 90-degree bend that fits in a slot for extra resistance to pulling open.

For demanding work in salt water, several excellent types of snaps are available. A choice among them can come down merely to personal, or regional, preferences. Atlantic anglers largely stick to the traditional coastlock or tournament snap. Many Pacific Coast anglers like the McMahon snap. Scattered users of the corkscrew snap may be found anywhere. Some of these snapswivels offer a choice between single-ring and double-ring make-up. Both are strong enough, but the double rings often make for easier and more positive rigging.

Ball Bearing Swivels

These swivels really do have tiny ball bearings in their innards, and you can readily tell it by their performance. However, there is a sharp line of delineation within the ball bearing types.

For most fishing, regular bulk pack snapswivels are fine. For really demanding work, especially in offshore angling and for the most severe twist challenges, you really should go to an expensive, stainless steel top-quality, ball-bearing swivel . The price may shock you on first reading but, when absorbed within the overall cost of ocean angling, it's little enough to pay for virtually foolproof reliability. In ball bearing models, a No. 1 is the smallest, and the numbers rise with the size of the swivel. Sizes 1 to 3 fit the bill for casting and light trolling. Sizes 3 to 5 are mid-range sizes for general use. Sizes 6 to 8 are the big-game sizes.

Once again anglers have the choice of using more expensive stainless steel which can achieve similar strength in much smaller sizes. Size designations in snapswivels generally run the same as for their non-snap counterparts.

An alternative to conventional snaps is a Tactical Angler clip, used to switch out lures in seconds without having to pinch a wire to lock in place.

CHAPTER 4

Angling Knots

Lots of us learned our knot tying from our time as Boy Scouts. I'll bet most of us remember the bowline, the square knot, a few different hitches and that's about it. We can tie them in our sleep, and they are enough for dozens of applications. Learn a few knots—especially the uni-system—and you'll be covered for just about anything.

Fair warning though. There are no compromises when it comes to tying knots. Imagine just putting together a jug line for each of your eight grandkids to leave out overnight for catfish, with a Toys"R"Us gift card on the line for the biggest catfish. Then imagine a 4-year old baby girl bawling her eyes out because her giant catfish got tangled in a tree, and while you're trying to drag it out, YOUR knot fails.

I'll bet you'll only let that happen once.

Learn a few knots—especially the uni system—and you'll be covered for just about anything.

Good knots are essential for pulling fish out of heavy cover. Several varieties are illustrated on the following pages.

Uni Knot

Rules of Good Knot Tying

Moistening knots in monofilament will make it much easier to draw them down.

Smooth, steady tension after moistening both lines will make it much easier to draw down and tighten the knot.

Reliable knots are vital to fish-catching success—with all kinds of tackle and all sizes of line, from the heaviest to the lightest. All the knots listed here are tried-and-true ties for the fisherman. They are not the only ones in common use, by any means, but they do represent a complete selection that covers any and every need in sportfishing. Even the simplest knot can't be tied just by glancing at an illustration. The proper way to go about learning a new knot is to sit at home with an assortment of lines and leader material, then study the drawings and study the instructions, printed or animated, step by step. All knots

should be drawn down snugly. With lighter lines, hand pressure alone can be depended on to tighten the knot sufficiently. When you tie heavy monofilament, however, you often have to grip the hook with pliers to obtain sufficient pressure. And when tying heavy monofilament leader directly to a lighter line, you may have to take a couple of wraps around your hand (use a glove or handkerchief to avoid cuts) before you can draw the knot snug.

Also, with heavy monofilaments, the wraps may not "lay up" close together unless you prod them with a fingernail or blunt instrument as you tighten the knot.

No matter what difficulty you might be having with a particular knot, never try bringing it to final form by jerking sharply. If things aren't going right,

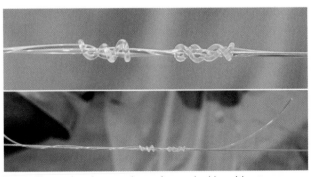

Two uni knots drawing together to form a double uni-knot.

What Makes a Good Knot?

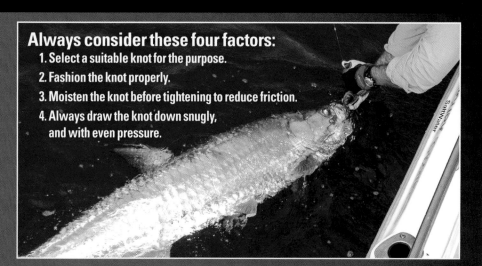

Always consider these four factors:

1. Select a suitable knot for the purpose.
2. Fashion the knot properly.
3. Moisten the knot before tightening to reduce friction.
4. Always draw the knot down snugly, and with even pressure.

That last step is too often neglected by fishermen. The majority of angling knots are likely to slip and fail unless they are drawn tight to begin with.

Be aware, too, that even if you "understand" the instructions for a new knot, you should practice its tying a number of times—to train your fingers and to help make sure you'll remember it the next time you go fishing. It's much easier to perfect your knots in the garage, than on the boat, in the heat of battle.

start all over. If you jerk while making the knot it will probably break on the spot, and if it doesn't, then failure is almost sure to come later at a more unwelcome time. Moistening the knot with your lips will make it easier to draw down.

In addition to the following knots, note that crimped sleeves are sometimes used to secure monofilament leader material—particularly in heavy offshore tests. Crimping procedures are the same as described in Chapter 5 for wire cable.

The closer to the boat your catch gets, the more strain the knot comes under.

VIC DUNAWAY

Uni Knot

For most fishermen, the uni-knot system is the only thing they really need to learn.

This unique system of knot-tying enables you to learn just one simple knot formation and adapt it to virtually any knotty need—everything from tying a hook to light line, all the way to joining lines that vary by 10 times in test.

Not only is this system the first and only unified approach to knot-tying, but it also provides close to 100 percent knot strength in most of its applications. The few finished ties which do not test near 100 percent still test consistently at 90 percent or higher. Moreover, the strength of the uni-knot isn't diminished when the line is broken with a jerk, rather than with steady pressure, unlike some other knots which test 100 percent on a steady pull but break at 50 or 60 percent if subjected to severe and sudden jolts—such as might be administered

by a big fish striking close to boatside, or by the angler himself, if he gets too muscular in trying to set a hook. The spider hitch and Palomar are examples of apparently top-strength knots which break all too easily on a severe shock.

The practiced knot-tying expert will simply add the uni-knot system to his personal inventory of ties, using elements of it for particular applications, and other knots, at times, for certain specialties. But for most fishermen, who are simply looking for the easiest way to handle their knotty needs, the uni-knot system is the only thing they really need to learn.

The uni-system works beautifully with braided lines as well as monofilament, and is by far the best way to tie those high-strength/small-diameter braided lines discussed in the preceding chapter.

Learning the Uni-Knot System

The one requirement basic to all fishermen is the need for tying a line to the eye of a hook or swivel. Familiarize yourself with the simple procedure of using the uni-knot here and then all other uni-knot applications become quite easy.

1 Turn the end back toward the eye to form a circle.

With thumb and finger of the left hand, grasp both strands of line and the crossing strand in a single grip just forward of the hook.

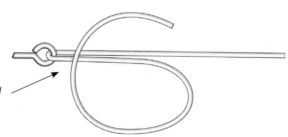

2 Make six turns with the end around both strands of line and through the circle. (With light lines—say 2- to 12-pound test—you should make five or six turns. If using heavier line, four turns will be sufficient.)

Pull

Learning a good loop knot can give just the extra action needed to fool a good fish.

A clip tied with a clinch knot can provide the benefits of a loop knot in addition to a quick-change system for lures.

3 Maintaining the same grip with the left hand, pull on the end of the line in the direction shown by the arrow until all the wraps are snugged tight and close together. Snugging down tightly at this stage is essential to maximum knot strength.

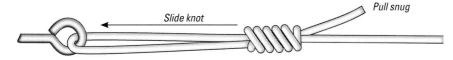

Slide knot

Pull snug

4 Finally, moisten the entire connection and slide the finished knot tight against the eye of the hook by dropping the tag end and pulling solely on the standing part of the line. The excess end can be trimmed flush with the knot after final positioning.

Trim here

Pull line

Line to Line

Tying line to line is actually done the same way as tying line to hook, even though the two parallel strands involved are from different pieces of line, rather than from the same piece doubled back.

This application replaces the blood knot, which is one of the most unwieldy of all knots to handle. Breaking strength of this tie is less than 100 percent, but over 90 percent and consistently stronger than the blood knot. It can be increased to 100 percent if you double both strands of line before tying the pair of uni-knots, but the single tie is strong enough for all practical purposes, and is trimmer.

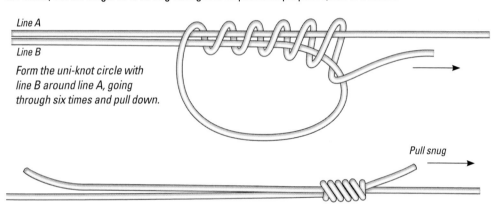

Line A

Line B

Form the uni-knot circle with line B around line A, going through six times and pull down.

Pull snug

The knot is formed and tightened. Now, tie another uni-knot (below) with line A around line B. Moisten area between and including connections.

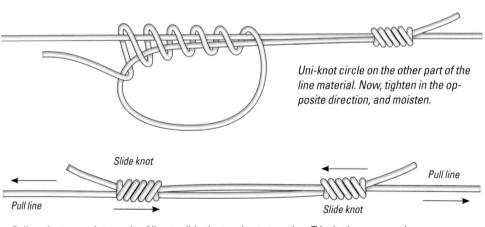

Uni-knot circle on the other part of the line material. Now, tighten in the opposite direction, and moisten.

Slide knot

Pull line

Pull line

Slide knot

Pull on the two main strands of line to slide the two knots together. Trim both excess ends.

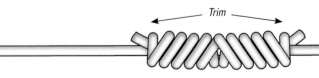

Trim

Line to Leader

Tying light line to heavy leader is not much different from the preceding application. It may seem awkward at first because the end of the light line must be doubled to gain maximum strength. But the doubled portion is treated as a single strand and is actually easier to draw down.

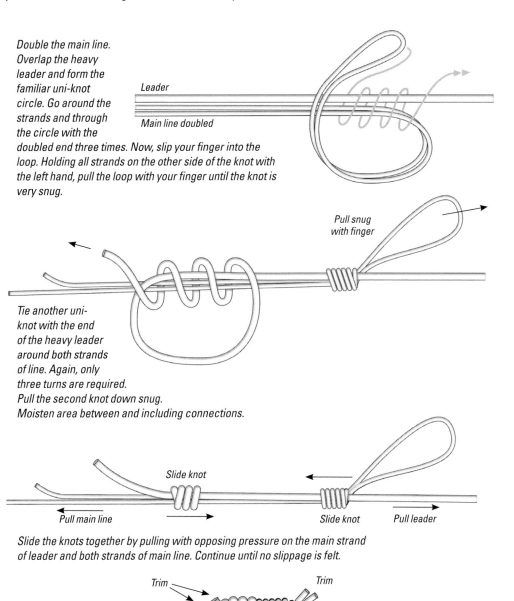

Double the main line. Overlap the heavy leader and form the familiar uni-knot circle. Go around the strands and through the circle with the doubled end three times. Now, slip your finger into the loop. Holding all strands on the other side of the knot with the left hand, pull the loop with your finger until the knot is very snug.

Leader

Main line doubled

Pull snug with finger

Tie another uni-knot with the end of the heavy leader around both strands of line. Again, only three turns are required. Pull the second knot down snug. Moisten area between and including connections.

Slide knot

Pull main line

Slide knot   Pull leader

Slide the knots together by pulling with opposing pressure on the main strand of leader and both strands of main line. Continue until no slippage is felt.

Trim   Trim

For final tightening, you will probably have to grip the line with a full-hand grip, instead of using thumb-finger grips. This tie will consistently provide close to 100 percent of line strength if the first uni-knot is snugged completely tight, and if final tightening is done carefully and with steady hard pressure.

Uni-Bimini Twist

To form a double line, you must use a simple but back-door approach. First you cut off enough line to form the desired length of double line, and tie the ends together with an overhand knot. Then you proceed to tie the double line back onto your line. The overhand knot is for convenience only and will be trimmed away later.

Double the end of the standing line. The procedure that follows is just the same as the line-to-line. The obvious and only difference is that you're working with two double strands instead of two single strands.

After the two knots are pulled together until they just touch, the final tightening must be done by pulling with both strands of double-line, but only the main strand of regular line.

The application of the Duncan Loop started the research leading to the uni-knot system.

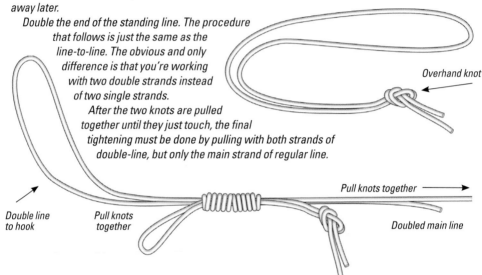

Overhand knot

Pull knots together →

Double line to hook

Pull knots together

Doubled main line

Uni-Nail Knot

You can tie a leader to your fly line in seconds with the uni-knot, achieving the identical result as with the tedious nail knot that requires a tapered nail or tube for tying.

Pull the leader knot down around the fly line. You'll have to do it in three or four stages, prodding the wraps together with your thumb in between the stages. This is because the fly line's soft coating does not allow the wraps to be pulled together in a single sweep. Moistening the connection is helpful.

Once you have pulled and prodded the wraps together, grasp the tag end of the leader with pliers. Holding the main strand of leader with your left hand, pull hard with the pliers to make the knot "bite" into the fly line's coating. This is what holds the knot in place. A second uni-knot isn't necessary. Trim off the excess ends of leader and fly line as close to the knot as possible, and you have the neatest of all fly leader ties, done in a few seconds.

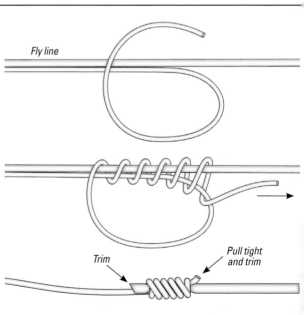

Fly line

Trim

Pull tight and trim

The Uni-Loop

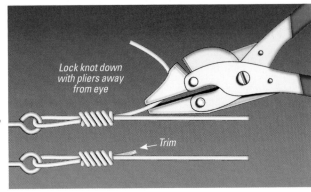

Lock knot down
with pliers away
from eye

← Trim

It takes just one slight variation to transform the hook tie into a loop arrangement which provides more freedom of action for artificial lures.

Instead of sliding the finished knot all the way to the eye, just slide it to the size loop desired. Then, gripping the loop just forward of the hook eye, take hold of the tag end with pliers and pull very hard. This locks the knot around the standing line (or leader) at that point. If it slides down at all it will only be under heavy pressure when fighting a fish. Meanwhile, the loop position is maintained while casting and retrieving. It was this particular application, by itself called the Duncan loop, that originally planted the seed for development of the uni-knot system.

Snelling a Hook

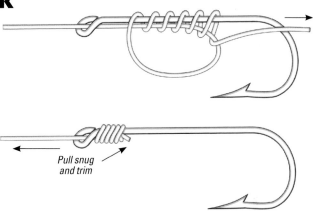

Pull snug
and trim

Snelling is a snap with the uni-knot. Thread line through the hook eye, pulling through at least six inches. Form the familiar uni circle and hold it tight against the hook shank with thumb and finger. Make several turns around the shank and through the circle. Pull on the tag end to draw the knot roughly closed. Finish by holding the standing line in one hand, the hook in the other, and pulling in opposite directions.

Start with
bail open

Draw knot
up to spool

Spooling Line

For a spinning reel spool, simply make a large loop in the end of the line with a uni-knot, drop the loop over the spool, and draw it up by pulling on the standing line. In either case, use only two wraps to form the uni.

To affix line to a revolving spool reel for filling, pass the end of the line around the spool, grasp the tag end and the standing line with thumb and finger of left hand, and tie a uni-knot. Trim the knot close, then pull gently on the standing line to snug the loop tight to the spool.

Improved Clinch Knot

The improved clinch long has been the most widely recognized of all fishing knots, and works well for tying monofilament, braided line or titanium wire. Use it for tying snugly to a hook, swivel and certain artificial lures, such as jigs, spinners and any lure with a split-ring permanently attached to the lure-eye. Plugs and spoons work best with a loop knot. A lot of fishermen also prefer a loop when using leadhead jigs.

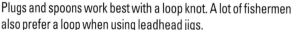

Thread the line through the hook eye.

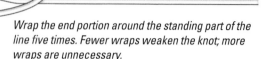

Wrap the end portion around the standing part of the line five times. Fewer wraps weaken the knot; more wraps are unnecessary.

Bring the end back through the opening between the hook and the first wrap.

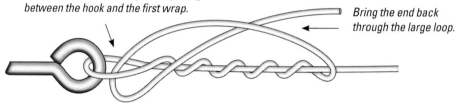

Bring the end back through the large loop.

Draw the knot tight by pulling on the hook and the line simultaneously. As soon as you're sure the end will not back out of the large loop, you can turn it loose and finish the job of drawing tight. Trim so that a short end is visible. It should not be trimmed flush with the knot.

Trilene Knot

The Trilene knot is a simple variation of the clinch knot in which the tag end is run through the eye twice and then passed through the resulting double opening just forward of the eye. Going through the eye twice, regardless of the knot used, will improve the knot strength of any line.

Twice through

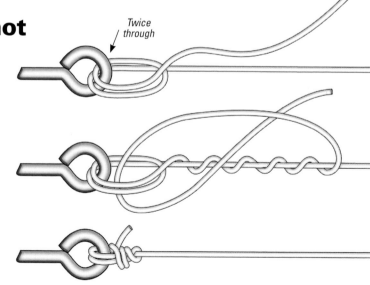

Blood Knot

Best uses for the blood knot are to retie a broken spinning line, to add more line to your reel spool, or to join tapered sections of fly leaders. In other words, the blood knot is useful mainly for joining together monofilaments of the same, or only slightly differing, diameters.

Overlap both sections of line, end to end and then wrap one section around the other five times.

Wrap the remaining end around the other section— also five times but in the opposite direction.

Insert both ends back through the center opening, again in opposite directions.

The knot is pulled tight by drawing on the lines at either side of the knot. Care must be taken at this point to prevent the ends from backing out of the center insert. Trim, leaving a short end.

VARIATION: This knot can also be used to make dropper lines for such applications as the homemade sabiki rig in Chapter 6. To make a dropper, just be sure to work with an excessive length of tag end on at least one of the two lines being joined. After the knot is drawn tight, this excess—perhaps six inches long—becomes the dropper. The other tag end can be trimmed close.

Albright Special

When you wish to tie a light monofilament line directly to a very heavy monofilament leader (for instance, 10-lb. to 80-lb.) this is the knot to master. It has the added advantage of being a slim and neat tie that will generally slip through the rod guides so you can crank the knot past the rod tip.

The Albright special also is used for tying light line directly to wire cable, nylon-coated wire or even to single-strand wire leader in the smaller diameters. It is excellent for joining braided line to monofilament leader material.

This knot is tricky at first, and may take some practice. However, it really isn't very difficult once you get the hang of it.

First, double back a couple inches of the heavy material.
Insert the line through the loop which is thus formed. Pull 10 or 12 inches of line through to give yourself ample line to work with.

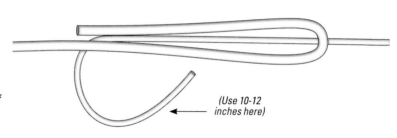

(Use 10-12 inches here)

Now you must wrap the line back over itself, and over both strands of the doubled leader. While doing this, you are gripping the line and both leader strands together with the thumb and finger of your left hand, and winding with your right. Make 15 turns (about half as many if using double line), then insert the end of the line back through the loop once more at the point of the original entry.

Before turning loose your thumb-and-finger grip, pull gently on the standing part of the line to remove slack; then pull gently on the short end of the leader to close the loop; then pull gently on the short end of the line to remove more slack.

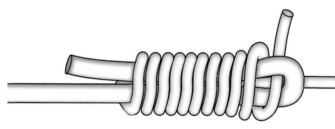

Finally comes the last stage of tightening. Pull the short end of the line as tight as you possibly can. Then pull the standing part of the line tight.

Clip off the excess line, leaving about an eighth-inch end. Clip off the excess from the leader loop, again leaving a very slight protrusion.

SPECIAL NOTE: The Albright special, in particular, is a knot that must be tied with great care. Practice it thoroughly at home. But, as mentioned before, once you learn it, it seems surprisingly quick and simple.

Quick Nail Knot Snell

Here's a very strong method for making a stiff, straight connection to a hook using monofilament or fluorocarbon. It's especially useful for up- or turned-down eye hooks, but may be used with other styles. In fact, it's not even necessary to pass the line through the hook eye—though many anglers choose to do so.

Some fishermen might recognize this as a modification of the nail knot. Here, there's no need for a nail or tube to serve as a stiffener during the tie; the shank of the hook functions as the nail.

Note that the illustrations show the knot being tied from the back of the hook to the front. Many anglers will find this method easiest, but it can be tied in the other direction, too.

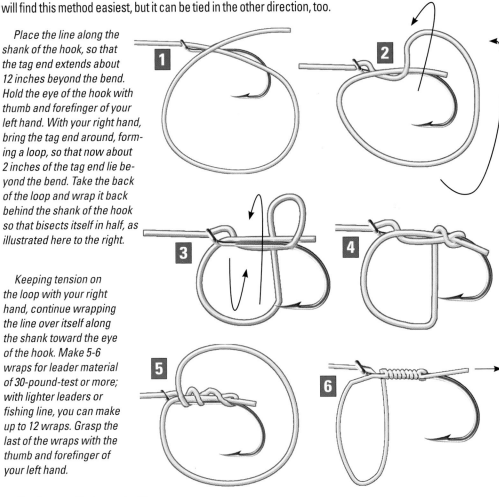

Place the line along the shank of the hook, so that the tag end extends about 12 inches beyond the bend. Hold the eye of the hook with thumb and forefinger of your left hand. With your right hand, bring the tag end around, forming a loop, so that now about 2 inches of the tag end lie beyond the bend. Take the back of the loop and wrap it back behind the shank of the hook so that bisects itself in half, as illustrated here to the right.

Keeping tension on the loop with your right hand, continue wrapping the line over itself along the shank toward the eye of the hook. Make 5-6 wraps for leader material of 30-pound-test or more; with lighter leaders or fishing line, you can make up to 12 wraps. Grasp the last of the wraps with the thumb and forefinger of your left hand.

Gently grasp the tag end with your teeth and pull until the loop disappears inside the wraps. Moisten the knot with saliva, but do not use your teeth to tighten the knot. Slide the knot up to the eye of the hook. Now pull on both the standing end and the tag end while holding loops tightly, to finish the knot.

Two-Wrap Hangman's Knot

This knot is sometimes called the figure-eight knot; however, it is different from another and more commonly used knot which is also called the figure-eight, but which can be used only with certain types of wire. See Chapter 5 for that one.

The two-wrap hangman's knot results in a slipping loop, which can be tightened at any point to provide the size loop-opening desired. The loop will remain open while casting, but will close tight against the eye when a fish is being fought. After the catch, it can easily be opened again (and should be retied if the leader has been frayed even slightly).

This knot can be used with either heavy or light monofilament, and is preferable to the end-loop knot (page 102) when no heavy leader is being used, because it retains a much higher percentage of breaking test.

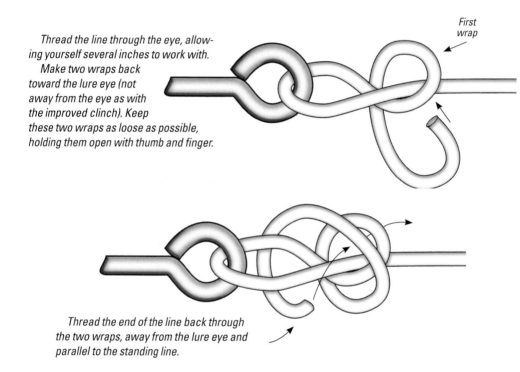

First wrap

Thread the line through the eye, allowing yourself several inches to work with.

Make two wraps back toward the lure eye (not away from the eye as with the improved clinch). Keep these two wraps as loose as possible, holding them open with thumb and finger.

Thread the end of the line back through the two wraps, away from the lure eye and parallel to the standing line.

Stick the lure into something rigid (such as a boat cleat, tree branch, etc.). After the hook is so fixed, grip the tag end of line with a pair of pliers.

Now pull simultaneously on the standing line with your hand, and on the tag end with the pliers. You'll note that the knot now slips up and down. Position the loop as you want it, then tighten firmly with extra pressure from the pliers.

Trim

Surgeon's Knot

The surgeon's knot makes a fast, easy and reliable connection for tying a heavy monofilament leader, or shock line, directly to either monofilament or braided fishing line. It can be used for line and leader of greatly differing diameter, although the practical limit, because of bulkiness, is no more than about three times line test—that is, 4-lb. line to 12-lb. leader; 8-lb. to 20-lb.; 10-lb. to 30-lb., etc. If your diameters differ more than that, it will probably be better to use the Albright special, which results in a trimmer product that flows more easily through the rod guides.

Even though this is one of the easiest of all knots to tie, it is difficult to illustrate plainly. So don't be alarmed. Follow both the illustration and instruction, and you'll be tying it in a few seconds.

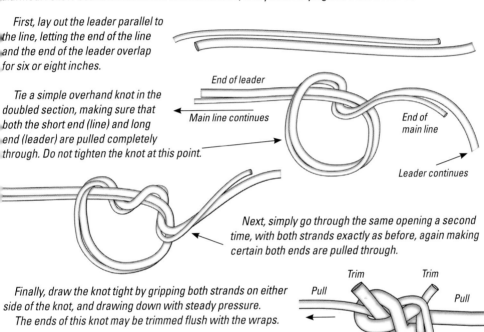

First, lay out the leader parallel to the line, letting the end of the line and the end of the leader overlap for six or eight inches.

End of leader

Tie a simple overhand knot in the doubled section, making sure that both the short end (line) and long end (leader) are pulled completely through. Do not tighten the knot at this point.

Main line continues

End of main line

Leader continues

Next, simply go through the same opening a second time, with both strands exactly as before, again making certain both ends are pulled through.

Trim   Trim

Finally, draw the knot tight by gripping both strands on either side of the knot, and drawing down with steady pressure. The ends of this knot may be trimmed flush with the wraps.

Pull   Pull

Surgeon's End Loop

The surgeon's knot can also be used to make an end loop (or a longer double line). The only difference is that you work with two strands of the same line, rather than with line and leader.

For making a double line, the surgeon's isn't as strong a tie as the Bimini twist but, like the spider hitch, it makes a fairly decent substitute for folks who refuse to learn the Bimini.

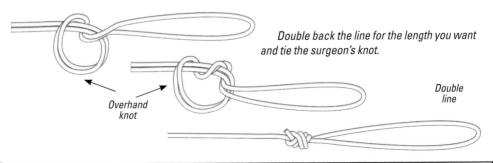

Double back the line for the length you want and tie the surgeon's knot.

Overhand knot

Double line

Dropper Loop

When making multiple-hook rigs, you can tie dropper lines of various lengths to these loops. Or you can fix a hook directly to the loop itself simply by threading the loop through the eye, then bringing it completely over the hook and pulling it back snugly against the eye.

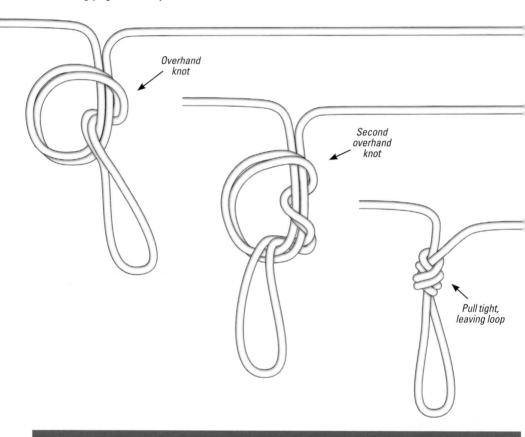

Overhand knot

Second overhand knot

Pull tight, leaving loop

▶ PRO TIP

Anglers using a high number of dropper loops will often build a rig maker to make their life easier. Using a piece of plywood 12 x 30 inches long and ¾" thick, insert an open eye hook in each end, and drill a triangle of 3 ¼-inch holes in the middle. Insert 3 ¼-inch dowels (pegs) in the triangle holes, and glue them in place.

Tie a swivel to your line and place it on either open eye. Then wrap your line around the triangle once, and overlap past the first two legs. Twist the overlapped lines around each other six times, and open the middle wrap. Remove the twist from the pegs. Bring the single loop through the middle wrap, and drape it over a peg. Pull each end of the mainline, and tighten down the wraps. Using the loop you just made to start the process, again drop it over the open eye, and repeat the process. Tie a surgeon's loop in the end of the line to hold your sinker, and you're ready to go.

Advanced Dropper Loop

Another method of forming a loop in line above the sinker is an advanced dropper loop. This knot will hang off the line at a right angle. The loop can be made to have a hook threaded on it.

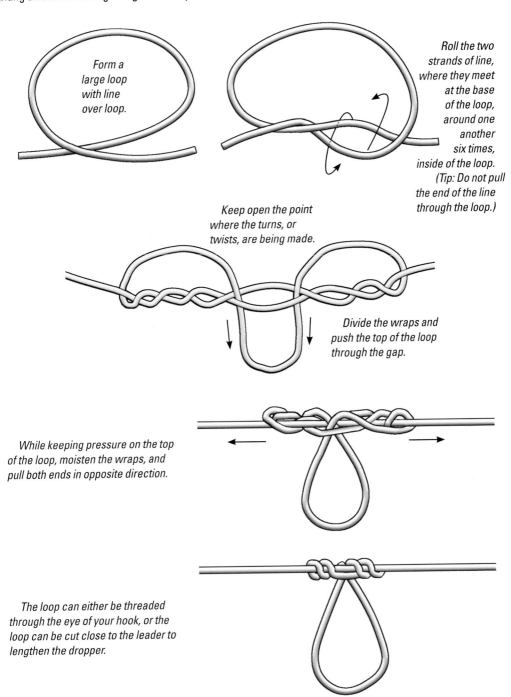

Form a large loop with line over loop.

Roll the two strands of line, where they meet at the base of the loop, around one another six times, inside of the loop. (Tip: Do not pull the end of the line through the loop.)

Keep open the point where the turns, or twists, are being made.

Divide the wraps and push the top of the loop through the gap.

While keeping pressure on the top of the loop, moisten the wraps, and pull both ends in opposite direction.

The loop can either be threaded through the eye of your hook, or the loop can be cut close to the leader to lengthen the dropper.

Palomar Knot

For tying on a hook or lure, the Palomar is a quick, slip-proof and dependable tie that usually will test at 100 percent on a testing machine, but when shocked—such as by a powerful strike at boatside—it can break far below line test. Therefore, it should be used only with leaders or fairly heavy lines— say 20-pound-test and up. If tying a hook or lure directly to light line, the uni-knot and improved clinch knot are much to be preferred.

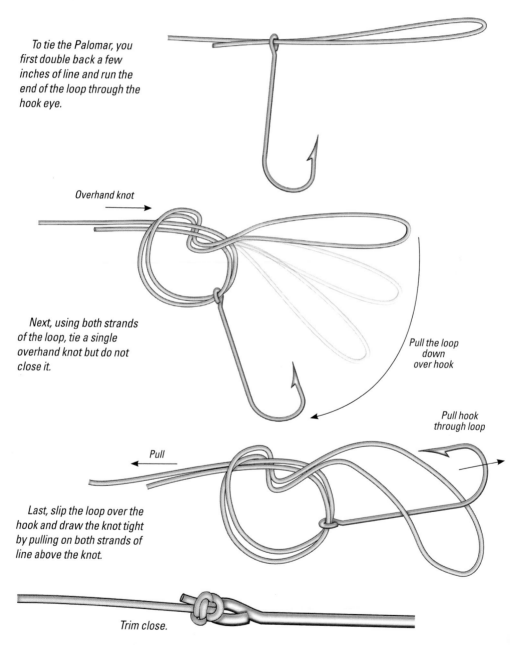

To tie the Palomar, you first double back a few inches of line and run the end of the loop through the hook eye.

Overhand knot

Next, using both strands of the loop, tie a single overhand knot but do not close it.

Pull the loop down over hook

Pull hook through loop

Pull

Last, slip the loop over the hook and draw the knot tight by pulling on both strands of line above the knot.

Trim close.

Spider Hitch

For making a double line, this knot has often been touted as a good alternative to the Bimini twist. But there really is no good alternative. The spider hitch often tests at 100 percent on a machine, but gradually weakens during a long fight, while the Bimini does not.

Double back the desired amount of line and grip the two strands with thumb and finger near the tag end, make a small loop near the tag end and take the base of this loop in the same thumb-finger grip.

Small loop

Wrap the doubled line around your thumb (and around the small loop too) for three to five turns.

One more wrap around thumb and loop

Slip the end of the long loop through the little loop. Pull the entire long loop through, allowing the wraps to slide from your thumb.

Back around and through the small loop

Tighten the knot as much as you can with hand pressure and trim the tag end.

Tube or Nail Knot

This one is used to tie a leader butt directly to your fly line. Originally, a nail was used to tie this knot—with the leader being inserted in the small space between nail and line.

By using a small tube instead of a nail, it is much easier to insert the leader back underneath all the wraps. Any small-diameter tube can be used—a hypodermic needle, the refill barrel of a ballpoint pen (cleaned out, of course), etc.

First, lay out the fly line and leader as in the illustration.

Grip all three (fly line, leader and tube) with thumb and finger of left hand.

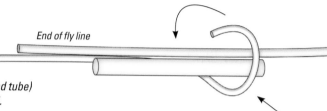

End of fly line

Take the leader with your right hand, and wrap back toward the end of the fly line, making five snug wraps.

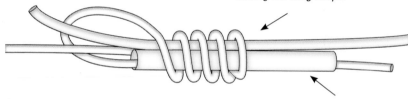

Run the end of the leader through the tube.

Slide the tube out and tighten the knot by pulling on both ends of the leader.

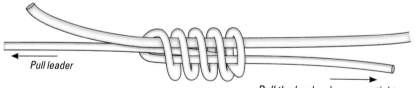

Pull leader

Pull the leader down very tight—using pliers to grip the short end if necessary.

Do not pull on the fly line until after the leader is pulled down so tightly that it bites into the coating of the fly line!

Once the knot is tight, the excess ends of the fly line and the leader can be trimmed short.

Perfection Knot

This knot is used mostly for making loops in the butt end of fly leaders, so that leaders can quickly be changed or replaced. The drawings are in condensed style so that the formations are shown more easily. For convenience, leave yourself a longer length of tag end than shown in the drawings.

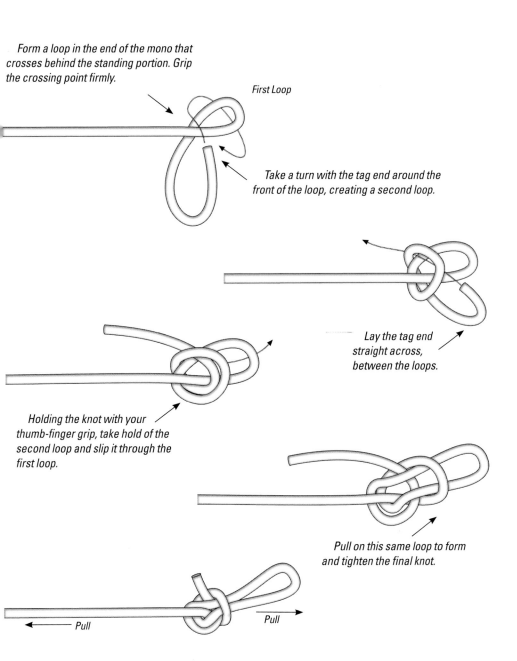

Form a loop in the end of the mono that crosses behind the standing portion. Grip the crossing point firmly.

First Loop

Take a turn with the tag end around the front of the loop, creating a second loop.

Lay the tag end straight across, between the loops.

Holding the knot with your thumb-finger grip, take hold of the second loop and slip it through the first loop.

Pull on this same loop to form and tighten the final knot.

Pull

Pull

Tying the Bimini Twist

This is one knot which really is difficult for the fellow who hasn't tied it before. But, once learned, it can be tied in less than a minute—and take heart at the knowledge that hundreds of fishermen now tie it routinely and quickly, even in a rocking boat. You can too, if you practice and master it at home.

1 *Double the end of your line, making the doubled portion about three feet long.*

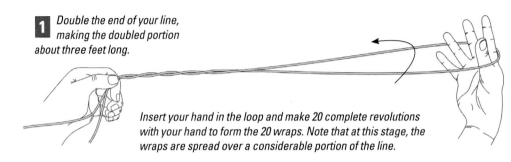

Insert your hand in the loop and make 20 complete revolutions with your hand to form the 20 wraps. Note that at this stage, the wraps are spread over a considerable portion of the line.

The one most important thing to remember when tying the Bimini is to keep constant pressure on all three points.

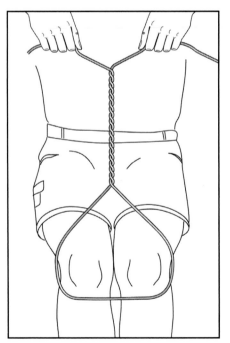

2 *Sitting erect, hold your knees tightly together and place the loop over them. Maintain pressure, as shown, with your hands on both the standing line and the short end.*

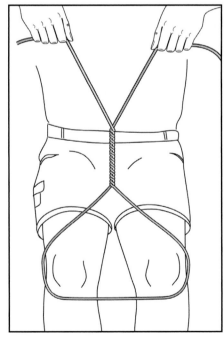

3 *Spread your knees slowly, maintaining very tight hand pressure in opposing directions, as before. This will draw the wraps tightly together.*

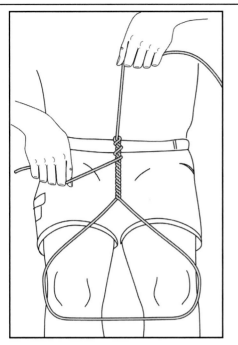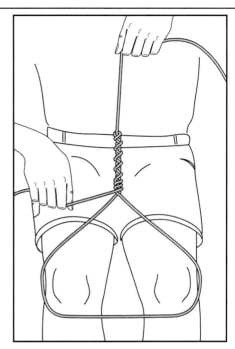

4 *Once the wraps are very snug, pull slightly downward with the short end while relaxing tension slightly at the same time. Be sure to keep up the tension, however, with the left hand and with the knees. The line should then roll easily over the wraps, all the way down to the end.*

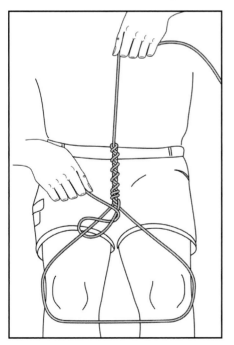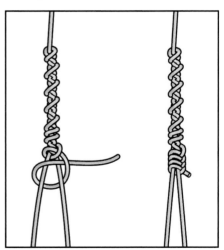

6 *This shows detail of finishing half-hitches: the first around a single strand, and three others around both strands. Instead of making three separate finishing hitches, you can make just one—and go through it three times with the tag end instead of only once. Trim, leaving about an eighth-inch end.*

5 *This shows the completed rollover before it is anchored with a half-hitch around one strand, and several half hitches around both strands.*

No Name Knot

Here's a nifty way to attach heavy mono leader to a double line. It's simple, quick and strong, but why it has no name is anyone's guess.

Double line by using the Bimini twist, spider hitch, surgeon's loop or uni-knot. The Bimini is the strongest.

Lay the leader and double line parallel. Wrap the end of the leader four or five turns around the two strands of line, working up the line toward the double-line knot.

Turn the end of the leader back and bring it through the loop at the end of the doubled line.

To finish the knot, hold the double line with one hand as you pull on the tag end of the leader with the other.

Trim the leader fairly close where it projects from the knot, but leave a tiny end to allow for possible further drawing down under the pressure of fishing.

Variation: A variation on the "No Name Knot" became the favorite of the crews fishing Cancun and Isle Mujeres, Mexico, and became known as the Yucatan knot. They both join double line to leader, however when tying the Yucatan knot you wrap the doubled line around the leader instead of the leader around the double line. Both are finished by placing the end of the leader through the double line to tighten.

Offshore Knot

This connection is used to affix an offshore snapswivel to the double line, so that trolling leaders and their pre-rigged baits can be quickly changed. The uni and improved clinch knots will serve the same purpose very well, but the offshore knot is neater.

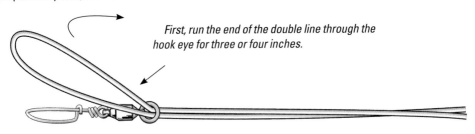

First, run the end of the double line through the hook eye for three or four inches.

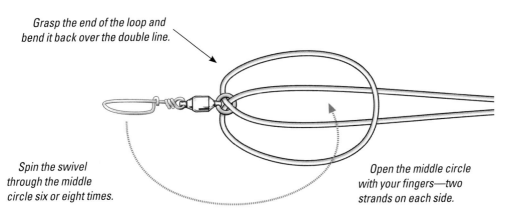

Grasp the end of the loop and bend it back over the double line.

Spin the swivel through the middle circle six or eight times.

Open the middle circle with your fingers—two strands on each side.

Holding the swivel with one hand, pull on both strands of double line. This will begin to draw down the wraps.

To complete the draw-down, tension should be kept on the double line while you use both hands to pull and prod the wraps carefully until they snuggle evenly against the eye of the swivel.

Best way to obtain the needed tension is to place the rod in a holder and keep the reel drag tight. If using heavy monofilament line, pliers may be needed for final tightening.

Work knot down with fingers.

End Loop Knot

A fast knot to tie, and it affords the necessary freedom of lure action which is so vital to the productivity of many plugs. Do not use this knot for tying a lure directly to light line, because it weakens the line-test too much. Instead, use the two-wrap hangman's knot or the uni-knot loop.

Before you put the line through the eye of the lure, tie a simple overhand knot several inches from the end, but do not close the overhand knot at this point.

Go through the eye and insert the end of the line back through the overhand knot.

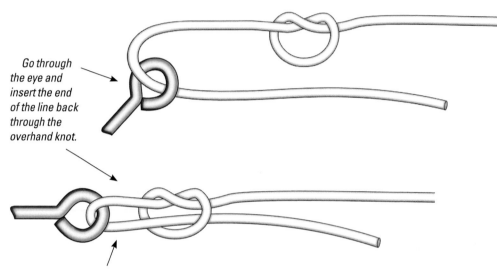

The final end loop is determined at this stage by drawing the overhand knot as close to the lure as you want it.

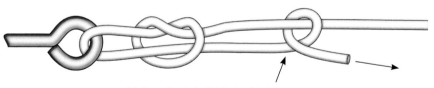

Make a simple half-hitch with the end of the line around the standing part of the line after the overhand knot.

Pull tight with pressure on the lure and on the line.

World's Fair Knot

This easy-to-tie knot tests nearly 100 percent. It got its name from being introduced at the Knoxville World's Fair in 1982 as the winning entry in Stren Line's "Great Knot Search."

Pass the doubled end loop through the eye.

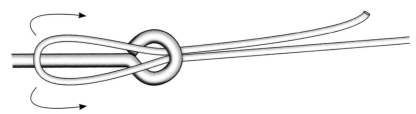

Fold the loop over and pull the double line up through the loop.

Run the tag end through the doubled strands and over the loop.

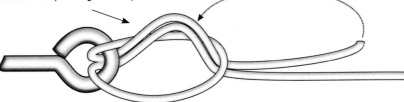

Run the tag end through the new loop formed from previous step.

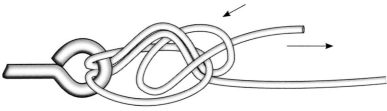

Draw the knot up to the eye.

CHAPTER 5

Wire Matters

Wire leader keeps even the sharpest toothed fish on the line. Lots of pros view it as a necessary evil and only use it when they are apt to run into a wahoo, shark or mackerel. It comes in several different materials, the most popular being the single strand stainless steel. Whereas it's very rare for a fish to actually bite stainless wire in two, it's very common for it to fail if not wrapped properly with a "haywire twist."

Live bait fishermen are encouraged to learn how to fish non-coated stainless cable. It's more flexible, and your bait will swim much more naturally. However, titanium wire stretches and doesn't kink nearly as badly as stainless. It's just about the only wire you can tie with a clinch or uni-knot.

Whereas it's rare for a fish to actually bite stainless wire in two, it's very common for it to fail if not wrapped properly.

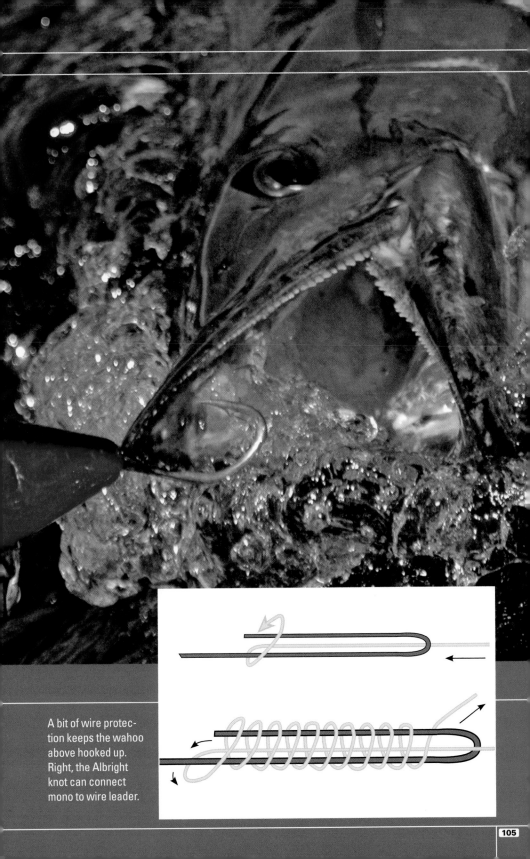

A bit of wire protection keeps the wahoo above hooked up. Right, the Albright knot can connect mono to wire leader.

How to Wrap Fishing Wire

SINGLE-STRAND WIRE SIZES
(For Multi-Strand Cable, See p. 115)

No.	Diameter	Lb. Test Stainless	Lb. Test Titanium
2	.011	28	--
3	.012	32	20
4	.013	39	--
5	.014	54	30
6	.016	61	40
7	.018	72	50
8	.020	88	70
9	.022	108	--
10	.024	127	--
12	.029	184	--
15	.035	258	--
19	.043	352	--

There are several types of fishing wire, and the purpose of this section is to give instruction as to how each type should be wrapped onto a hook, lure or swivel.

Instructions on how to choose among the various types and sizes of wire, and their uses as fishing leaders, are covered in Chapter 3.

These are the types of wire in regular use:
1. Stainless steel single-strand leader wire.
2. Titanium single-strand leader wire.
3. Monel single-strand trolling wire (wire line).
4. Wire cable, formed of twisted wire filaments.
5. Wire cable, coated with plastic.

When working with single-strand stainless wire, all diameters are wrapped in exactly the same way; however, the larger the wire, the more difficult it will be to wrap. When working with the larger sizes, it will be necessary to grip your loops of wire with pliers as you make the wrap.

Titanium wire is entirely different from most stainless steel wire in handling characteristics. It is supple and, therefore, is rigged by means of knots instead of wire wraps.

Cable wire, whether plain or coated with nylon, is normally rigged with crimped sleeves, although the smaller diameters can be effectively knotted too.

Cutting pliers, obviously, are a necessity when working with wire. They will be needed to cut the desired length of wire from your coil or spool. In some cases (mostly with cable) cutters are used to trim the end after the wrap. But single-strand wire should be BROKEN, not cut, or a tiny sharp end will be left that can rip a careless hand.

A light wire stinger rig on a pilchard will catch toothy fish.

KINGFISH The king mackerel is often caught on medium ocean gear with lines of 20- to 40-pound test. Wire leader helps to keep the king connected, though many are taken with heavy mono and fluorocarbon leader.

The Haywire Twist

For strength and reliability in virtually all types of saltwater fishing, the haywire twist should be the standard wrap with single-strand stainless wire or Monel wire line. Experience has proven that simple overhand wire wraps will invariably pull out under heavy pressure. For that reason, anglers new to wire leaders are strongly encouraged to learn the haywire twist from the start. A failed leader is a horrible way to lose the fish of a lifetime.

Here's how to wrap the haywire twist:

Start by forming the desired size loop. You may simply make a loop for later attachment to a snap, or you may run the wire through the eye of hook or swivel. In either case, the procedure is the same.

Cross the strands as shown. Hold loop tightly with fingers of left hand, or with pliers. Using right hand, press DOWN at point A with forefinger, and at the same time press UP at point B with thumb. If it's done correctly, you can easily see how BOTH strands of wire are wrapped together instead of one being wrapped around the other.

The second illustration shows how the wire should look after the first twist. Using exactly the same procedure, repeat three or four times if making a wire leader, or 10 to 12 times if wrapping the softer Monel trolling wire. After making the series of haywire twists, finish off by wrapping the short end around the standing wire as snugly as possible several times. This finishing wrap does not add strength, but is necessary to keep the haywire from unwrapping. Unless the wraps (called barrels) are snugged tightly against each other, you will have trouble breaking the wire, as described next.

BREAK WIRE by bending a "crank handle" in the surplus end, as shown. Then, while holding the loop tightly in the left hand, crank this handle in a full circular motion. The surplus will snap off neatly at the last wrap. If you have difficulty breaking the wire in this manner it is probably because you are making the circular motion in the same direction as you made the wrap. You must let your circular sweep run PARALLEL to the standing part of the wire—not AROUND the standing wire. One way to make sure you are cranking in the right direction is to make your circle in such a way as to let the "elbow" of your little handle brush the standing part of the wire as it goes by.

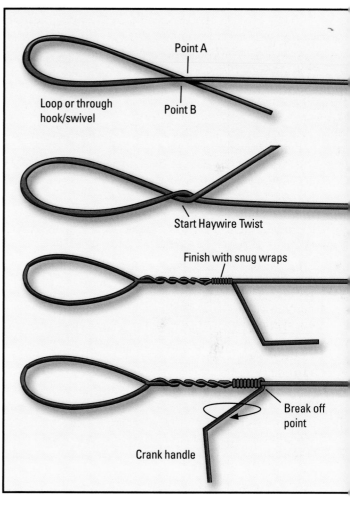

Loop or through hook/swivel

Point A

Point B

Start Haywire Twist

Finish with snug wraps

Break off point

Crank handle

BARRACUDA
Light tackle fishermen love the great barracuda. You can catch one longer than your leg on light line, but without a wire leader chances are you'll never get it to the boat.

The Greene Twist

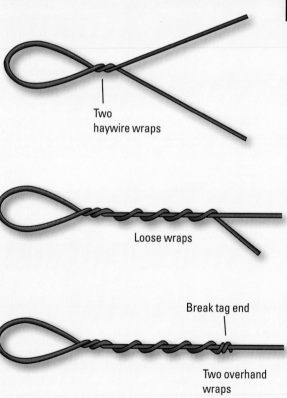

Two haywire wraps

Loose wraps

Break tag end

Two overhand wraps

This wire twist, amazing as it seems, gives an extra measure of breaking safety over the traditional haywire twist. This extra margin means little in routine angling, especially with light and medium tackle, and when fish are netted or gaffed. However, in big-game fishing, when the leader must be handled by a mate to bring the fish within range of a flying gaff or the tagging stick, the Greene twist is a surer bet to withstand the extra pressure.

First form the loop or run the wire through the hook eye, as the case may be, and then begin the wrap exactly the same as for the haywire; however, you make only two haywire wraps. Next, wrap the tag end around the standing wire five or six times very loosely—so loosely that it would unwind if you let it go. Last, make two—and two only—overhand wraps as with the haywire, and break off the tag end.

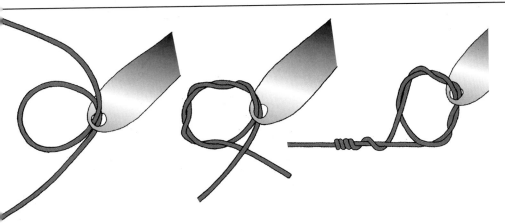

Special Spoon Wrap

Here's a nifty system for attaching a trolling spoon to your wire leader. It gives the spoon much more action in the water, and is widely used by commercial king mackerel fishermen and by many charterboat crews. Run your leader wire through the eye of the spoon, pulling several inches of wire through. Turn the end of the wire and go through the eye a second time.

Now you see that a circle of wire has been formed. Run the end of your wire in and out through this circle several times, until you go completely around the circle and get back to the standing part of the leader wire. Now make your haywire twist, finish with the regular barrel wrap and break off the surplus wire as usual.

NOTE: Immediately after forming the circle, adjust the size of the circle to desired diameter by pulling on the loose end of wire. The diameter usually is about a half-inch.

The special spoon wrap is widely used by king mackerel fishermen and by many charter boat crews when the kingfish are running in local waters.

► PRO TIP Wire

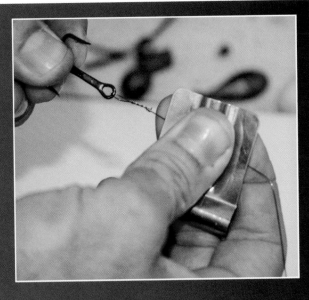

Of course it's best to have a new stainless wire leader ready after catching a fish. When numbers start to stack up, such as for commercial kingfish fishermen, this can be difficult. That's why many boats carry stainless wire straighteners to rub the kinks out of a used leader. If you find yourself running short on rigs, they are a handy tool to have around.

You only need to pull the wire tight and press the tool tight to the wire and rub it back and forth to straighten it.

Rigging Multi-Strand Wire

Sleeves must be chosen to match the diameter of the wire you use.

Multi-strand twisted wire is commonly used for leader material in both light tests for inshore fishing, and heavy tests for big-game applications. Some braided wire has a nylon coating.

There are no strict rules to follow in choosing between multi-strand and single-strand wire for your metallic leaders, although general guidelines are offered at the beginning of the chapter on "Leaders."

All of the connections to be described here may be used with either plain or nylon-coated cable.

Sleeve and Crimper

This is probably the most widely used method of attaching cable leader, particularly 60-pound and above, to a hook, trolling lure or swivel. Sleeves can also be used to make monofilament leaders, but they seldom are, except in heavy tests for offshore trolling, where special monofilament sleeves are required to avoid weakening the crimps.

Sizes of both the sleeves and crimping tools vary widely and are sold at most saltwater tackle shops. Sleeves must match the diameter of the wire or monofilament you plan to use. Any dealer who

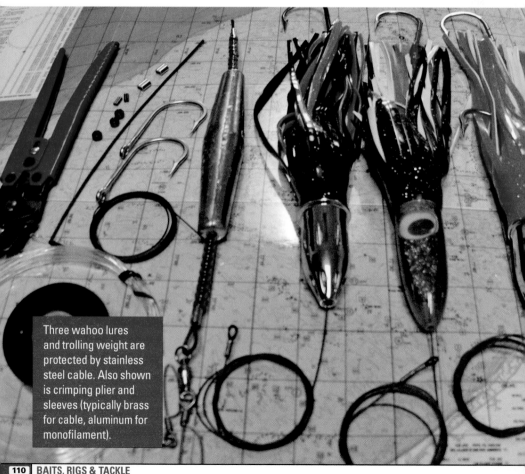

Three wahoo lures and trolling weight are protected by stainless steel cable. Also shown is crimping plier and sleeves (typically brass for cable, aluminum for monofilament).

sells sleeves should have a chart detailing appropriate sizes for the brands and tests he stocks. Most sizes can also be matched by studying the chart on the sleeve package.

When crimping large sleeves on heavy monofilament leaders for offshore trolling, special crimping devices or swagers are available that provide a positive crimp, yet do not bruise and weaken the leader material. These tools are expensive—but still relatively cheap in the context of overall big-game fishing costs.

Crimping plier compresses a double-barrel sleeve around steel cable. Elements are size-matched for dependability.

SINGLE SLEEVE RIG

One sleeve may be used with light cable wire for light-duty fishing. To rig,

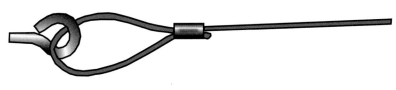

simply thread the sleeve onto the wire, then run the end of the wire through the eye of your hook, and then back through the sleeve. Adjust to the desired size loop, crimp the sleeve, and trim off excess wire. Remember, when attempting to crimp the sleeve, the object is to close the two strands of wire or monofilament together, not flatten the crimp. It's also recommended to not crimp all the way to the end of the sleeve when using mono. This prevents damaging the mono.

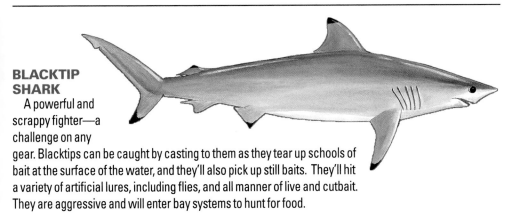

BLACKTIP SHARK

A powerful and scrappy fighter—a challenge on any gear. Blacktips can be caught by casting to them as they tear up schools of bait at the surface of the water, and they'll also pick up still baits. They'll hit a variety of artificial lures, including flies, and all manner of live and cutbait. They are aggressive and will enter bay systems to hunt for food.

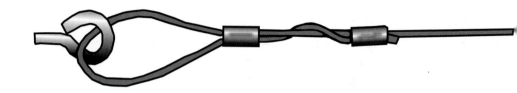

DOUBLE SLEEVE RIG

For added protection against failure (and especially with larger sizes of cable), use two sleeves. Start by crimping on the first sleeve as described on the preceding page. Then wrap the excess end once or twice around the standing part of the leader and thread it through a second sleeve. Last, crimp the second sleeve and trim off excess wire.

FIGURE-EIGHT KNOT

Light cable or nylon-covered cable can be tied directly to lure, hook or swivel by using this simple, yet strong, clinch knot. You merely wrap the end once around the leader, then thread it back through the first opening—as shown in the illustration. Use pliers to hold the tag end as you pull on the standing piece of wire to tighten the knot.

Titanium wire, and even extra-supple cable, might be tied to hook or swivel with either this knot or the improved clinch knot. Preference should be given to the improved clinch if it forms up well with your chosen kind and size of wire. If at first it doesn't, try reducing the number of turns—one at a time—until the knot can be snugged neatly and tightly.

If sharks are your target, you better become expert at rigging wire leaders.

You merely wrap the end once around the leader, then thread it back through the first opening.

Wire Fly Leaders

There's a slim chance that you'll be able to land a shark, barracuda or any of the other sharp-toothed species without a trace of wire on your leader. Not to say that it can't be done of course—just that if you're fishing for these species and want a high hookup-to-capture ratio, wire is required. These species' teeth are so finely-honed with a cutting edge that barely even a glancing touch from them will sever any other kind of leader but one of the varieties of wire, straight or tieable, available to anglers.

Options among materials for a wire leader include the standard single-strand stainless steel, and coated or uncoated stainless steel cable. As on

The trace of wire on this fly leader helped to catch this hefty mackerel.

Selection of wire leader material for fly and other light tackle fishing.

other gear, single-strand will be tied on with a haywire twist. Look for No. 2 wire for smaller species and larger diameter wire for big sharks—but for those fish, cable might be an even better choice.

The word "trace" is used to describe the length of the wire for good reason. Its length amounts to no more than a short fraction of the entire length of the leader. A few inches is all—the least length that can be handily tied for small mackerel, which would be two or three inches—up to about six inches for big sharks and 'cudas. Obviously for those big fish you'll need a length long enough to extend out of the danger zone of teeth when the hookup occurs. But at more than six inches

long, the wire will distort the performance of the leader and line and disrupt the casting. Still, wire kinks—which when fighting a big fish for some duration of time can become a liability.

For that reason, for the bigger fish most anglers use seven-strand plastic-coated stainless steel cable, which won't kink. The cable can be tied to the fly with a snell—as long as the fly is prepared for a snell—or with a figure-eight knot or a melt-the-plastic knot. For that last knot, the wire goes through the eye of the hook and out, and then is wrapped around itself toward the leader at least five times. Then the plastic coatings are fused by heat, say by the light of a cigarette lighter.

For big-game fishing, many anglers use 49-strand stainless steel cable, uncoated, which is a bit less visible than cable with plastic coating.

One of the more attractive options is to use the knottable, plastic-coated cable leader materials. A few are made by Rio, Tyger Wire and Surflon. These are easy to handle, very flexible and with them you can tie the knots which you normally would, both to the fly and to the leader.

Also, a titanium-alloy leader material is available which affords some stretch, much as a shock leader does. These are made by a few companies including American Fishing Wire and knot2kinky. Finally, pre-built leaders including that trace of wire can be purchased. One maker of these leaders is Scientific Anglers.

TYING MONOFILAMENT TO WIRE LEADER

For casting, light tests of conventional single-strand wire can be joined directly to monofilament or braided line by using the Albright special knot. You simply double back the end of the wire about one inch, squeeze the loop

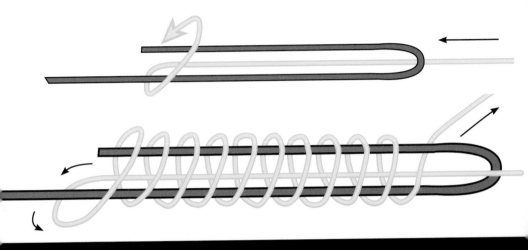

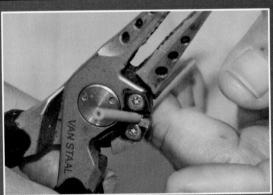

Chafing loops are plastic tubes or sleeves that protect leader material from abrasion where loops meet connections or might suffer weakening from rubbing against hooks or swivels under pressure.

Loops come in different styles, including stainless steel as well as clear nylon tubing. It is recommended to use a chafing loop on all big game lures, especially if you plan on reusing the leader multiple times.

Start by cutting the tube of chafing guard to fit the size of the loop you want to protect.

Slide the sleeve into position against both sides of guard and crimp sleeve closed, with no slack between guard and sleeve.

is tightly as you can, and then tie the Albright to it, as described in the knot chapter.

Some kinds of wire are more flexible than the old single-strand and can therefore be tied to a line with the uni-knot, as well as the Albright. If the uni is your choice, proceed as for the line-to-line application shown in the preceding chapter, making four or five turns with the line around the wire, but only one turn with the wire around the line. After the opposing wraps are pulled together, finish off by using pliers to draw down the wire very tightly before clipping off the excess. Types of wire for which this adaptation of the uni-knot is suitable include cable, coated cable and titanium.

While a direct tie makes the joint less bulky than if a swivel were used, be sure to consider the fact that the absence of a swivel can lead to severe line twist with certain lures or baits.

Use a chafing loop on all big-game lures, especially if you plan on reusing the leader multiple times.

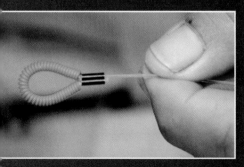

A well-protected loop should hold up for many battles with big gamefish.

MULTI-STRAND WIRE (CABLE)
Sevenstrand – non-coated

Size (pound test)	Diameter
18	.011
27	.012
40	.015
60	.018
90	.024
135	.029
170	.033
250	.039

Sevalon – nylon-coated

Size (pound test)	Diameter
18	.018
27	.020
40	.024
60	.034
90	.048
135	.058
170	.065
250	.075

Tyger Wire

Size (pound test)	Diameter
2	.006
5	.010
15	.014
30	.019
50	.024
70	.030
120	.037

49-strand – uncoated (aircraft cable)

Size (pound test)	Diameter
175	.036
275	.042
400	.053
600	.067
800	.092

CHAPTER 6

Leaders & Rigs

Fishing is all about tradeoffs. For instance, every time you select a bait for a certain species you're after, you're costing yourself a bite from something else.

Nowhere is that dynamic a bigger dilemma than when it comes to selecting the rig and leader you're going to use. Remember, the less terminal tackle you put in the water the better, but it's not enough to just get the bite, you've got to have what it takes to get the fish to the boat.

There are plenty of choices to make between what kind of line you use and what kind of hook and tackle you put on it. Do your homework.

There are plenty of choices to make between what kind of line you use and what kind of hook and tackle you put on it. Do your homework.

When you get a prize like the cobia, aka ling, above, you want to be sure your leader can handle it. Right, a table swager for crimping connections.

Leader Selection

For snook of this size, you'll want a stout leader but one that is also as invisible as possible in the water.

Fishing leaders can be divided into two broad classes:

1. Leaders designed for low visibility to avoid spooking wary fish.

2. Leaders designed to protect the line from shock, abrasion, sharp teeth, or from being cut by the fins or tail of exceptionally large fish.

The perfect leader would be one that is virtually invisible, yet strong enough to resist even the jaws of a shark, bluefish or barracuda. Unfortunately, there is no kind of leader material which comes close to providing the advantages of both extremes; therefore, any leader you make up, for any kind of fishing, is necessarily compromised to some extent.

Low-visibility leaders are generally made of either monofilament or fluorocarbon, and are used in both fresh and salt water. In fact, for most freshwater fishing the angler needs no leader at all, IF he is using monofilament line. The line serves as its own low-visibility leader, and nothing heavier is usually needed; however, the angler who uses braided line is advised to use a low-visibility leader, even if the breaking test is the same as that of his line. He can, of course, use either lighter or heavier leader as conditions dictate. Many anglers fishing in extremely heavy

(say 6-pound test and under), and so the ultralight angler may find it advisable to tie on a mono leader of around 12- or 15-pound test, even in open water. And with the typical size range of bass-fishing lines—12 to 25 pounds—it is not a bad idea to tie on a 30-pound-test monofilament leader when fishing in or near thick weeds or other obstruction. Heavier leaders are also useful when live-baiting for bass, unless your line tests 20 pounds or more. If you hook the big one you're always hoping for, he just might manage to fray your 12- or 15-pound line before you can get him to the net.

All flyfishing leaders, of course, fall into the low-visibility classification. A fly line is very thick, and so a monofilament leader must be used to form a less visible connection to the fly. Sometimes (mainly in salt water) additional protection is also needed at the fly, and this is accomplished through a heavy

> ## The perfect leader would be one that's virtually invisible, yet strong enough to resist the bite of sharks, barracuda and bluefish.

cover will use a lighter-test leader to make sure the line breaks near the lure if they get hung up.

Still, there are many freshwater situations when a monofilament leader heavier than the line is called for. Pike, muskellunge and gar are species that come immediately to mind. Even the small teeth of a bass might wear through extremely light line tippet, attached to the regular thin fly leader.

Except when fishing for gar and larger members of the pike clan, the freshwater angler is not apt to need a mono or fluorocarbon leader heavier than 30 pounds, or a wire leader. But leaders designed for protection, rather than for low visibility, are necessary in just about every area of saltwater fishing.

and anything else that makes your presentation more natural increases.

And now back to the original question: monofilament or wire?

Monofilament leaders should get first call over wire in the great majority of applications. Use wire only in cases where monofilament can easily be cut, such as by the teeth of bluefish, mackerel or barracuda. Even then, monofilament will usually result in more strikes, and so you will have to judge for yourself whether the switch to wire is likely to produce enough additional action to justify it. In a

Should you use monofilament to increase the number of bites or use wire to eliminate bite offs? That's the tradeoff.

Monofilament or Wire?

For purposes of this discussion, the terms "monofilament" and its short form "mono" will refer to both nylon and fluorocarbon material, to distinguish those soft materials from wire. But, of course, the angler must also make his own personal choice of the soft materials.

A much more recent addition to the fishing scene than nylon, fluorocarbon is, diameter-for-diameter, less visible in the water. That's because its refractive index is close to that of water itself. Fluorocarbon leader material also is stiffer and has a harder finish than most nylon monofilaments, which makes it more resistant to abrasion; however, various grades of nylon are available, and some that are marketed as leader material are nearly as stiff and hard-finished as fluorocarbon. See "Fishing Lines" in Chapter 3 for additional notes on nylon and fluorocarbon. Because of variations in water color, light level and angle of the fish's approach to a lure, it is difficult to guess just how much difference fluorocarbon's lower visibility will make to overall success. But, at times, it is likely to add at least a few more strikes to the day's total. A good rule of thumb is, if the water is clear, and the fishing pressure heavy, the need for fluorocarbon

More often than not, big king mackerel, like this, will sever monofilament leaders. Wire is often used when kingfish are targeted.

A few species, though possessing no visible teeth, have extremely raspy or bony jaws.

Live crab on a strong leader, left, presented on a long cast with a big spinning rod is a good setup for putting a tarpon in the air, as above.

"hot bite," wire probably will not be a disadvantage. Anglers using natural baits also need to consider hook-up ratio. Consider fish like billfish, mahi, and tuna. With no teeth to bite their prey into pieces, they almost always turn a baitfish in their mouth to swallow it. Many offshore trollers believe they get a better hook up ratio on mono leaders that make the bait easier to get completely into the fish's mouth when the bait is dropped back after a strike.

Snapper, grouper and seatrout are a few examples of fish that possess formidable-looking teeth, yet they do not seriously threaten monofilament leaders because their teeth are not designed for shearing or clipping. Monofilament is a better choice than wire for any of those species.

A few species, though possessing no visible teeth, own exceptionally raspy or bony jaws. This group includes the tarpon and snook. Monofilament leaders can and should be used for both species (when casting, anyway), but it must be heavy enough to withstand the raspy jaws over a considerable length of time. Mono as heavy as 100-pound

test is needed when seeking large tarpon—say 75 pounds and heavier. For smaller tarpon, and for snook, 40- to 60-pound leaders are about right, while 30-pound test is the minimum practical size, even for snook that average less than 10 pounds.

Why not use thinner wire, rather than thicker monofilament, for such fish as snapper, grouper, tarpon or snook? Because it seems obvious from the cumulative experience of many anglers that even the thinnest wire is more likely to spook a fish than is monofilament of considerably greater diameter. Also, the supple monofilament is not subject to some of the pitfalls that accompany the use of wire—kinking, spiraling, etc. And an important benefit for the caster is the fact that the soft mono allows much better action with almost every sort of artificial lure.

Wire seems less objectionable when trolling than when casting—possibly because most fish approach a trolled bait from the rear, or possibly because the wake of the boat helps camouflage the leader.

Stainless, Titanium, or Cable Wire?

In those instances where wire leader is a necessity, the angler still must select between single-strand wire and cable or twisted wire.

Both stainless and cable wire have their place and each excels at certain applications.

Stainless steel has long been the standard material for single-strand wire, but now anglers have an option in titanium, which (somewhat like monofilament) is supple and slightly stretchy, although not translucent. Titanium would be a particularly good choice for the angler who rigs with wire leader when he casts artificials, because its flexibility allows better lure action, particularly with stop-and-go or up-and-down retrieves. Another advantage of titanium is that it does not kink like stainless wire. Its main drawbacks are a sharply higher price than stainless, as well as lower breaking strength, diameter for diameter. The angler who uses light lines and short leaders might not be dissuaded by either factor, but the offshore fisherman who uses many leaders, all several feet long, may have to watch his budget.

There are no ready rules, or even a standard set of suggestions, that will help you in making your own selection from among stainless, titanium and cable. The only thing that can be done here is to discuss the merits and demerits of each, and mention a few popular applications.

Single-strand stainless leader wire is less expensive than cable. Cable is more flexible in the smaller diameters, and has become a favorite among live-bait kingfish fishermen. Each angler must weigh the advantages that titanium might give him over stainless steel against its higher price.

The main drawback of single-strand stainless wire, compared to either cable or titanium is that it can far more easily be deformed after a catch, and, even more serious, that it can kink and drastically weaken the leader. You must inspect it frequently for such kinks, and if any are observed, they must be cut out and the leader rewrapped or replaced. Do not attempt to "unkink" the leader by bending it in the opposite direction, as this will weaken it even more. However, minor offset bends or spirals that develop in stainless wire can safely be straightened without appreciable loss of strength. It is difficult to do, but many tackle dealers carry small wire-straightening tools that make the job easier.

Cable and titanium are both more supple than single-strand stainless, and so either is a logical choice for casters who like a short wire leader. Nylon-covered cable

Without a wire leader, you can almost always kiss a wahoo like this one goodbye.

is more supple yet, and many casters prefer to use it instead of plain cable—however, sharp-toothed fish can quickly shred the soft coating, and so leaders may need to be changed more often.

Heavy cable leaders are still used in some big-game fishing, particularly for sharks. However, heavy monofilament (mostly 200- to 300-pound test) has largely replaced cable for marlin fishing. At any rate, cable is resistant to kink-breakage, which stainless wire is not. It is often a tradeoff as to which tackle to use for your purpose.

Each angler must weigh the advantages that titanium might provide against its higher price.

Leader Length and Connection

For all kinds of casting applications, the heavier monofilament leader should be tied directly to your line, using the appropriate uni-knot, the surgeon's knot or the Albright special. If the line is doubled first with the Bimini twist, the connection of double line to leader should prove close to 100 percent strength, regardless of which knot you choose. With single line, the surgeon's knot will reduce strength by 15-20 percent, but both the uni and Albright will hold at 90 percent or better.

Even for the lightest fishing, the mono leader should be at least two feet long. This allows a few inches of leader to be cranked inside the tip guide when you cast, and means that the leader—not the light line—will be absorbing the strain and chafe from the tip guide during the cast.

Much longer mono leaders are required for certain heavy-duty types of casting, such as surf fishing and ocean casting with lures weighing two ounces and up. Your mono must be long enough so that it will go through all the guides and wrap a couple of times around the reel—and still leave the necessary casting length outside the tip guide. This arrangement is sometimes referred to as a "shock line" or "shock leader."

As a matter of fact, this shock-leader arrangement is a good one to use as your basic leader rig for just about every kind of saltwater fishing with spinning tackle or light-line classes (under 30-pound) of general tackle. Here's how it works: Tie several feet of 30- or 40-pound-test monofilament directly to your line. Most of the time this will be all the leader necessary, and because you have a goodly length of it, you can change lures frequently, cutting the leader back a number of times before it gets so short you have to change it.

Now, if you get into toothy fish such as blues,

you simply add a short length of wire, 12-18 inches, to the end of your shock leader, using a small black swivel as a connector (with titanium, the connection can be direct, without a swivel, using the Albright special). If you want to go after big tarpon, tie 12 inches of 80- or 100-pound mono to your shock leader, using the uni-knot or Albright special. Or, when you take a yen for bottom

The shock absorbing quality of mono lines and leaders help play fish boatside, where many fish are lost when a fish shakes its head with little slack in the line.

fishing, slip your sinker onto the shock leader, then tie on a swivel and add the desired length and size of additional leader.

The long shock leader has numerous advantages, of which shock absorption is only one. It acts as a safeguard against a large fish wrapping up in the leader and breaking the line; it guards against a big fish reaching past a short leader and breaking or cutting the line with sweeps of its tail; it better takes the abrasive punishment of underwater obstacles, such as coral or oysters. For offshore fishermen having 30 feet of leader makes it much easier to handle near the boat. For a tuna fighting to the last gasp, or a big mahi turned sideways in the current, it's much easier for a mate to handle the fish hand to hand. It's also much easier to get a quick release on a billfish before he is overstressed by fighting light tackle for the last 30 feet.

Mono Leader Suggestions

Type of Fishing	Leader Length	Leader Test (Pounds)
Most freshwater	2-3'	none to 20
All-around inshore	2' to rod length	20-40
Snook, tarpon	rod length	30-50
Deep jigging, reef or bottom fishing	rod length	50-60
Ocean casting (surface and mid-depth)	rod length	30-60
Ocean trolling (sails, small tuna, dolphin, etc)	6-12'	40-80
Ocean trolling (blue marlin, giant tuna)	12-15'	80-300

NOTE: Add a short tippet of 80 or 100-pound mono to your basic leader when fishing for big tarpon. Add a short tippet of wire if likely to be getting strikes from bluefish, mackerel, barracuda, or shark. A short wire tippet at the end of a mono leader also helps in rigging certain trolling baits. In any case, the wire need be no more than about 12 inches long.

Wire Leader Suggestions

Type of Fishing	Leader Length	Wire Size
Inshore casting, trolling, light bottom fishing	6"-3'	2-5
Offshore trolling, drifting (sails, tuna, dolphin, etc.)	6-9'	3-7
Offshore trolling (billfish, big tuna)	12-15'	9-12
Bottom fishing, deep trolling	3-9'	7-9
Shark fishing (large shark)	12-15'	9 and up

Leaders for Heavy Tackle

Pre-Made Wire, Mono and Cable Leaders

To make line ready for instant attachment or change of leaders, first form the desired length of double line, then tie to the end of the double line a heavy-duty snapswivel, preferably ballbearing. The basic uni-knot, improved clinch knot or offshore knot may be used to tie on the swivel.

Prepare single-strand wire leaders by forming a small loop on one end using a haywire twist. For mono and multi-strand cable leaders, slide a sleeve onto the leader, form a small loop, insert tag end into the sleeve and crimp shut. Attach your hook or rigged bait to the other end, also using a haywire twist or crimped-sleeve loop. Refer to the table of Wire Leader Suggestions for size and length of wire.

Several of these leaders can be made up in advance, coiled neatly, and kept ready for quick change simply by unsnapping and re-snapping the snapswivel.

You can either rig your baits to the leaders as needed, or you can rig several baited leaders in advance and keep them coiled and ready in an ice chest.

You may, of course, use an ordinary swivel instead of a snapswivel. In this case, you would not make the wire loop, but merely leave the end of the leader as is, so it can be wrapped to the swivel.

Stiff Rigs

These rigs are for running lures without ballyhoo or strip baits. The goal is to set the hook in the upright position, with the bend of the hook just barely sticking out of the back of the skirt. Rigging the last section—the part from the back of the lure head to the hook—is often done separately with 49-strand wire. Or you can use mono, but wire is stiffer. The connections are crimped and the rig wrapped with heat-shrink material to stiffen it.

Fishing concave or slant head lures enables you to increase speed and cover territory. They often use stiff rig hooks.

Offshore Leader - Wire and Monofilament

Many anglers use heavy monofilament leaders for offshore trolling—with only 12 to 24 inches of wire at the end. The short length of wire is ample to guard against cutting by sharp teeth, and it also makes bait-rigging easier when using J-hooked ballyhoo. Ballyhoo and other trolling baits are sometimes more difficult or time-to rig with monofilament.

This leader arrangement is especially helpful to anyone who fishes offshore in a small boat, or even a large boat with a cramped cockpit. The monofilament is much easier to control in tight quarters than is a long length of wire, and offers other advantages as well.

Again, start with a snapswivel tied to your double line. Prepare the monofilament leaders in advance. The monofilament will form all but a couple of feet of your overall leader and can test as little as 40 pounds when you use light lines (20-pound or less) for dolphin, small tuna and sailfish; or anywhere from 100 to 300 pounds when using heavier tackle.

Use either a perfection loop knot or for heavier tests crimp a loop to form one end of your mono leader. If your leader is less than 60 pounds tie a loop, or tying any connection for that matter is fine. For heavier tackle you need to learn how to crimp properly. For foolproof crimps, make sure you start with a quality crimping tool, called a swager, or a "swag." You can generally count on quality sleeves to have a chart on them telling what sized

Fresh ballyhoo (clear eyes, good color) rigged on light mono leader will get you maximum bites.

Learning proper "wiring techniques" when handling billfish is mandatory for safety. Many things can go wrong when it comes to getting hands on these fish.

mono or cable matches the size sleeve. It's important to learn how to line up the sleeve so it fits in the proper slot in the crimping tool. Your goal is to line up the crimp in the tool so the two pieces of mono are crimped into each other, not flattened out. It's also important to not crimp the end of the sleeve into the mono to prevent weakening it.

Monofilament is much easier to control in tight quarters than is a long length of wire and offers other advantages as well.

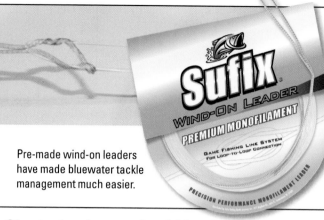

Pre-made wind-on leaders have made bluewater tackle management much easier.

Short wire tippets should be made in advance. When the bite turns on, you don't want to get caught rigging more baits.

Most anglers leave the other end of the leader clear until ready to deploy. You can make up dozens of short wire leaders in advance. Simply haywire twist your hook to one end, slide any feathers, chugger heads etc. you want in front of your bait, and haywire a small swivel on the other end. As the leaders are used, cut the end of the mono, and tie or crimp a new wire trace on.

The short wire tippets should be prepared in advance. They are easy to store, and you can rig plenty of baits in advance. When the bite turns on, don't get caught rigging more baits.

The heavy mono section of leader will not need changing until and unless it becomes nicked or heavily frayed.

Bent-butt rods meant for fighting fish from chairs can tackle marlin, big tuna and big swordfish.

Offshore Heavy Tackle Leaders

Big game trolling has been made much easier because of heavy wind-on mono leaders. Most anglers purchase their wind-on leaders pre-made. They are built by splicing a loop of hollow core braid to one end of a 20- to 30-foot mono leader. To join the leader to your line, first tie a Bimini twist to form a loop on the end of your fishing line, then use a loop-to-loop connection to add the leader.

Some experts recommend passing the coiled leader through the joined loops twice to increase the strength of the connection. Having attached the wind-on, your baits or lures can be rigged on much shorter and more manageable leaders. Double crimp a quality ball bearing snapswivel to the end of your wind-on leader and finish with a short (3- to 5-foot) leader holding the bait. Refer to the general discussion on leaders at the beginning of this chapter for more information on the cable leader. Refer also to the instructions for rigging big-game trolling lures in Chapter 9.

Heavy cable is preferable to single-strand wire leaders for the following fishing specialties: giant marlin, giant swordfish, big sharks, big bottom fish at extreme depth (for instance, warsaw grouper).

Present-day big-game anglers exhibit a wide preference for heavy monofilament over cable when seeking swordfish, marlin and big tuna, but the option to use cable remains.

Sailfish, like this one nearing the boat for release, are commonly fought on 20- and 30-pound outfits with all-knot connections in the line and leader rigging.

Leaders for Light Tackle

All-Purpose Straight Monofilament

This is the simplest of leaders and the most widely useful, consisting of nothing more than a length of heavy monofilament tied directly to your line.

For freshwater and light saltwater fishing, make the tie with the uni-knot or surgeon's knot.

For any kind of saltwater fishing where your line is apt to be put to the full test of its strength, make a double line first, then tie your leader to the double line, using the uni-knot, surgeon's knot or Albright special. If the leader is more than twice the thickness of your line, the Albright will prove best, because it is the trimmest tie and will clear the rod guides more easily. Only with a double line can you be sure of getting 100 percent knot strength.

All purpose mono leader

As indicated by the two illustrations, most lures should be tied to the heavy mono with a loop knot—the uni-loop or end loop. Hooks for fishing with bait can be tied with the basic uni-knot, the improved clinch or the Palomar.

Recommended lengths of mono leaders are discussed at the beginning of this chapter. Recommended strengths are shown in a separate table.

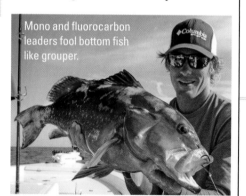

Mono and fluorocarbon leaders fool bottom fish like grouper.

Wahoo are known for striking brightly-colored lures pulled fast.

Mono Leader with Heavy or Wire Tippet

In some cases (as has already been discussed) it is desirable to add an additional short leader of stronger material (called a tippet) to your basic leader.

You can add heavier mono by tying it on with

Main line

Leader to line knot

Main line   Heavy mono leader

Straight Wire Leaders

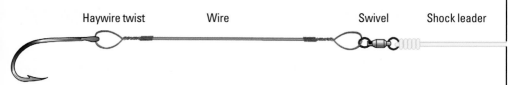

Haywire twist   Wire   Swivel   Shock leader

With lines under 20-pound test, it is seldom advisable to use a straight wire leader without a shock leader of monofilament. Though you can often get by without it, the added strength of the shock leader is highly desirable.

However, if you wish to use a stainless wire leader up to three or four feet long without the shock leader, rig it as follows:

Wrap your wire to a swivel, using the haywire twist. Wrap the other end of the wire to your hook or lure, also by means of the haywire.

Tie the swivel to your line with the uni, improved clinch knot or palomar.

If you choose titanium wire, both swivel and lure must be attached with knots instead of wraps; use the improved clinch knot. Or the swivel can be eliminated and the wire tied directly to the line with the Albright special.

the uni-knot or Albright special knot.

You can add light cable or nylon-coated cable, by tying it on with the Albright special OR by using a swivel as a connector. The swivel should be tied to the leader with the uni-knot or improved clinch. The wire tippet can be attached to the swivel by means of the figure-eight knot or a crimped sleeve.

If you wish to add single-strand stainless wire, a swivel is the best way. Your line can be tied to titanium wire—or to very light stainless wire—with the Albright special. Be sure to use the haywire twist in wrapping your wire to a swivel.

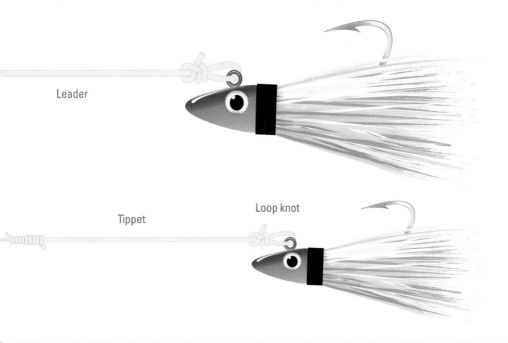

Leader

Tippet   Loop knot

Sinker Rigs

The Splitshot

Splitshot sinkers are the smallest type available—and by far the handiest to use. Splitshots require no special leader or rigging but are merely pressed onto whatever rig you're using, if and when a small amount of weight is needed to improve casting ease, or to sink your bait a bit faster.

The splitshot has long been standard in freshwater fishing, but is sadly overlooked by many saltwater anglers. It can be just as helpful to folks who fish the coast. The saltwater fisherman who keeps splitshot handy will find many instances when he is able to add just the right amount of added weight without having to re-rig with a different type of sinker—which likely as not is bigger than he really needs.

Press the splitshot to your leader, using pliers. The shot can be positioned about six inches from the hook, or right at the eye of the hook.

If more than one shot is used, do not place them close together but keep them about an inch apart.

CAUTION: Crimping a splitshot directly to light line may severely weaken it at that point. Best use shot on leaders only.

Clinch or Rubbercor Sinker

The clinch is a tapered sinker, with a full-length groove and soft "ears" at either end. You attach the clinch simply by laying your leader in the groove of the sinker, folding the "ears" over the line, then pressing the groove closed with pliers.

The Rubbercor is a patented sinker, which works in much the same way as the clinch. But it is a much-improved design and considerably easier to use, because it can be taken off and put on at will—with no pliers and without bruising the line or leader.

Instead of the lead ears, the Rubbercor has a center insert of rubber, which protrudes at both ends of the sinker. You lay your line in the groove,

Splitshot sinker

Egg sinker

Rubbercor sinker

Having the right size and style sinker can make the difference between catching and fishing.

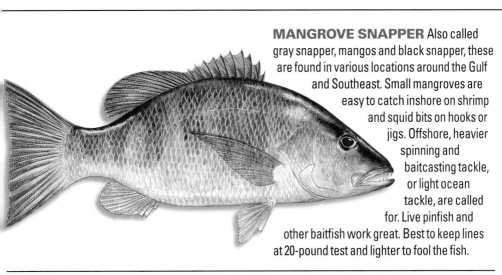

MANGROVE SNAPPER Also called gray snapper, mangos and black snapper, these are found in various locations around the Gulf and Southeast. Small mangroves are easy to catch inshore on shrimp and squid bits on hooks or jigs. Offshore, heavier spinning and baitcasting tackle, or light ocean tackle, are called for. Live pinfish and other baitfish work great. Best to keep lines at 20-pound test and lighter to fool the fish.

twist the rubber ends and your line is secured. To remove, twist the rubber ends in the opposite direction.

Clinch and Rubbercor sinkers come in various weights, and are especially useful in weights of one-quarter ounce and heavier, where they replace several splitshot.

Sliding or Egg Sinker Rig

This is pretty much the standard sinker used for saltwater fishing. Egg sinkers range in size from one-quarter ounce to several ounces, but the basic rig shown here is widely used with all of them—whether you're using a half-ounce sinker on a spinning rod for inshore channel fishing, or a two-ounce (or heavier) sinker on a boat rod for reef bottom fishing.

For inshore, or offshore waters shallower than 60 feet, you slide the sinker onto your line (or, preferably, your shock leader), then tie on a swivel, using the uni or improved clinch knot; then add your leader and hook.

As you can see, the egg sinker is free to travel

When gag grouper like this head for the rocks, any weak link in your rig will break.

If your light line is tied directly to the swivel, your knot may be weakened and a breakoff result.

along your line but is stopped well above your hook by the swivel. When a fish bites, he can take out line without feeling the weight of the sinker. It is advisable to use a shock leader, or double line, above the swivel, because the free-running sinker often bangs hard against the swivel while you're fishing. If your light line is tied straight to the swivel, your knot might be quickly weakened and a breakoff can occur.

Pyramid Sinker Rig

The egg sinker just doesn't hold position on smooth bottom if there is any current or wave action. That's why pyramid sinkers are the standard weights for surf and ocean-pier anglers, who fish mostly over sand.

The rig shown here is built around a three-way swivel: that is, a swivel with three eyes instead of the standard two. Tie your line or shock leader to one eye, using the uni or improved clinch knot. To the second eye, tie a short piece of heavy monofilament, and to the other end of the monofilament, tie your pyramid sinker. The same knots serve for all those ties.

The third eye, of course, is the one to which you attach your leader, with hook and bait. Monofilament generally is the leader choice, but you might wish to use wire if expecting bluefish, shark, etc.

Sputnik Sinkers

For surf fishermen there are conditions where even a heavy pyramid is just not enough. Stripers, big redfish and even big whiting are sometimes most active when the surf is churned up by a rough ocean. When that happens, the "Sputnik" sinker is the only way to hold bottom. The Sputnik has crossing heavy wires attached to the bottom of the sinker. Upon hitting bottom, one or two wire prongs digs into the sand holding the bait in place. Once enough pressure is applied by the angler the prongs spring free allowing the angler to reel in and reset them.

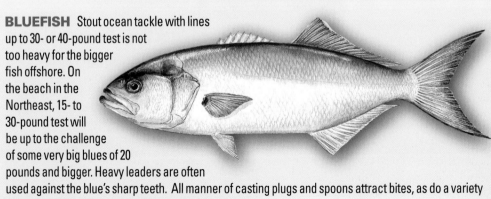

BLUEFISH Stout ocean tackle with lines up to 30- or 40-pound test is not too heavy for the bigger fish offshore. On the beach in the Northeast, 15- to 30-pound test will be up to the challenge of some very big blues of 20 pounds and bigger. Heavy leaders are often used against the blue's sharp teeth. All manner of casting plugs and spoons attract bites, as do a variety of baits, including live and cut fish, cut squid and shrimp.

Pyramid Fishfinder Rig

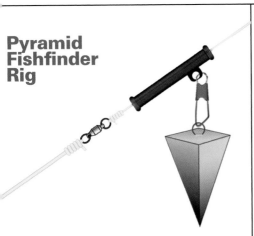

Another basic rig for the pyramid sinker is the fishfinder or sliding-sinker arrangement. It works much like the egg sinker rig, in that the pyramid sinker is allowed to slide freely up and down the line or shock leader above your swivel.

This could be accomplished simply by threading your line through the eye of the pyramid sinker, but such an arrangement really isn't satisfactory. It is far too easy for the line to get twisted up if the line runs through the eye of the pyramid, causing it to fail at the worst possible time. You should use a SINKER SLIDE, which can be purchased at most tackle stores in beach country.

The sinker slide is simply a small accessory which has an eye on one end (for your line to run through), and a snap on the other, to which your sinker is attached.

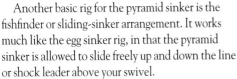

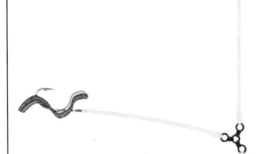

Double Drop Rig

The double drop rig employs three-way swivels to suspend baits outwardly from a fixed position where it is held by a weight heavy enough to hold in the existing conditions. The rig is popular on party boats where it is important that everyone fish straight up and down to avoid line tangles with their neighbors along the rail, and it is also popular among surf anglers because it can be easily cast straight out in the surf and the weight adjusted for conditions.

Use pyramid sinker or Sputnik sinkers in sandy areas, bank sinkers in rocky areas. Select hook size for the bait and the fish you are seeking and try two different baits on the hooks to see what the fish want: cut shrimp and squid strip, for instance. You can switch all baits to the desired one when you find the pattern.

2-Swivel Rig

When fishing deeper water offshore for bigger fish, it's wise to place your egg sinker between two swivels on a piece of heavy mono 18 to 24 inches apart. If you leave your sinker on the main line, dropping it in deep water will cause problems. The sinker will fall much faster than the bait. Not only will that cause the line to get twisted, but when your sinker hits bottom, your bait is apt to still be high in the water column.

If you want to keep the sinker away from your hook, pinch a small split-shot to the leader at the desired point.

Egg Sinker with Splitshot Stopper

The egg sinker can be used without a swivel if you prefer.

If you're using a shock leader tied directly to a heavy tippet simply slide the sinker onto your shock leader before you tie on the tippet. The knot will be plenty large enough to assure that the sinker won't slide over it to your hook.

If you wish to use a shock leader without a heavy tippet, slide the egg sinker onto the leader before tying on your hook. Now, if you want to keep the sinker away from your hook, just press a tiny splitshot to your leader at the desired point a foot or so away from the hook to keep the sinker from sliding farther.

VARIATION: **Knocker Rig**

Although tradition calls for using a swivel or a splitshot as a "stopper" to keep the sliding sinker separated from the hook, many bottom fishermen now eliminate the stopping device altogether and allow the sinker to slide all the way down to the hook. This arrangement, sometimes called a "knocker rig," makes for easier casting and tangle-free sinking. When the rig is resting on bottom, the closeness of the sinker seldom, if ever, seems to keep fish from biting. Many offshore anglers prefer using a knocker rig with a live bait hooked in the tail. Once the bait hits the bottom simply freespool to allow the bait to swim away from the sinker.

The Trolling Sinker

Trolling sinkers generally weigh several ounces and are used mostly with medium or heavy tackle, including wire line outfits, for deep-reef and ocean trolling.

Some trolling sinkers are torpedo-shaped, while others are kidney or keel shaped to reduce line twist. Some have a planing head that helps attain

a greater depth. All have an eye (or bead chain) at either end for ease of rigging.

Regardless of shape, they are all rigged as follows:

1. Tie a heavy-duty swivel to your line or double line.

2. Wrap about three feet of leader wire to the swivel and wrap the other end of the wire to the forward eye of the trolling sinker.

3. Take a second length of leader wire, 3 to 6 feet long. Wrap one end to the rear eye of the trolling sinker, and the other end to your hook or lure.

VARIATION FOR WIRE LINE: If using wire line, it is advisable to substitute heavy braided nylon line, at least 100-pound test, for the wire mentioned in Step 2. This is a safeguard against the effects of electrolysis.

For this type of deep trolling, you can use either a rigged bait (ballyhoo, mullet, strip, feather-strip), or else a large lure, such as a spoon or feather. Make sure you use an extra heavy duty hook for this rig. Pulling trolling weights, and/or wire line through the water puts huge pressure on a hooked fish.

Breakaway Sinkers

The obvious use of breakaway sinker rigs is to get your bait to the desired depth in situations which require so much weight that the sinker would be a disadvantage after a fish is hooked.

The simplest and most effective method is to run a length of soft copper wire (such as you buy for rigging ballyhoo) through the eye of an egg sinker. This leaves some of the wire protruding from either end. Wrap one end lightly to the eye of your swivel and wrap the other end around your leader with two or three wide spirals.

This will hold the sinker firmly enough in place so that you can drop it down. When a fish is hooked, the soft wire lets go, usually on the first dash.

Variation: You can also fold the line through the sinker until it protrudes and then slip a length of flat rubber band into that loop and pull the line

tight to pull the band into the sinker until the line comes back out and the band, still in the sinker, holds it there. The band will hold the sinker in place, until the fish strikes, when the force of the strike will pull the line out of the sinker or even slice the rubber band and free the sinker.

A weight can be rigged to pull off the line either by using a band of light rubber pulled into the weight's center, above, or by wrapping it by wire to the rig, below.

Swordfish Rig

There are two basic kinds of swordfishing rigs used by recreational anglers and many variations among them. The first is for drifting at night, when swordfish rise up from the depths. The second kind of rig is for daytime swordfishing. It is designed to fish depths of up to 2,000 feet where the fish stay during the day. The rig illustrated is a daytime rig meant to be fished while clipped to another rod outfitted with a weight, which acts as a downrigger to bring this fishing rig with it. When the fish takes the bait, this line comes out of the clip and is free. The fishing outfit is a 70 International, filled with 65-pound braid, with a 150-foot, 80-pound topshot, a 20-foot wind-on leader and an 8-foot bait leader. The bait goes at least 100 feet from the weight so you put a wax loop on the 80-pound topshot of mono, put that in the big clip on the line of the outfit that acts as a downrigger. You fish this rig either manually or with an electric reel.

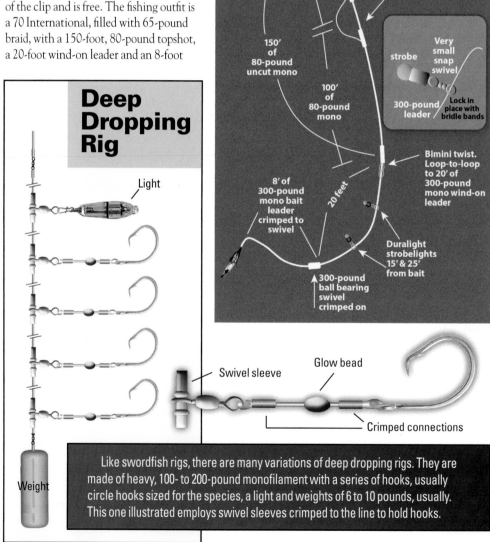

MAINLINE: 2,500 yards 65-pound Stren Invisibraid

8-turn uni-knot in braid to mono to 3-turn uni-knot in mono to braid

50' of the 80-pound mono to 50-pound waxed-thread loop

50'

150' of 80-pound uncut mono

100' of 80-pound mono

strobe — Very small snap swivel

300-pound leader — Lock in place with bridle bands

Bimini twist. Loop-to-loop to 20' of 300-pound mono wind-on leader

8' of 300-pound mono bait leader crimped to swivel

20 feet

Duralight strobelights 15' & 25' from bait

300-pound ball bearing swivel crimped on

Deep Dropping Rig

Light

Weight

Swivel sleeve

Glow bead

Crimped connections

Like swordfish rigs, there are many variations of deep dropping rigs. They are made of heavy, 100- to 200-pound monofilament with a series of hooks, usually circle hooks sized for the species, a light and weights of 6 to 10 pounds, usually. This one illustrated employs swivel sleeves crimped to the line to hold hooks.

Heavy Ball Sinker Rigs

Perfected in the San Francisco Bay area for getting baits down to striped bass when they are at depths which pretty much prohibit the usual rigs, heavy ball sinkers—sometimes weighing two pounds or more—are useful, too, in such specialties as plumbing extreme ocean depths for cod, snapper, grouper and tilefish. For economy, the balls can be of cast iron instead of lead.

One illustration shows the ball rigged as a three-way sinker as in preceding rigs with other types of weights. This would obviously require extremely heavy tackle and a lot of muscle to crank the ball back up, either with or without a fish attached. It's best used with a motorized reel.

The detailed drawing shows a device popular in the Pacific northwest to release the ball once a fish is hooked, so the quarry can be fought on lighter tackle without the heavy weight. The sinker release is spring-loaded. You draw back the spring, insert the eye of the ball sinker into the aperture, and release the spring. When a bass or salmon hits, the spring is depressed and the sinker falls free. The sinker release is not used on a dropper line, but is simply tied into the leader by means of the swivels at each end.

STRIPED BASS

All categories of casting tackle—spinning, casting and fly—are used on small and medium stripers. Stout surf outfits get the call along beaches, and in the ocean, light to medium ocean outfits are best. Spoons, squids, feathers and large surface or swimming plugs all have their uses, and a huge array of productive baits include various small fish, live and dead, plus eels and marine worms.

Chunk Float Rig

For surf casting or fishing from an anchored boat, the chunk float rig holds the bait in position and also suspends it up and away from the rig, higher in the water column with the float. Fish can find the bait first, apart from the rig. Use a sinker slide or a three-way snap with pyramid sinker heavy enough to hold bottom. Add small float ¾ of the way down leader to keep bait off bottom, away from crabs. Use 1-inch wide chunk of menhaden or other bait.

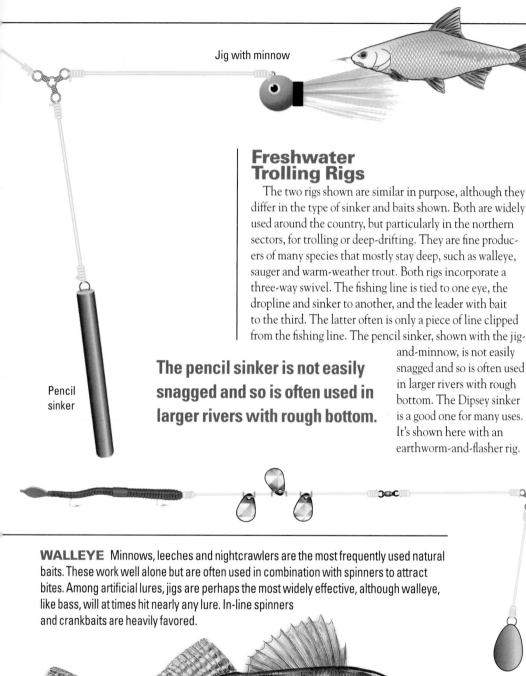

Jig with minnow

Freshwater Trolling Rigs

The two rigs shown are similar in purpose, although they differ in the type of sinker and baits shown. Both are widely used around the country, but particularly in the northern sectors, for trolling or deep-drifting. They are fine producers of many species that mostly stay deep, such as walleye, sauger and warm-weather trout. Both rigs incorporate a three-way swivel. The fishing line is tied to one eye, the dropline and sinker to another, and the leader with bait to the third. The latter often is only a piece of line clipped from the fishing line. The pencil sinker, shown with the jig-and-minnow, is not easily snagged and so is often used in larger rivers with rough bottom. The Dipsey sinker is a good one for many uses. It's shown here with an earthworm-and-flasher rig.

Pencil sinker

The pencil sinker is not easily snagged and so is often used in larger rivers with rough bottom.

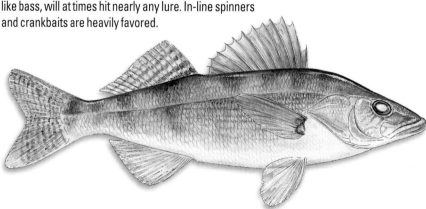

WALLEYE Minnows, leeches and nightcrawlers are the most frequently used natural baits. These work well alone but are often used in combination with spinners to attract bites. Among artificial lures, jigs are perhaps the most widely effective, although walleye, like bass, will at times hit nearly any lure. In-line spinners and crankbaits are heavily favored.

SUMMER FLOUNDER

Also named fluke and northern fluke, this fish is an aggressive feeder that will chase down baits and artificials. Finger mullet and other small baitfish make the best baits, although shrimp, crabs and worms are also good. Jigs and swimming plugs, retrieved slowly, are productive. Spinning, baitcasting and light saltwater outfits are all appropriate.

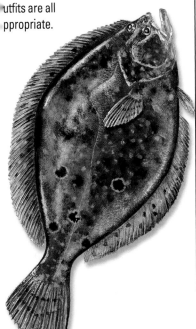

Versatile Bottom Rig

This is one of the most popular of bottom rigs, and can be used by varying the size of hook and sinker in virtually every area of saltwater fishing—in bays, from bridges and piers, in the surf, and in deepwater partyboat angling. As you can see, it differs from the preceding pyramid sinker rig (page 132) only in that a bank sinker (or Dipsey) is used instead of the pyramid. Also two or more three-way swivels may be incorporated into the leader for additional dropper lines with extra hooks.

Bank sinker

Spinner Fluke Rig

The spinner fluke rig is good for drift fishing in open water. Add squid strip or live killifish to hook. The spinner and beads will increase visibility, especially useful for discolored water. Snap sinker to bottom of rig, just enough weight to hold bottom.

Bank sinker

Spreader Bottom Rig

Though used primarily for fluke and flounder fishing in bays, the spreader rig is a good one for fishing on any comparatively smooth bottom and for many types of fish.

While most anglers purchase them ready-rigged in tackle shops, it's not too difficult to fashion a spreader, using stiff, springy wire. Dropper lines for hooks and sinker are of monofilament. Your fishing line, of course, is tied to the swivel at the center of the spreader.

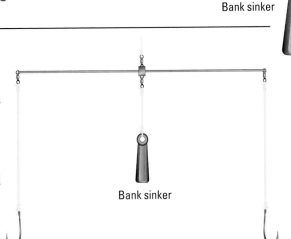

Bank sinker

Sabiki Rigs

There are tricks to removing the sabiki without tangling it.

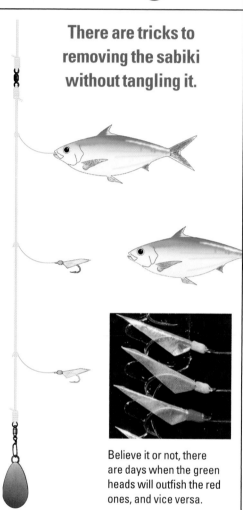

Believe it or not, there are days when the green heads will outfish the red ones, and vice versa.

end of the rig. To use a sabiki, you tie the top end to a swivel at the end of a fishing line—usually rigged on a spinning outfit—and the bottom end to a sinker. The whole rig is then lowered into a school of baitfish that has been spotted by sight or on a depth sounder. It is not necessary to impart much jigging action to the sabiki; simply lowering

Tie on the sabiki while it's still in the package, above, to avoid tangling. Then fill pack with water to soften cardboard. Pull it out. Tie on sinker, below.

and raising the rod generally provides enough to attract the little fish. (Tip: To easily remove sabiki rigs without tangling, first tie your line to the swivel while rig is still in package. Second, fill the bag with water, softening the cardboard. Then pull the rig out. It should come out tangle free.)

Should you wish to rig your own sabiki, proceed as follows:

Using the blood knot, tie two pieces of 12- to 15-pound-test monofilament together, but allow

Sabiki rigs—multiple small hooks or lures that dangle from a section of leader—are used to catch thickly schooling baitfishes, such as various species of herrings and small jacks. They will, however, take many other small fish when worked at or near the bottom. Commercially rigged sabikis are widely available and are the choice of most anglers. The models offered for sale vary greatly in hook size and lure type. Typically they are supplied with loops or swivels at either nough tag end to remain on one side of the knot so that it protrudes about 6 inches. This long tag end becomes a dropper, to which you will tie one hook. The other tag end can be trimmed close to the knot.

Next, tie several more lengths of monofilament together in the same way, thus creating the number of droppers you want to employ. Tie your chosen hooks or lures to the droppers.

Although configurations vary, commercial sabiki rigs usually have six hooks, rigged with three droppers on each side of the line, as in drawing No. 2; however, you probably will do just as well—and with much less fouling—if you rig only four hooks, with all of them on the same side of the leader and enough space in between so they cannot foul on each other.

After completing your chosen number of droppers and hooks, use the surgeon's or perfection loop knot to tie loops at both ends of your completed rig. Your line is tied to the top loop, and a sinker is attached to the bottom. By using loops instead of swivels or snapswivels, you are less likely to lose your rig to cutoffs from such toothy fish as mackerel and small bluefish, which often strike anything metallic.

The lures you select should depend on the size of the baitfish you want to catch. For small schooling types like herrings and sardines, shiny little silver or gold hooks, No. 6 or smaller, are enough in themselves to attract strikes, without being dressed or baited. A tiny fluorescent bead—available at craft shops and many tackle outlets—will add color and appeal when threaded on before the hook is tied. If you can't convince yourself that bare hooks will work just fine (but they will!), you can sweeten the hooks with tiny dabs of cutbait—or use old or cheap fishing flies. For larger and stronger baitfish such as blue runners, you can use small jigs, 1/16th of an ounce or so. These should be deployed with a fairly heavy spinning outfit so the hard-fighting baits can be landed with as little delay as possible.

Avoid handling your baits at all costs. Removing their slime with your hands makes it harder for them to swim, and they tire too easily. Always use a dehooker, always dip them from the well one at a time with a monofilament dip net, and always store them in an oblong or round live well with plenty of circulation.

A sabiki rig full of live baits is a good thing, but care must be taken of the baits in how they are handled.

Bait dehooker for catching baits on a sabiki rig.

Float Rigs

How do you select the proper size and type of float? Follow these guidelines:

Pole fishermen should use a very small float, or one of the slender designs. (Many still like the old turkey quill, of which there are numerous manufactured successors.) Larger floats are for bigger baits and, hopefully, bigger fish. The design is not actually too important. Just try to use the smallest size which will support the bait you're using. This is especially important with live baits. You don't want a float which can be easily pulled under by your bait, making it difficult to tell when the strike comes.

Fixed Float Rig

This is the standard setup for fishing with a float. The rig remains basically the same, although it can be used with a wide array of floats—in various sizes and designs. The float is placed at a predetermined depth, and fixed there so it will not move. The manner in which it is fixed depends on the design of the float. Many have a hollow center and a peg. Some feature a spring-loaded clip. The latter, however, often tend to slip, and they can weaken a light line at the point where attached.

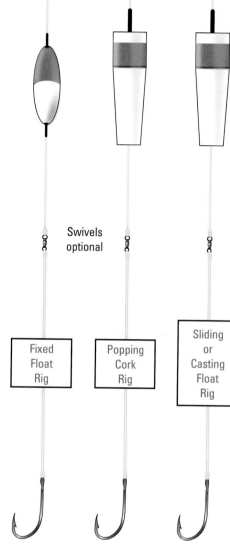

Kn
an
bea

Swivels optional

Fixed Float Rig

Popping Cork Rig

Sliding or Casting Float Rig

SPOTTED SEATROUT Light gear is a must to feel the tussle of a smaller trout, and can be used to handle even the biggest of the species, which weigh in the 10-pound range, though the record fish weighed 17 pounds, 7 ounces. Nearly all popular natural baits work well, and seatrout will eagerly hit jigs, spoons, topwater plugs, subsurface plugs and flies—well, just about anything that you throw at them.

Popping Cork Rig

This is the same as the fixed-float rig, the only difference being that you use a float which is specifically designed to pop the surface of the water when you twitch the tip of your rod.

Just like an ordinary float, the popping cork supports your bait at the desired depth, and signals a strike. But it also helps attract fish to your bait. Instead of letting the cork lie still, you pop it at frequent intervals; be sure to take up any slack line which results. The noise is attractive to many predatory fish.

Sliding or Casting Float Rig

It can be awkward, or even impossible, to cast with a fixed float—especially if your float is several feet above the bait. To achieve this, you must use a sliding float in conjunction with a plastic, hollow bead.

Many anglers tie a knot, or better a tiny rubber band, in their line at the point where they want the float to stop, then thread the bead onto the line below the band, then thread the float onto the line below the bead. Last, they tie on the leader (or hook and sinker, if using no leader).

The hole in the bead is too small to permit passage of the band, therefore the bead stops at the band. And the bead, of course, stops the float. Beads can be purchased at tackle counters. If necessary, you could use a small button instead of the bead. A better option is to wrap a bit of tape or thread tightly around your line at the desired stopping point. There also are tiny manufactured stopping devices of plastic, sold either alone or in a complete sliding-float kit.

A kid's balloon can take the place of an expensive float. Right, mackerel on a float for stripers.

Balloon Float

One of the most versatile and easily carried of floats is an ordinary toy balloon. A package of balloons can be tucked away in a corner of your tackle box, out of the way until one is needed. A balloon can be inflated to whatever size is needed to support your particular bait. Make a single knot in the balloon's lip to hold inflation, then tie the lip to your swivel or leader at the chosen depth, using a bit of light line for the purpose. The fight of a husky fish will burst the balloon, so that there is no added pressure on your rod as you tussle. Tie the balloon on tightly so that it does not become litter in the water after it breaks.

Stinger Rigs

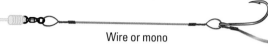

Wire or mono

Stronger hook
(often used with treble)

Here's a rig that can be used effectively with both live and dead natural baits, even plastic worms, and is a snap to make. It's called the "stinger" because the trailing hook nips short-striking fish, or those which usually clip a bait in the middle and avoid a single, forward-placed hook.

The rig can be made with either monofilament or wire leader, and in a variety of hook sizes for such diverse purposes as swordfishing with whole squid and 14/0 hooks and rigging a sandworm to 1/0 hooks.

You can choose to use a swivel to connect the

whether they be kite-flown, drifted, slow-trolled or freelined.

The stinger hook is often left to swing free, which is a deadly arrangement but not considered sporting by most anglers. It also is prohibited by the International Game Fish Association, which requires that the trailing hook be attached to the bait and positioned at least a shank's length behind the first hook.

When used with dead baits, such as strips, ballyhoo, cigar minnows or squid, the front hook is inserted at the front of the bait, in at the bottom and out the top, and the second hook placed wherever it happens to reach. The front hook now serves the same purpose as the "pin" in a regular trolling-bait rig.

When grass is a problem, you would not wish to use a stinger rig for trolling—but it could be done. And the stinger is the best of all rigs for drifting dead baits.

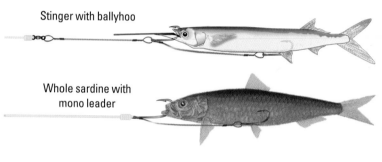

Stinger with ballyhoo

Whole sardine with mono leader

stinger hook to the main leader. The swivel allows the stinger hook to turn easily to hook into the bait. With the swivel method, in rigging, when you run the leader through the eye of the forward hook, run it through the eye of the swivel before tying or wrapping off. Then take a separate short length of leader, tie or wrap it to the other eye of the swivel, and then wrap the second hook to the end of it.

Many anglers routinely use the stinger rig with live baits,

If you're looking for a bite from a monster, you may want to use a multi-stinger rig.

Light Cable Stinger Rig

One of the most effective offshore livebait rigs ever is the stinger rig or "30-second kingfish rig."

It's made with either 29- or 40-pound non-coated cable. It's extremely light, flexible, and easy to tie cable. For a compromise between mono and hardwire, it may well be the best of both worlds.

The rig itself is also extremely easy and fast to tie and to learn. There's no excuse to ever lose a fish because you put a leader out that was weakened from an earlier battle.

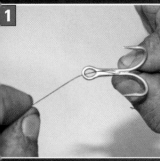

1 Grasp a No. 4 4X treble hook by the extra welded-on hook. Push the end of leader up through eye.

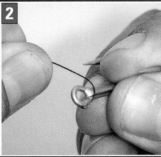

2 Hold end of leader down against the flat side of the hook's shanks. Wrap wire snug against shank.

3 Start at eye and wrap six times down shank. Push other end through the eye and pull tight.

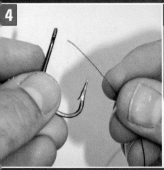

4 Slide single (3/0 livebait hook) onto cable and position near treble for size of bait you'll use.

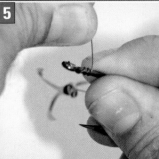

5 Repeat step 2 and 3 for this hook to wrap hook to cable. Leave enough leader to tie swivel.

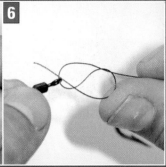

6 Secure swivel with figure-8 knot. Trim excess cable. Store in smallest ziploc bags.

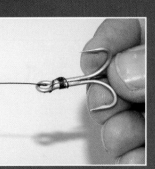

Fly Leaders

Fly leaders can be bought already tapered or can be connected in a series of descending line tests.

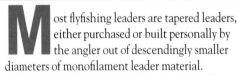

M ost flyfishing leaders are tapered leaders, either purchased or built personally by the angler out of descendingly smaller diameters of monofilament leader material.

Tapered leaders cast much more efficiently than do level leaders. If properly matched to the fly (and if the mechanics of the cast are good) a tapered leader will always turn over neatly and deposit the fly at leader's length from the fly line.

When making tapered leaders, use the same brand of monofilament for all sections, since diameters may vary from brand to brand. For optimal knot strength, avoid mixing monofilament and fluorocarbon—choose one or the other.

The sections may be tied together with either the double uni-knot or blood knot. When a heavy tippet is used, it usually is tied on with the Albright special, although the uni or surgeon's knot can be used.

First step in making tapered leaders is to tie a short piece of stout monofilament directly to the end of your fly line, using the uni-knot's nail

The peacock bass, native to South America, have been a boon to South Florida freshwater fly anglers.

knot application, or the traditional nail knot. Make a loop in the end, using the perfection loop, or end loop knot.

This short piece of mono with its loop serves as a convenient connector for your fly leaders, which can be attached and removed with interlocking loops. Of course, the connector could be eliminated and the leader tied directly to the fly line, but the connector is a huge convenience.

The length of the mono connector can vary according to personal whim. Freshwater fly fishermen often keep it very short—just a few inches—and attach their entire pre-made or manufactured tapered leaders to it.

Saltwater anglers, on the other hand, are more inclined to make the connecting length out of 30-pound mono from three to six feet long, thus treating it as the actual butt of their leaders. They make up the rest of the leader, including clas tippet and heavy tippet (if any) as a unit, then make a loop on the heavy end of the leader for interlocking with the loop on the butt.

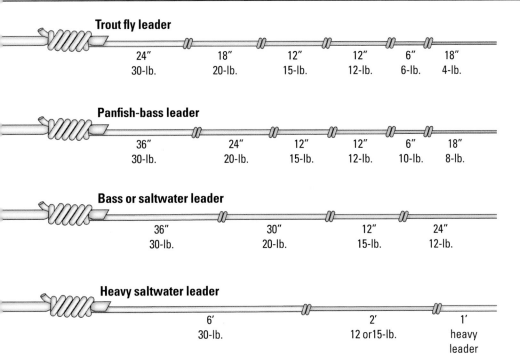

Trout fly leader

24"	18"	12"	12"	6"	18"
30-lb.	20-lb.	15-lb.	12-lb.	6-lb.	4-lb.

Panfish-bass leader

36"	24"	12"	12"	6"	18"
30-lb.	20-lb.	15-lb.	12-lb.	10-lb.	8-lb.

Bass or saltwater leader

36"	30"	12"	24"
30-lb.	20-lb.	15-lb.	12-lb.

Heavy saltwater leader

6'	2'	1'
30-lb.	12 or15-lb.	heavy leader

Trout Fly Leader

You can have a lot of fun fishing with this leader and small trout flies (dries, wets or nymphs) for panfish, such as bluegill and crappie. Sometimes you can clobber pannies with dry flies when they are reluctant to hit the usual popping bugs.

For trout fishing you can use this leader as your starter, but leaders for trout fishing vary greatly in length, strength and makeup, depending mainly on the character of the water being fished and the size and type of the flies used.

Panfish-Bass Leader

(Open water; small streamers or poppers)

This leader serves the same purposes as does the level leader to be described, but will prove much more satisfactory than the level in the long run, and should be chosen by anyone who wishes to become a practiced and proficient caster.

Bass or Saltwater Leader

(Large streamers; large bugs)

This is the workhorse leader for inshore saltwater angling, as well as for bass fishing with big lures. Use it for stripers, seatrout, redfish, jack, and many other types. For snook and small tarpon, you can add an additional one-foot heavy tippet of 40-pound-test monofilament. Tie this to the 12-pound material with the Albright special or surgeon's knot.

For mackerel, barracuda or bluefish, you can add a one-foot heavy tippet of light wire cable, either plain or nylon-coated. Tie the cable to your 12-pound material with the Albright special. Tie your fly to the cable with the figure-eight knot.

Heavy Saltwater Leader

This is the leader used for big-game fishing with the saltwater fly rod—giant tarpon, shark and various offshore species such as kingfish, amberjack, blackfin tuna, sailfish and other huskies. (If you're fishing specifically for dolphin, you can safely use the general-purpose saltwater leader described earlier.)

The makeup of this leader is simple, but you must prepare it with considerable time and care.

First, use the nail knot, fast nail knot or uni-knot-nail version to tie a leader butt of 30- or

40-pound-test monofilament to your fly line as described earlier. Six feet is the usual length. Second, take a six-foot length of "class tippet"—most often 12-pound or 16-pound-test monofilament— and make a double line in both ends. Tie one of the double-line ends to the leader butt, using the Albright special. Tie the other double-line end to your heavy tippet, again using the Albright special.

After you get through doubling both ends of your light material, and tying them to butt and heavy tippet, your section of light material will measure somewhere around two feet long. If it comes out longer, you're okay. Nor is there anything to worry about if it comes out slightly shorter than two feet. But if it comes out shorter than 15 inches, redo it.

If tarpon fishing, make your heavy tippet of 100-pound-test monofilament. If offshore or shark fishing, make it of cable, or nylon-coated cable.

Tournament, club and International Game Fish Association rules all require that the light material ahead of the heavy tippet be no less than 15 inches long. The same rules require that the heavy tippet itself be no longer than 12 inches, and this measurement must include the knots.

If your heavy tippet is of stout monofilament, tie it to your fly with the two-wrap hangman's knot. If using cable, tie on your fly with the figure-eight knot.

For mackerel, barracuda or bluefish, you can add a one-foot piece of hard wire, or cable, plain or nylon-coated. Tie the cable to your 12-pound material with the Albright special. Tie your fly to the cable with the figure-eight knot.

A rainbow trout on fly calls for a light leader to fool the cautious fish in clear water.

When making tapered leaders, use the same brand of monofilament for all sections.

Stealthy poling to fish on the flats for maximum concealment.

Level Leader, No-Knot Eyelet

Although trout fishermen would shudder, the most common fly leader used by southern freshwater anglers is simply a level length of monofilament, usually in 6-, 8- or 10-pound test, and seldom any longer than 6 or 7 feet.

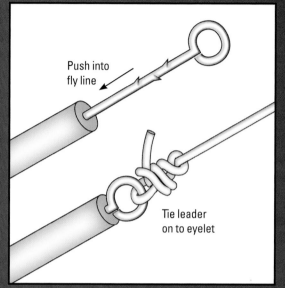

Push into fly line

Tie leader on to eyelet

Panfish and average-size bass are not very sophisticated, so the short level leader normally does an adequate job, and it casts well enough with poppers and plastic molded insects, which are the main lures used.

Simplest method of attaching the level leader is to tie or loop it to the short monofilament connecter described previously.

You might also use a manufactured no-knot eyelet, which is sold in most tackle stores. This is nothing more than a barbed straight pin with an eye in the end of it. Push the barbed pin carefully into the hollow core of your fly line. Tie your leader to the eye, using the improved clinch knot. The no-knot eyelet is very strong and not apt to fail in light freshwater fishing if carefully installed.

Minimize the impact of your presence and let your line and leader perform by keeping your distance from the fish.

The angler keeps his distance from the pool where he drifts his fly to minimize the impact of his presence and to let his line and leader perform well.

CHAPTER 7

Freshwater Baits

Crickets and worms are the most popular baits just about everywhere panfish are sought, but it's their availability because of farm raising that makes them a crowd favorite. Truth be told, anywhere you can overturn a log imbedded in warm, moist soil, whatever lies beneath it is probably a delicacy to most freshwater fish.

Certainly bass, muskies, and many species of trout and salmon are very picky eaters. Bass for example may crush a native shiner, while ignoring one raised in a hatchery. Trout will often only eat perfectly presented imitations of exactly whatever insects are hatching on the water's surface at that moment. But if it's a fried fish dinner you're looking for, just turn over a log, grab whatever's wiggling (be careful), drop it near some cover and watch your bobber go down.

If it's a fried fish dinner you're looking for, just turn over a log, grab whatever is wiggling, drop it near some cover and watch your bobber go down.

Fisherman at right nets a crappie that bit a slow-trolled live minnow. Above, large-mouth bass have a very diverse diet.

Live Baitfish

Live Shiners

Live shiners, chubs and similar forage are the standard natural baits of fishermen seeking bass and other predatory species. They can be purchased at bait shops and fishing camps. Many independent local tackle shops will sell bait indigenous to the local area. Generally speaking, these baits will outperform hatchery baits because of their hardiness and natural scent.

Avid seekers of trophy-size bass, especially in the South, prefer to catch their own native shiners, using pole, light bobber and No. 10 hook with bread balls for bait. Liberal chumming with watered bread helps attract shiners to the bait.

Native shiners often run six or eight inches in length, and sometimes 9 or 10 inches. They don't come too big to suit bass anglers who seek huge largemouths.

Naturally, more action can be expected with the small shiners, and some very big bass often hit little baits.

Smaller, bait-store shiners should be used with about a 3/0 hook. With big native shiners, tie on at least a 5/0 hook, and don't be afraid to use hooks as large as 8/0—preferably in a bronzed freshwater pattern.

When you're using a float rig, it's usually best to hook the shiner lightly through the dorsal surface. However, when drift fishing or slow trolling (with a bobber or without) you'll get more natural swimming action by placing the hook in the shiner's mouth, and out through its nostril. This makes it possible for the shiner to keep breathing and live longer. In weedy areas, a large weedless hook can be used, and the lip hookup is best for this.

This big bass may well pass on a smaller hatchery shiner, only to nearly choke himself on a jumbo wild shiner.

Front dorsal area

Lip hookup

Weedless hook

To send a shiner under floating cover, hook it in front of the dorsal. To troll it, hook through the lips, at left.

Live Panfish

Small panfish (bluegill, pumpkinseed and other species of sunfish) make excellent baits for bass and other game species in states where their use is legal.

As with shiners, larger panfish are apt to lure bigger bass. Hook them in exactly the same ways as described for shiners.

There's absolutely no doubt that shiners are much preferred for bass bait by fishermen in general. However, quite a few specialists use native panfish by choice. There will be times when shiners are scarce, but a few panfish can almost always be taken by fishing with worms or bread balls.

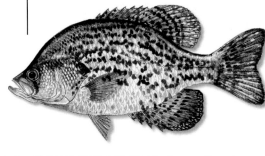

SPECKLED PERCH Nothing beats a live minnow, but dead minnows and cut strips of fish are pretty good baits for speckled perch, also known as crappie, papermouth and a list of other names. Worms, shrimp and insects will work, too. Tiny jigs lead the artificial pack, but spinners are productive, too.

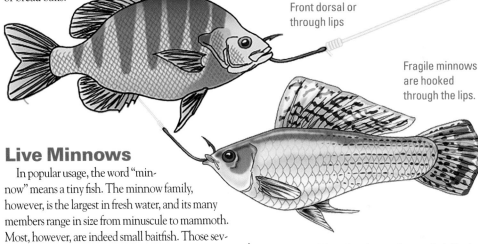

Front dorsal or through lips

Fragile minnows are hooked through the lips.

Live Minnows

In popular usage, the word "minnow" means a tiny fish. The minnow family, however, is the largest in fresh water, and its many members range in size from minuscule to mammoth. Most, however, are indeed small baitfish. Those several inches long can be hooked up as recommended for shiners and used to attract medium to large gamesters.

Perhaps the majority of small live minnows used in freshwater fishing are dunked by anglers seeking walleye, perch or crappie. But, as all devoted sweetwater anglers have long since learned, little minnows will entice every predatory fish that swims, including sauger, rock bass, warmouth, pickerel, white bass, striped bass, black bass, trout and even catfish.

Occasionally a crappie fisherman will miss out on his primary target, but return to dock with a nifty string of bluegills or warmouth—all caught on minnows. And stories are legion concerning panfishermen who find an 8- or 10-pound hybrid or largemouth bass wallowing around at the end of their poles.

Because of their fragility and size, it's difficult to hook most small minnows through the back without doing them serious injury—even with very light hooks. Therefore, the most common hookup for small minnows is through both lips.

Use only the tiniest of splitshot sinkers when fishing a minnow. This is a fragile bait that can't carry around much weight.

Should you run out of live minnows, dead ones can often be used with success. Sometimes the prey is more hungry than picky, but if liveliness seems important, then you can twitch your pole or rod to make the dead bait look like merely a dying bait. Even frozen and preserved minnows take fish in many situations.

Warm days and blooming lilies means peak time for frogs—and their predators.

Live Frogs

Everybody knows that live frogs make great bait for bass. Members of the pike family are especially fond of frogs as well. Still, frogs are not used too often anymore because of the difficulty in procuring and handling them in fishable quantity. Some anglers go to frogs as a last resort—only when other baits aren't working. Then they chase down a frog or two. More often than not, the frog produces action.

The frog can be hooked lightly through one leg. Frog skin is tough and the hook seldom pulls out. If presented with no sinker or other terminal tackle, the leg-hooked frog really kicks up a commotion and attracts fish. Another common

Frogs can be hooked through their lips, as well as in leg.

In clear water, a leg-hooked frog on a light mono leader with no terminal tackle may well produce when all else fails.

hookup is through both lips, as with a shiner or minnow.

In a clear-water situation, where perhaps you can see bass—and they can see you—a leg-hooked frog, presented on a light monofilament line with no other terminal tackle, will draw a strike when all else fails.

Sometimes you'll encounter a great number of very small frogs on the bank of a lake or river. These are easily caught and make fine bait for panfish. Use No. 8 hooks on pole or light spinning tackle, and hook the frogs in exactly the same way as already described.

Crawfish (Crayfish)

Many river and creek fishermen swear by crawfish, using the larger specimens for bass—particularly smallmouth—and the smaller ones for rock bass, trout or panfish. Lake fish will eat crawfish too, of course, but this bait is at its best when allowed to drift along with the current of a stream.

The easiest way to get crawfish is at night with

a light and dipnet along the shallow edges of a stream. They roam and feed at night and are easily spotted with a light. You can get some in the daytime by turning over rocks and limbs in shallow water or small pools. Watch out for the

pinchers—they nip painfully, but do no serious damage to your fingers.

Like live shrimp in salt water, crawfish can be hooked lightly through the top of their hard forward shell (carapace). Most anglers, however, prefer to hook them through the tail as shown in the illustration. This helps a lot in keeping the crawfish from backing under a rock or root.

Toss the crawfish upstream, using a sinker just heavy enough to get you down near bottom. Let the current tumble the bait downstream.

You may remove the claws without harming the bait's appeal but folks who use crawfish often quickly learn to handle them and hook them without getting pinched.

Clear water makes you visible to the fish. In those conditions, light line and long casts are called for.

Earthworms

Spinner rigged with worm

From tiny red wigglers to huge night crawlers, earthworms have been used by more freshwater fishermen than all other baits combined. And so it probably always will be, because worms just catch fish—not only panfish and catfish, but also the more glamorous types like walleye, trout and bass.

There are many ways of hooking worms, but the one illustrated is very productive and very commonly used. Hook once through the center section, then turn the hook and go through the center section once more. If the bend of your hook is large enough, go through a third time.

This arrangement leaves both long ends of the worm free to wave around in the water—and the action attracts trout, bass and those big panfish just as much as whatever smell and taste appeal the worm might have. Seldom do you miss hooking a fat panfish with this hookup, because they tend to grab the worm in the middle. Small fish will sometimes grab the end of the worm, but you probably don't want those anyway.

Kids, of course, often use a small piece of worm and thread it on the hook. That's because they don't want to miss those nibbling little fish. And if you wish to catch some little fellows for bait, then you can thread a tiny piece of worm too.

If you're going for catfish or carp, you'll want to use a "gob" of worms. Probably you'll select a No. 1 or 1/0 hook. Start with one worm and hook it two or three times through the middle as described previously—but then hook it two or three more times. Now push

Hook through worm a few times.

the worm all the way up the hook shank to the eye of the hook; take another worm and hook it several times in the same fashion, then push it close against the first worm.

Use as many worms as it takes to cover the hook completely, from barb to eye, with just what the name implies—a real gob of worms. Naturally, the number of worms needed to make a gob will vary according to the size of your worms and the size of your hook.

COMMON CARP Many natural baits are used to trick carp, including doughballs and secret recipes made by anglers. Worms and crayfish are about the best producers, and for artificials, try jigs and sinking flies.

Red wigglers are thin and smaller than crawlers and make great panfish baits.

your lawn—or a lawn belonging to your neighbor, for that matter. What you can do is search the lawn at night with a flashlight, especially after a rain. Worms often come out at night—thus earning their name as night crawlers—and can simply be picked up.

For an experience Jr. anglers won't soon forget, try "grunting" your worms. Find some soft fertile ground (near a garden) and drive a wooden stake in the ground. For ultimate grunting success this should be done just after daylight, while dew is still on the grass. Rub a rasp or concrete brick over the top of the stake making a grunting noise. Believe it or not, worms will start crawling out of the ground. Your leg isn't being pulled. Grunting works!

Procuring Worms

There are many ways to get worms—the easiest way being to go into a bait store and buy them.

If you prefer to dig your worms, look for them in soft, moist earth. Generally they can be found near a spring or well, or near an outside faucet where the ground stays wet. If no water source is nearby, you can tell good worm territory by examining the ground for the tiny hills of dirt that worms leave on the surface.

Most lawns in good condition are excellent worm territory but naturally you don't go around digging up

Night crawlers can get big and fat and easily hide a hook to fool a big bass or catfish.

Leeches

Leeches, like earthworms, are classified as annelids. The very obvious difference is that earthworms won't latch on to you and suck your blood, as some leeches do in certain waters. Generally, though, most leeches are parasites of fish, not people. And fish take revenge, by feeding avidly on leeches whenever they get the chance to turn the tables.

As bait, leeches are particularly good for trout and walleye, but will also take panfish, bass and other species. You can purchase them in many bait shops in northern states, or order them by mail. Fortunately, those you buy are types that do not grab you and suck your blood when you handle them.

Bait leeches average 1-3 inches long, and are usually hooked up by running the hook through once.

Crickets and Grasshoppers

While crickets are selected as bait far more often than grasshoppers—for the simple reason they are widely sold in bait shops, while grasshoppers are not—both insects are effective producers of panfish and trout and are hooked in the same way.

Both can be hooked through the thorax, which is the forward, crusty half of the body, or even threaded though the head and thorax. The rear portion is soft and tears loose easily.

Hook just under the thorax shell to keep grasshopper lively.

Grasshoppers and crickets can be fished on the surface or below it. Right, a genuine Cajun panfish bobber made of a porcupine quill has little resistance in the water when a fish hits it.

There is no way to hook a cricket or grasshopper so that it will stay alive for any great length of time. But if the hook is carefully inserted between the head and the thorax of a large grasshopper, and run just beneath the shell as illustrated, they will remain lively for a reasonable period. However, when fished beneath the surface, a dead cricket is often just as effective as a live one. Many people do all their fishing with crickets below the surface—using a small hook, splitshot and a very light cork or bobber.

An excellent method in rivers and creeks—whether the target fish are panfish or trout—is to fish the grasshopper or cricket with no terminal tackle of any kind except, of course, the light hook. It will float along, kicking at the surface for a while, then will begin to settle slowly. Hungry insect eaters seldom can resist such a natural presentation and they may strike anywhere from

Lily pads by a bank with plenty of structure make great habitat for bass and panfish. Below, a cricket tube to keep your baits alive.

Regardless of color, species or size all crickets seem to produce equally well.

the surface to the deepest depth the unweighted cricket can attain.

Crickets and grasshoppers are widely considered to be among the leading stream baits for panfish, but they work in lakes and ponds too.

As mentioned, crickets are sold at most bait stores. It is possible to catch your own—but don't waste fishing time by doing it the same day you fish. It's much better to set aside an afternoon, catch your crickets, and keep them until the day of your trip. They will stay healthy and happy indefinitely in any mesh box or cage, with a few potato peelings to feed on.

Commercially raised crickets, the kind sold at bait counters, are light in color and referred to as gray crickets. The ones you catch in the wild will be somewhat larger and much darker, deep brown or black. Regardless of color or species or size, they all seem to produce equally well.

Look for wild crickets in

pastures or open fields, especially those liberally strewn with fallen limbs and other things the crickets can hide under. They almost always stay hidden during the day.

While you hunt for crickets, you'll kick up grasshoppers from grass and low brush. Catch them if you like, for they make just as good an offering to the fish. However, catching grasshoppers requires more effort, since they often must be chased. Crickets don't move nearly as fast, or in such long hops.

RAINBOW TROUT Rainbows take a wide range of artificial and natural baits. They eat things from canned corn to cheeseballs, in addition to the normal menu of worms, grasshoppers, insects, bees and small fish. They'll hit dry and wet flies, streamers, spinners and small spoons, too.

Insect Larvae

A great many common insects undergo a metamorphosis: that is, a change from one form to another during their life cycle. These insects begin life in a worm-like stage, when they are called larvae. Next, they go into a dormant or pupal stage, during which they change into adult form. Well-known examples of larvae are the various caterpillars, which become moths and butterflies, and grubs, which become beetles.

So much for the lecture on entomology. The point for fishermen is that many, many types of larvae make excellent bait. Some larvae are commonly sold in bait shops; others are not, but can easily be obtained in the right place and right season.

Worms and insects are great for most panfish but crappies are more susceptible to jigs or live minnows. Oak worms, lower right.

Caterpillars

Fishermen generally refer to fish-bait caterpillars as "worms," and identify the various species to their own satisfaction simply by tacking on the name of the tree on which the worm is found: for instance, "catalpa worm," "oak worm," "pecan worm," "camphor worm."

The catalpa worm is perhaps the most widely popular of bait caterpillars, and some fishermen keep catalpa trees for the sole purpose of raising a yearly crop of good bream bait.

When small, catalpa worms are used whole on

Most fishermen refer to caterpillars for bait as "worms" and identify them to their own satisfaction.

the hook. When they get big (and they get real big) they are often broken in half, and sometimes turned inside-out before going on the hook—not a procedure for the queasy, obviously, but darn good bait for both big panfish and catfish.

Oak worms appear in great number on small oak trees, notably the blackjack oak, in early fall. Camphor trees get their crop of bait worms in late summer. Of course, these seasonal appearances vary slightly in different sections of the country.

Actually, just about any kind of caterpillar makes good bait. There are exceptions, of course, and they can be painful exceptions. Shy away from stinging kinds, such as the saddle-back caterpillar, and all species which are covered with thick fuzz. Some very good bait species, however (including the oak worm and pecan worm), have small but soft bristles which are harmless.

When small caterpillars are used for bait, they can be threaded on your hook as the illustration shows. Larger ones should be hooked once or twice at the tail end. If the skin of the caterpillar is tough, bring the point and barb of the hook outside the skin for easier hooking of the fish.

panfish baits.

Commercially sold grubs include those called golden grubs, right.

Most grubs are small and should be threaded onto the hook as in the illustration.

Grubs

Thread grub onto hook.

Most insect larvae referred to as "grubs" or "grub worms" are white or yellowish in color and have prominent hard heads with visible mandibles or pinchers. The majority are larvae of various beetles, and are found either in soft ground or under the bark of trees—usually dead trees but sometimes, as in the case of pine, in living trees as well.

Those aforementioned pinchers can indeed pinch. But you can safely use the bait simply by keeping your fingers away from the business end. One type of grub is called a "sawyer." You'll sometimes find a rotting pine log in the woods so full of sawyers that you can hear them grinding away from several feet. Their noise sounds like sawing, hence the name. Sawyers are excellent

Maggots

The larval baits called "maggots" represent a variety of insect species, only one of which is the common housefly. That should make you feel better! Anyway, the unsavory public reputation of the housefly maggot is due not so much to the bug itself as to the carrion on which it usually is observed. Bait maggots are grown on less offensive foods, such as grain, and are sold by bait stores throughout the country. In addition, various small maggots may be bought in tins, both in local bait shops and from mail-order houses. Some of these are even dyed in various colors—maybe to appeal to style-conscious fish. Maggots or not, they are cleaner and easier to use than most other larval baits.

REDBREAST SUNFISH Crickets and larvae may work best, but worms are also a top bait for catching these sunfish. They'll also hit plugs, in-line spinners and grub-tipped spinnerbaits. Popping bugs and flies work, too.

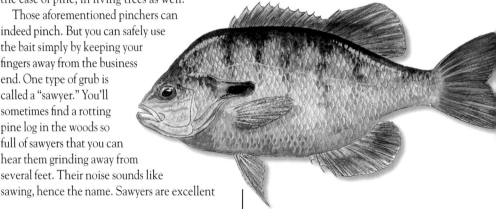

Bonnet Worms

Actually, bonnet worms are caterpillars and should perhaps have been included in that category. But most fishermen don't think of them as caterpillars because of their habitat. They are found in the stems of spatterdock, a water lily called "bonnet" in the South. Look for bonnets that have a hole in the stem, right in the center of the pad. Pull up the stem and slit it carefully, and you'll find the worm (unless, of course, it has already attained adulthood and departed). An awful lot of bream fishermen say bonnet worms are the very best baits of all.

An awful lot of bream fishermen say bonnet worms are the very best baits of all.

Hellgrammites

Hellgrammites are the larvae of dobson flies and rank among the best all-around baits for river fishing, inasmuch as they are greedily snapped up by largemouth and smallmouth bass, trout and a variety of panfish. They are tough to corral, but can be taken by overturning logs and driftwood in slow-moving sections of streams. Careful—they can nip painfully. They are best fished by hooking once through the segmented body, then bumping them with the

Hook near the head or near the tail.

current along the bottom. In the rural South, hellgrammites were once called "gator fleas," and a few folks still believe that the hellgrammite goes out and catches the fish, instead of vice versa. This myth developed because the hellgrammite defensively grabs hold of any fish that bites it, and occasionally a panfish will be landed even though unhooked, because the "gator flea" is hanging on to its lip or gill.

Grass Shrimp

Small shrimp inhabit many fresh waters and are commonly called "grass shrimp." Many bait stores carry them, and if you know your waters you can dipnet or seine them from grassy areas.

Grass shrimp are small and it often takes two or three to make a suitable bait, even on a small panfish hook. The illustration is deliberately magnified in effect, so you can see how several grass shrimp should be hooked at one time. Of course, any suitably large specimen you might find in your bait supply can be used singly.

Like saltwater shrimp, grass shrimp can be kept alive for a long time without being kept in water. They should be kept in a cold container, moist, but protected from actually sitting in water. You can keep them in a can, or a waxed paper cup which, in turn, is placed in you portable ice chest.

If you don't carry an ice chest, keep them in a can on a bed of moist weed, cloth or newspaper.

Gar Roe

South of the Mason Dixon line, there is a magical, top-secret bluegill bait spoken of in hushed tones around many campfires. It's actually used more for chum than bait, but bluegills will come from as far away as the scent of gar roe reaches. If you're hardcore, you can gig your own big female gars, and remove their roe, but if you are fortunate enough to deal with a fish camp that sells it, don't leave the dock without it. Then just anchor in a bluegill-rich environment, and spread a handful around. Thread a little on your hook and get the grease warmed up. If there are bluegills around you won't be going home empty handed.

BLUEGILL The bluegill's natural diet is made up largely of insects and crustaceans, so baits such as worms, crickets and grass shrimp are widely used. Bluegills will take almost anything in their environment and many things from the angler's house, like bacon, bread and corn.

Salmon Eggs

Salmon eggs are a natural food of trout and are taken avidly by many other fish—including varieties that have never seen a salmon egg except for the processed kind sold in jars as bait.

The eggs can be fished singly or in globs. A single egg obviously requires a very small hook and a careful hookup. The egg should be allowed to drift as naturally as possible along bottom in imitation of an egg swept along by the current. Globs of eggs must be aided in staying on the hook. If you use a snelled hook, then push the snell knot down on the shank, until a bulge of line is formed. A portion of the egg cluster can be inserted under this bulge, which is then tightened. Or additional line can be pulled from

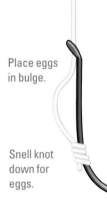

Place eggs in bulge.

Snell knot down for eggs.

STEELHEAD The steelhead is a strong fish and usually challenged with fairly heavy fly fishing equipment—No. 8 or 9. They'll also hit spinners and spoons, and salmon eggs rate as the top natural bait.

Thread salmon eggs on small hook.

above the knot and looped around the hook and the cluster. Another method is to tie the eggs in very fine netting. Artificial salmon eggs often work very well, and when fish are really gorging on eggs, they will also impulsively hit small spinners and other artificials which are colored orange or deep pink.

When fish are really gorging on eggs, they will impulsively hit small spinners.

Pools below waterfalls are a perfect setting to try for trout using salmon eggs, above.

Catfish Baits

Since catfish will bite just about anything, it's surprising to see how many catfish fishermen go to the trouble of preparing special baits made out of blood, or smelly cheese or other unsavory substances. But they do catch catfish, and so you can't argue with them.

You don't even have to create and manufacture your own recipe for catfish bait any more. Numerous commercial offerings are available in jars or tubes—so many, in fact, that you can experiment with various types to determine your own favorites, just as you probably do with different baits and artificial lures for other kinds of fish.

Many catfish enthusiasts keep their frying pans well supplied even though they never use any bait except plain old earthworms (See the category headed "Earthworms" for instructions on making a catfish worm-gob.)

Cats also will happily bite any of the other panfish baits mentioned in these pages, and channel cats seem to

FLATHEAD CATFISH Many small flatheads are caught on light spinning and casting gear, but the big cats require heavy lines and stouter tackle. Live fish are best for the big ones, and smaller flatheads will take worms and the range of panfish baits, including dough and premade baits.

Flathead catfish, left, can be targeted with big, live panfish baits, right, one of their favorite prey.

Downed trees and the stumps of old, rotted trees make the perfect haven for catfish.

show a special fondness for fat catalpa worms and other caterpillars.

If you want bait particularly for catfish, but don't wish to go in for elaborate preparations, you can hardly do better than to slice up some beef or pork liver. For that matter, any kind of liver works.

Another popular catfish bait is a piece of frozen shrimp. Chunks of cutbait, from any kind of fish you can get your hands on, are also fine catfish producers, and are probably the most-used baits on trotlines and bush lines.

Trophy-size catfish may hold out for live shiners or other baitfish of the kinds and sizes used for bass.

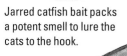

Jarred catfish bait packs a potent smell to lure the cats to the hook.

If you want good catfish bait, but don't want an elaborate preparation, you can't do better than slicing up some beef or pork liver.

BLUE CATFISH These cats, especially when bigger, call for heavy baitcasting, spinning and even light saltwater gear. Many are caught on trotlines, too. Live baits are good, including fish and crawfish, and large cutbaits and meat chunks work, too.

CHAPTER 8

Saltwater Baits

Saltwater baits are all about duplicating what predators are feeding on, but there's actually a lot more to it than that.

Several types of natural saltwater baits are actually better when fished dead, totally out of their environment. Ballyhoo, for example, have never been seen on a rip in 3,000 feet of water where a wahoo will crush one on sight. Live, you can only pull a ballyhoo at maybe 2.5 knots, whereas once you brine them and rig them you can troll one at nine knots and cover four times more ground. It's also doubtful whether a giant bluefin tuna has ever seen a black mullet, but there's been many a monster deceived by a swimming split-tailed mullet.

Brine them and rig them and you can troll ballyhoo at nine knots and cover four times more ground.

When you're on the fish, nothing instills confidence like a livewell full of live baits, right.

Live Fish

A lip-hooked mullet is a good bait in saltwater shallows—and in the depths for that matter, too.

Every coastal area has its popular types of live baitfish—anchovy, menhaden (mossbunker), mullet, sardine, silverside, spot, grunt, butterfish, pinfish, cigar minnow, chub, mummichog, blue runner and goggle-eye, to name just a few examples.

When you get right down to it, virtually any small fish of appropriate size can be used for live bait.

Stomach samples of deepsea fishes—from billfish to bottom feeders—prove they regularly eat such oddities as porcupine fish, trunk fish, file fish, or anything else they can inhale.

The whole point is this: use the popular baits whenever possible—after all, they're proven. But if you can't get the desired species of baitfish, don't hesitate to put out any small fish you can come up with. Chances are, the fish care less than you do.

Placement of the hook in a live bait is often important and can vary according to the species of baitfish and how you want it to act.

Saltwater baitfish ball up as a defense when predators attack them.

The two hook positions in the mullet illustrated are common ones, used with many different types of fish. One hookup is through both lips or else through the upper lip only; the other hookup is through the back.

Use the lip hookup when slow-trolling, or any time when boat motion or current would tend to pull a back-hooked bait through the water sideways, or in an unnatural way.

Many anglers feel that small-mouthed baitfish, such as mullet or pinfish, should not be hooked through both lips for fear of impairing "breathing" ability and shortening bait life. Mullet often are hooked by inserting the hook point into the mouth, then upward through the top lip only. Bait such as pinfish or spot may be hooked from side to side through the nostrils.

The back hookup generally is a better placement, since a striking fish is more apt to get the hook on its nitial hit. So hook through the back whenever it allows you to present the bait so that it swims in a free and natural manner. While slow trolling or fishing in a moving current, hooking through the upper lip or through the nostrils is a much more natural presentation. While fishing still waters, placing the hook forward in the back tends to keep the bait nearer the surface. Hook it toward the tail if you want it to swim downward.

Placing the hook just behind the anal fin, on the bottom of the baitfish will keep the bait struggling nearer the surface, and may also help thwart short-striking fish.

Hook placement in other portions of the bait's anatomy may be necessary because of the nature of the species. Shown are the two hook-ups most commonly used by California anglers with live anchovies. The hook can be stuck through either the tough "nose" of the fish, or through the bony "collar" just aft of the gills.

Similarly, some of the many baitfish species of the herring family, such as sardines, pilchards, white bait, etc., may be too soft-fleshed to permit a reliable hookup through either the dorsal or the lips. A solution, as illustrated, is to run the hook side to side through the eye socket, just above the eyeball, or in the area of the nostril.

Mesh bait pens let some anglers keep baits alive for extended periods of time.

Some Common Hook Placements

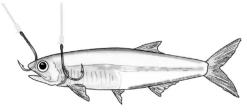

Anchovy can be hooked in nose or gill collar

Hook mullet through top lip or back

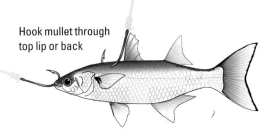

Eye-socket or nostril hookup for pilchard

Hook in rear underside for more depth

Side-to-side for small-mouth fish

Hook placements in other portions of the bait's anatomy may be necessary.

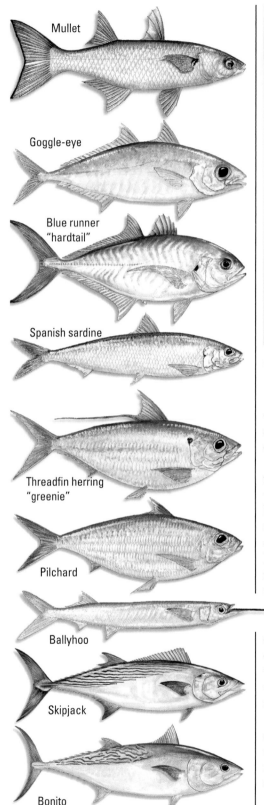

Mullet

Goggle-eye

Blue runner
"hardtail"

Spanish sardine

Threadfin herring
"greenie"

Pilchard

Ballyhoo

Skipjack

Bonito

Catching and Fishing Live Ballyhoo

Ballyhoo, also called balao or halfbeak, has been employed for many years by ocean anglers as a standard dead bait. It is rigged whole for trolling, or can be cut into strips and chunks.

Ballyhoo also make one of the premier live baits for many varieties of offshore gamefish, and are well worth the effort it takes to catch them. Live ballyhoo are never found in bait shops because of the difficulty of keeping them alive and in good condition for any length of time, though often in locations near where ballyhoo live, you might find fresh dead ballyhoo that are a grade above those that have been frozen.

While live-ballyhoo angling was developed in the Florida Keys and is still centered there, opportunities to catch these splendid baitfish and use them live exist in many warm waters of the world—in the Bahamas, throughout the Caribbean and tropical Latin America, and in many areas of the Pacific.

When disturbed, ballyhoo skitter across the surface of the water somewhat like flying fish, and this is how anglers often find them. Once skittering ballyhoo are located, the boat is anchored and a chumline begun. Ballyhoo respond to standard chums made from ground fish, and can also be chummed up with oatmeal or cracker crumbs. They stay at the top and can be spotted dimpling the surface of the water in the chumline. Once ballyhoo are near the boat, they can be either castnetted or caught by using very light line—no more than 10-pound test—to which is tied a No. 10 or No. 12 hair hook. The bait can be a tiny bit of cut fish or cut shrimp. Though an old fashioned fishing pole makes the best ballyhoo-angling tool, few salty anglers are so equipped and most use light spinning rods. (Some do, however, keep tele-scoping glass poles aboard just for bal-lyhoo.)

Hook through upper jaw.

Option: secure bill to hook with wire.

Regardless of what tack-le is used, the bait must be drifted at the surface or just under it, and kept in sight by the angler so he can see the ballyhoo take the bait. Many anglers use the freshwater style "quill corks" to let them now they are getting the light bite of a ballyhoo.

Soda straw

Hook down, through lower jaw.

Slide straw over hook and bill.

Even though it might be possible to catch a lot of them, you should resist the impulse to load up the baitwell with more than it can accommodate. Large, well-aerated wells on sportfishers—especially if their shape is round—can keep two or three dozen baits alive over a fishing day, but wells on most small boats often cannot effectively keep more than a dozen.

When trolled for sailfish and other offshore species, a live ballyhoo should be pulled at just above idle speed. This is probably the slowest pace used for any bait. Ballyhoo also can be free-drifted or used on a kite. For that matter, many good fish are caught simply by drifting out a live ballyhoo on the very spot where you are catching the bait.

Ballyhoo belong to the group of fishes known as halfbeaks, and when you get your first close look at

one it will surprise you to see that the "bill" is not an extension of the upper jaw but of the lower one. This curious physiognomy is the key to how you hook them.

Insert the hook into the mouth, point upward, and bring it out the top of the upper jaw. A small hook should be used, as a large one not only would tear out easily but would also diminish the action of the bait. Usual sizes are from 3/0 to 6/0, and in a rather light-wire hook, or a short-shank livebait hook. The hook shank can be secured to the beak with a bit of copper wire.

Many anglers use an alternate system of mouth-hooking. They thread a piece of ordinary soda straw, maybe three inches long, onto the leader. They affix the hook downward through the lower jaw at the base of the bill, then slide the soda straw forward, over both the bill and the hook shank, thus securing it firmly.

A mouth hookup is the proper one for trolling, drifting, or for freelining the ballyhoo in a current.

For kite fishing, or for freelining when current is not a problem, you may prefer to hook the bal-lyhoo through the dorsal surface near the mid-way point—taking care not to injure the spine.

Livebait Trolling With Light Tackle

It's hard to say where it all started, but somewhere around the first competitive kingfish tournaments during the early '80s, trolling live baits on light tackle took the offshore scene by storm. Starting in the Southeast, slow trolling with live baits soon spread like wildfire throughout the Gulf. Boats that had been either trolling rigged ballyhoo, mullet and strips, or fishing live baits under a cork, were mostly using heavy wire and triple strength 8/0 and bigger heavy-duty hooks. Suddenly they started seeing kingfish pros barely creeping along with "trout rods" and small extra smooth Teflon drag reels, attached to a live pogey, or sardine, by a relatively tiny (No. 4 3x) treble hook with a stinger hook in the bait's back.

Slow trolling live baits actually seems to have started with the south Florida sailfish fishermen, but once the tactic was adapted to using the tiny trebles and light wire for kings, and kingfish tournament checks started growing, the tactic became SOP for almost every pelagic imaginable.

There are only a few things you need to fine tune to become a successful livebait troller. The goal is to make your bait look unencumbered

Above, live baits dropped from a castnet being picked up off the deck. They'll make great baits when slow-trolled. Below, hardy live baits like the blue runner can be trolled with a skirt and stinger rig added.

by your rig. The bait has to appear completely natural or the very biggest, smartest fish in the neighborhood will be the one that turns away at the last second, avoiding striking a bait with hooks in it.

For your baits to look natural, you'll need a 6 ½- to 7-foot rod with a very soft tip, and a high speed reel capable of holding at least 300 yards of 12- to 25-pound monofilament. Eighteen inches of either No. 4 hardwire or 30- to 40-pound cable will allow your bait to swim longer and more naturally than heavier tackle.

The rig, nowadays fished with either single or treble hooks, is universal whether you're trolling with live pogies, mullet, sardines, threadfins, speedos or cigar minnows. Simply run the thin wire lead hook through the nostrils, and either bury the trailer though the bait's back or let it swing free.

Calling this method of livebait fishing "trolling" may be a misnomer. If you're "pulling" the baits through the water you're going too fast. Your baits have to swim naturally whether on the surface or on a downrigger.

Keep fresh baits swimming back and forth behind your boat, as you ever so slowly make your way across some structure. Pay constant attention to your baits, and your payoff will be a full fish box.

Bridle Rigging

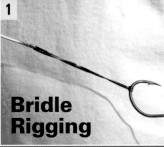

1
Secure No. 16 or No. 32 (for larger bait) rubber band with half hitch on hook. Other end to rig needle.

2
Using wet hands or wet cloth, hold bait by the head.

3
Run rigging needle through nostrils or eye sockets. Leave bands sticking out each side.

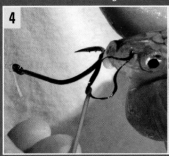

4
Pull rubber band through until bait is centered on rubber band.

5
Remove needle from end of rubber band.

6
Place hook through loop protruding from other side of bait.

7
Pull on hook until rubber band begins to stretch.

8
Start twisting rubber band.

9
Twist rubber band until almost all slack has been taken up.

10
Pull hook away from bait until you can place hook through loop directly next to bait's head.

11
Let bands pull hook tight back into place next to bait.

Slowly let bait back as boat creeps along. Bait must be able to swim freely to attract predators.

Rigging Live Bonito

A live bonito probably is the best of all baits for offshore trolling—small ones measuring a foot or less for sailfish and other relatively small offshore species with tackle up to 30-pound test, and larger live bonito for big marlin on heavy tackle.

Since live bonito of any size are often hard to procure, and because they don't live long in the average baitwell, they usually are picked up individually on a small trolling feather or spoons. Many hardcore bonito pullers use a No. 15 sabiki rig pulled behind a small planer to rack up multiples. To keep bonitos alive, tuna tubes are necessary. They are only

knots will do the job.

Now tie the circle of line in the middle, thus forming a figure-eight. Take the free end of the figure-eight and hitch it two or three times around your hook. The bait is ready to use.

If you're a serious marlin fisherman and want the

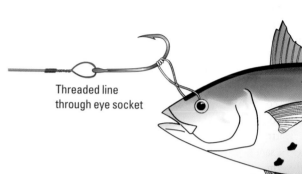

Threaded line
through eye socket

Metal figure eight

When a bonito comes aboard hold him firmly but gently with wet gloves.

practical on bigger boats, so catching bonito one at a time, and putting them out immediately is more practical.

In the interest of speed (when you aren't prepared in advance for a better hookup) hook your bonito through the lips and troll it slowly.

Properly, however, you should have a bait needle ready, threaded with about 6 inches of nylon or Dacron line (20- or 30-pound test). When the bonito comes aboard, have someone hold him firmly but gently with wet gloves, while you run the needle through the eye socket at about the 10 o'clock position. Remove the needle and quickly tie the ends of the line together to make a circle. The surgeon's knot, or simply a couple of overhand

best possible live bonito rig, get some preformed figure-eights made of brass. These are sold in most hardware stores (they're used as connectors for light chain).

To rig the metal figure-eight (shown above), use the bait needle as before to thread a line through the bonito's eye socket. Tie the line tightly to one loop of the figure-eight, as close as possible to the bonito's head. Now you simply fix the other loop of the figure-eight over the bend of your hook.

Obviously, when buying the figure-eights, you must be sure they are large enough to fit your chosen hook.

The metal figure-eight, because it is not bound tightly to the hook, allows the bait much more freedom of action. With this rig you can troll a little faster. In calm conditions, you can often raise your speed enough to add a couple well-rigged dead baits to your spread so you can attract different sized fish at the same time. Speed is of the utmost importance in getting a live bonito on the hook and back in the water. You should be able to rig in a few seconds, so practice rigging on dead baits until you can do the job efficiently but quickly.

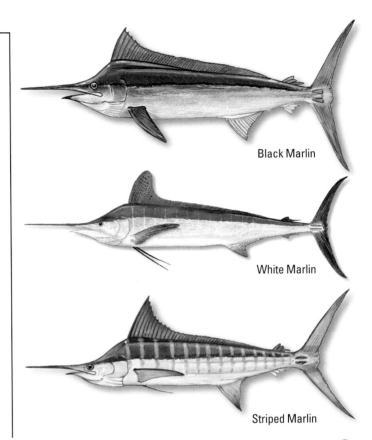

Black Marlin

White Marlin

Striped Marlin

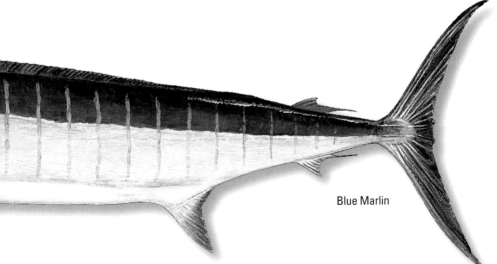

Blue Marlin

BLUE MARLIN Blue marlin are most often caught trolling, sometimes by drifting. Though they can be caught on lighter gear used for sailfish and dolphin, that's quite a challenge and usually by accident. The standard is a good, balanced ocean trolling outfit in the 50- or 80-pound class. Baits fall into three categories: 1. Artificial trolling lures; 2. Live, fairly large baitfish; and 3. Rigged natural baits, for instance mullet, mackerel and bonito. Lures are used most often because they allow more ocean to be covered.

Shrimp

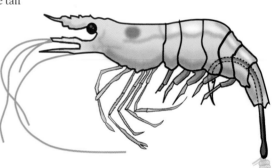

Live Shrimp

King of live baits for coastal fishing is the live shrimp. It will take anything from bottom feeders to tarpon and king mackerel.

Some anglers hook their shrimp lightly through the tail, but these are the two most common hookups:

1. Through the head, either by running the point of your hook lightly under the horny ridge atop the head, or from top to bottom through the head, taking care to keep the hook in front of the dark spot inside the head (as shown in the shrimp-and-jig rig, described later).

2. Threading. Insert the point on the underside of the tail, then work it the full length of the tail section and out in back of the head.

System No. 1 allows the shrimp to move about freely. It is a good choice in situations where fish are extremely selective. The obvious disadvantage is that the hookup is flimsy. This means the bait is easily stolen by smaller fish. Still, you must use this hookup whenever it appears the fish are insisting on the most natural, free-swimming presentation.

System No. 2—the threaded shrimp—is considerably more durable and equally productive in many kinds of fishing, such as simply letting the shrimp drift with a current or lie on bottom. A lot of anglers use the flimsy head hookup when it really isn't necessary, thus wasting much expensive bait.

The threaded shrimp is entirely satisfactory for seatrout, redfish, bonefish, most snapper, grouper and many other species. Your shrimp should be threaded when using the popping cork because a head-hooked shrimp can be popped right off your hook. And, of course, the threaded bait is given plenty of action by your popping motions.

If a threaded shrimp works so well, why not use dead bait instead of live? Well, sometimes you can and get good results. But experienced anglers know that the more desirable species of fish somehow prefer a shrimp with live appearance, smell and taste over a dead shrimp—even though the live one may not be moving about.

Live shrimp crawl forward with their legs and jet back with their tail.

Weedless Shrimp

When grass is thick and the water shallow, it's difficult to work most artificial lures—or even a natural shrimp that's hooked in the usual way. This rig, borrowed from the familiar Texas Rigged artificial worm, is a good solution. It can be still-fished on weedy bottom or else retrieved—very slowly—like an artificial lure.

Begin by pinching off the shrimp's fantail, which would add resistance in the water and contribute to spinning on the cast. Then proceed as follows:

1. Insert the point of the hook in the tail end of the shrimp for about a half-inch, then bring it out and pull the shank through almost to the hook's eye.

2. Spin the hook so that the point faces the body of the shrimp.

3. Curl the shrimp a little and stick the hook in as far down the body as the particular hook shank permits, then straighten the body so that it lies almost parallel to the shank.

This defies the usual advice of always leaving the hook point clear of the bait, but all species of gamefish can easily blast the point through the soft body of the shrimp on the strike.

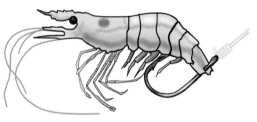

Steps 1 & 2

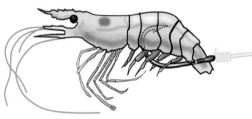

Step 3

Live Shrimp with Jighead

Although many rigs incorporate artificial lures with dead, cut or rigged baits, not many combine live bait with artificials. The reason is obvious: artificial lures must be given motion by the angler in order to produce efficiently; live baits are generally left to provide their own movement, which should be as natural and unfettered as possible.

A certain few lure-livebait combinations, however, rank among the best of all fish-catchers. In salt water one of the leading examples is the marriage of a live shrimp and a lead jighead. Some heads are marketed for just that purpose, but any leaded hook—whether salvaged from an old jig or purchased new—will serve well.

Since this rig does its best work right smack on bottom, the weight of the jig may have to be juggled in order to obtain the desired depth. In coastal shallows, one-quarter ounce is the

A jig's hook in the tail of a shrimp, when retrieved, will pull the shrimp backwards to imitate it escaping from attack.

usual size, but a half-ounce often is needed, and sometimes a head weighing up to an ounce is used in deeper channels and passes, particularly when there is strong current. Be aware however, when fishing in shallow water, you'll want to use as light a weight as possible. Not only will you want your bait to be able to move naturally, but in shallow

Certain livebait-lure combinations rank among the best of all fish catchers.

water your bait needs to land as lightly as possible on the surface.

Start the point of the hook under the shrimp's "chin" and bring it out the top of the head—taking care to avoid damaging the dark organ which is visible in the head of the shrimp.

1/4 oz. - 1 oz. for most coastal situations

Make a long cast either directly upcurrent, or upcurrent and quartering away. Be sure to allow the rig to sink all the way to bottom, then retrieve just fast enough to keep a tight line as it works down with the current. You will, however, have to help keep it moving at times by very softly lifting the rodtip a few inches and increasing your retrieve rate just slightly. With a bit of practice you develop a "feel" for crawling the gadget along bottom, and your lifts of the rod at intervals impart a natural up-and-down movement to the shrimp.

The rig also can be fished effectively where there is no current at all. In this case, simply make a long cast and, again, allow it to sink to bottom. Holding your rodtip right at the surface, turn your reel crank v-e-r-y slowly—more slowly, probably, than you have ever retrieved a lure in your life, even when using an artificial worm. Just a bit too much speed and the shrimp will go off keel and begin to turn. With a creeping pace, however, the shrimp will move upright and naturally, with its legs churning.

No need even to attempt listing the species of fish a jig-live shrimp combination attracts, since just about everything from large gamefish to panfish (and, unfortunately, trash fish as well) love a slow-moving shrimp.

REDFISH Redfish range along the Gulf Coast, along Florida's coasts, along the Atlantic Coast north to Long Island, and sometimes even farther north. They can be caught on all kinds of tackle, from surf gear to light rods. They feed aggressively on live baitfish, shrimp and crabs and they also take cutbait and artificial lures with gusto.

Keeping Live Shrimp

A good livewell, with re-circulating water or an aerator, is the most satisfactory repository for live shrimp. Resist the temptation to cover your shrimp with too much water. It's much easier for aerators to provide oxygen to a smaller amount of water.

Bait buckets with a removable perforated inner container work quite well. The inner container is kept on a line in the water while you're fishing. If you move, the bucket is filled with water and the container placed inside. But if you have a long distance to travel, be sure to change the water frequently.

An even better bucket is the one-piece type that provides all the advantages of the traditional two-piece. It has a solid bottom and perforated top. It lies on its side when in the water, thus permitting good flow, but retains water in the bottom when hauled up to deck or dock.

The Icing System

Keep shrimp alive without water, for several hours—even for a full day or more if you're careful. Here's how it works:

The shrimp must be transferred directly from the dealer's well into a water-tight container—a large waxed paper cup, an old coffee can, or even a plastic bag. This container then must be kept very cold, in an ice chest, but the shrimp must, at all times, be kept from coming in contact with water from the melting ice.

The colder you keep your ice chest, the longer your shrimp stay alive. It's best to have a separate small ice chest just for your shrimp. General-purpose ice chests are opened frequently for drinks, etc., and this brings up the inside temperature.

CAUTION: Don't transport your shrimp on ice, then remove them and place them in a livewell. If you use the icing method, stick with it all the way.

Using Live Eels

In many areas of the Gulf of Mexico, live eels are the preferred bait for sight fishing cobia. In that fishery, baits are usually kept chilled to keep them docile and easy to handle. The eels are then hooked in the shoulder and placed in a bucket of sea water until a cobia is spotted.

In the East Coast striped bass fishery, the live eel reigns supreme. They are drifted or slow trolled around likely structure. When fishing water shallower that 20 feet, the eel will find his way to the bottom. In deeper water a 3-way rig (weighted according to current) with at least 3 feet of fluorocarbon and a lip-hooked eel is dynamite.

You can keep shrimp alive without water, for several hours—even for a full day or more if you're careful.

Pink Shrimp
P. duorarum

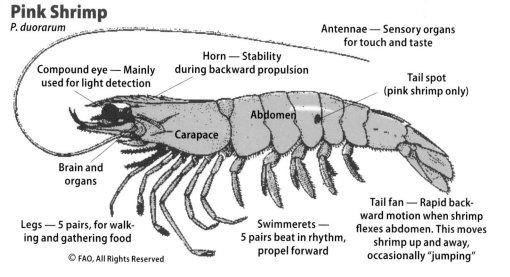

Antennae — Sensory organs for touch and taste

Horn — Stability during backward propulsion

Compound eye — Mainly used for light detection

Tail spot (pink shrimp only)

Abdomen

Carapace

Brain and organs

Tail fan — Rapid backward motion when shrimp flexes abdomen. This moves shrimp up and away, occasionally "jumping"

Legs — 5 pairs, for walking and gathering food

Swimmerets — 5 pairs beat in rhythm, propel forward

Live Blue Crab

The live blue crab is a deadly bait for many fish, including red and black drum, cobia, snook and a big variety of reef and bottom fish, such as grouper and snapper.

"Dollar crabs"—that is, crabs approximating the size of a silver dollar—are the choice for both permit and tarpon in Southern waters. Tarpon will take larger crabs, but seem to favor the smaller ones.

Large live crabs make an excellent bait for deep bottom fishing for snapper and grouper. Let's say you've been fishing a deep hole or wreck where you can't avoid hooking amberjack every time you drop a live fish, or even a strip. You want to get past the amberjacks and try for a big snapper or grouper. The live crab is your solution. Amberjack ignore it, yet the bottom fish love it.

No matter what size crab you use, remove the claws (for your personal safety), and hook as shown, through the tip of the shell.

Live Baitfish with Jighead

In certain situations, the combination of a jighead with a live baitfish can also be used with effect. One such instance would be for "hanging" a baitfish deep in a moving current where gamefish are foraging. Hook the bait through both lips, let it out in the current, and when the desired position is reached, lock the reel and then either hold it or place it in a rod holder.

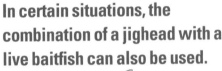

In certain situations, the combination of a jighead with a live baitfish can also be used.

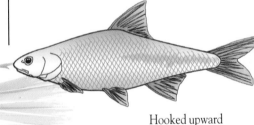

Hooked upward through the lips, the baitfish will hold a pretty normal attitude, facing into the current like a free-swimming fish, and the jighead helps hold it upright most of the time.

The bait will do a bit of swinging, and even turn on its side at times, but this is all to the good, since a sudden flash or a quick movement that simulates a fish in distress often touches off a strike.

Another application of the jig-baitfish rig is to cover a desired path of retrieve, as with the jig-and-shrimp. Cast the bait out and bring it back at a creeping pace over the selected course. Remember that a fast, or even a medium, retrieve rate will probably cause the baitfish to twist.

Sardines are excellent baits alone or paired with a light jighead.

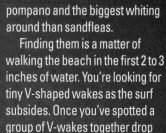

If there's a method of gathering bait that's fun for the whole family raking sandfleas is at the top of the list. Not only is it simple and free, but there is no better bait for pompano and the biggest whiting around than sandfleas.

Finding them is a matter of walking the beach in the first 2 to 3 inches of water. You're looking for tiny V-shaped wakes as the surf subsides. Once you've spotted a group of V-wakes together drop your rakes between them and the ocean, and push down on it to filter out the receding wave.

Stand in front of the opening to the rake and shuffle your feet in the sand to scare fleas into your rake. Store them in damp sand with wet cloth above.

Sandfleas

The sandflea is a specialized bait, used almost exclusively by surf and ocean-pier fishermen for pompano. It will take other surf species as well, but is unsurpassed as a pompano bait along the beaches.

Sandfleas (not really fleas, but crustaceans) are sold at many beachside tackle shops, or they can be caught by the angler. Look for them at the edge of the surf where waves roll up on the sand,

and then recede. As the wave recedes, look for V-shaped wakes in the soupy sand, made by the protruding antennae of the sand flea.

You must immediately scoop them out by digging under the "V" with your hand, to bring up a handful of sand which, you hope, has the sandflea in the middle of it.

Surf regulars build a special scoop, which can be compared to a shovel with a wire-mesh bottom.

They spot the antennae, dig out a big scoopful of sand, then let the sand filter through the mesh, leaving the fleas. Sometimes they get several baits in one scoop.

Hook the sandflea as shown in the illustration—once through from bottom to top.

POMPANO

Catch pompano stillfishing, drifting and casting from beaches, piers and around inlets. By far the best natural bait is a live sandflea, but pompano also eat hooked clams, squid, fiddler crabs and shrimp, eagerly. For artificials, use jigs that bounce on bottom and bonefish-type flies.

Fiddler Crab

A traditional bait for sheepshead, the fiddler crab can be found almost everywhere in tidal areas (though abundance varies with season). Besides sheepshead, fiddlers take snapper, redfish, grouper, drum—even an occasional snook.

You may find fiddlers on sandy shores, mud flats, or among mangrove roots. Sometimes they're in bunches that resemble waves moving across the sand. Unless they reach their holes, they are easy to chase and capture by hand.

Do not fear the one overgrown claw which gives the fiddler its name. Though it looks wicked indeed, it has little strength. The pinch of a fiddler crab can't break the skin, or even cause enough pain to make you say a very loud "Ouch."

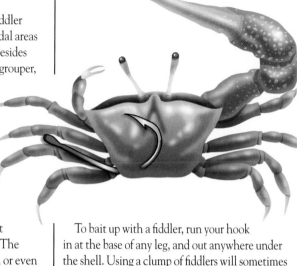

To bait up with a fiddler, run your hook in at the base of any leg, and out anywhere under the shell. Using a clump of fiddlers will sometimes attract a jumbo sheepshead, that may be hanging around a school of bigger fish.

Live Crawfish

A live crawfish (spiny lobster) of legal size makes a mouthful of bait indeed. As you can guess, it's used only for big fish—giant cubera snapper mainly, along the lower east coast of Florida and the Keys. Occasionally, the live crawfish is chosen as a bait for goliath or other big grouper.

Baby crawfish are good bait for many fish, but it is unlawful to use them in Florida waters.

The double-hook rig shown here is the most satisfactory for cubera snapper fishing. Use two heavy-duty hooks, at least 9/0 and usually larger, and wire them together with cable and sleeves (see the section on wire wraps for instructions on securing the cable). The hooks are about four or five inches apart.

As the illustration shows, the upper hook goes between the "horns" of the crawfish. The lower one is inserted into the soft underside of the tail section, and out again.

Always use gloves when handling live crawfish. They well deserve the adjective "spiny."

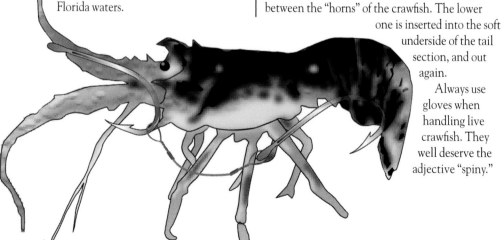

Marine Worms

Soft-bodied marine worms (sandworms, bloodworms, clamworms, etc.) are excellent all-around baits and one of the most popular along the Middle and North Atlantic coasts. As shown in the small illustrations, chunks, pieces or whole tiny worms can be used for panfish—perhaps even several tiny worms on a single hook. Larger worms, rigged to a single or double hook, or behind a spinner, make excellent trolling, drifting or stillfishing baits for larger prey, such as weakfish, striped bass and flounder. An easy double hookup is accomplished with the Stinger Rig, shown in Chapter 6.

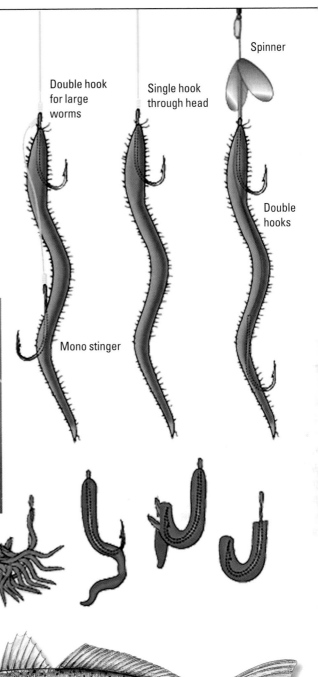

Double hook for large worms

Single hook through head

Spinner

Double hooks

Mono stinger

Sandworms can be globbed on a hook and drifted with or without weight, making a succulent bait for big fish.

WEAKFISH Spinning, baitcasting, light saltwater tackle and often surf gear are used for weakfish. Weakfish go after a variety of baits, including shrimp, marine worms, crabs and squid, as well as live small fish and strips of fish. Among lures, try spoons, tin squids, jigs and swimming plugs, among others. Jig-and-bait combos work well when fishing deep.

Rigged Trolling Baits

Ballyhoo (Balao)

The ballyhoo is the simplest and fastest-to-rig of all offshore trolling baits. This, combined with the fact that it is an excellent producer of everything from marlin to mackerel, makes the ballyhoo top choice among both professional and private skippers.

The rigged ballyhoo is most often trolled at the surface, skipping across the waves, or swimming just under. It is rigged in exactly the same fashion for deep trolling with a sinker in front of it, or for drift fishing, either with a freeline or with a sinker.

A key step in making a ballyhoo rig is to leave a "pin" in your wire leader after wrapping on the hook. The pin should be at right angles to the leader, and pointing in the opposite direction from the hook. The leader wrap, of course, is made with the haywire twist. Now take a piece of copper wire (which you buy in precut lengths at the tackle store) and wrap one end of it several times around the leader wire at the base of the pin.

To rig a perfect ballyhoo, be sure to use either a ¼-inch dowel, an unsharpened pencil, or a discarded arrow shaft to remove the ballyhoo's eyes. You can speed up your rigging by stringing multiple baits on the dowel at a time. Next step is to inspect your ballyhoo for pectoral fins that have been turned backwards by the way they went in the bait bag. If any fins are turned outward, cut them off. If not, your bait will lie on its side, and only skip instead of swim. Next take a small bait knife and

Ballyhoo Prep

Bright, fresh baits are always an advantage and will stand up to the preparation routine. They also troll far better than frozen bait.

1

By prepping baits you are trying to accomplish a few things. First, you're purging the stomach cavity of any waste and also popping out the inflated swim bladder. Some anglers expedite the purging by cutting a slit from the anal cavity toward the tail.

2

Holding the bait gently in your hand facing you and belly up, gently squeeze from the front of the bait's stomach and work from head to tail toward the vent. The stomach's contents will exit the bait through the vent.

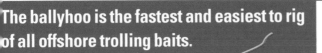

Wrap copper wire one third the way down bill and back a turn or two and break off remaining bill.

The basic ballyhoo rig, above, has many variations, as seen in the following pages.

3

Next, turn the bait over belly down in your hand and gently pinch the top of its back, working from head to tail. This action should loosen up the backbone. You will notice the depression down the top center on the fish's back "pop up" as you go.

4

Finally, rinse the bait off in salt water and flex it loosely in a snakelike motion to complete. Before you attach this bait to a leader you should also remove the eyeballs to keep them from bulging out. This also provides an easy hole to pass your rigging wire through during the final rigging stages.

make the tiniest of incisions from the anal cavity toward the tail. Then gently press the sides of the ballyhoo which will drain the stomach cavity. Then gently squeeze the bait from top to bottom forcing the meat away from the bone (as seen in Ballyhoo Prep).

Hold the ballyhoo in your left hand, and with your left thumb lift up the gill cover.

With your right hand, insert the hook point under the gills and into the body cavity. Work the point as far back as you can, and bring the point out on the underside of the bait.

When the point emerges, pull on it gently—just enough to bring the eye of the hook under the gill cover, and the leader pin under the "chin" of the ballyhoo, forward of the eyes. Insert the pin upward, through both jaws of the bait, and with your thumb, hold the leader wire flush against the underside of the "chin."

Take the copper wire and wrap it tightly behind each gill cover. Bring the copper wire under the gill cover, across his back and behind the second gill cover. Now wrap the copper wire around the pin under the chin, and around the pin from the opposite direction. Then wrap the copper around the bill 30% of the way out the bill. Cut off the extra wire, and cut the bill off squarely. Your bait is now ready, should both swim and skip.

Single-Hook Monofilament Ballyhoo

Always begin with the highest quality fresh bait, new leaders and sharp hooks. Small details make the difference at the moment of truth.

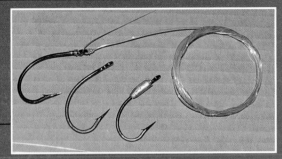

Insert your hook into the gill opening and exit the center of the belly, with the hook point while pulling the eye of the hook into the body cavity. Be sure the hook is lined up on the center line of the bait for straight tracking.

Keeping the wire tight, make two wraps around the lower eye socket and gills to anchor the hook in bait. Push the wire through the lower jaw and exit through the top jaw where it joins the head. Pull tight.

Make a couple of wraps down the beak and stop. Break the beak short. You may or may not choose to split the beak with your leader. (See closeup photos of steps in sidebar.) Wrap copper wire over beak forward to the end. Add lure in front of bait, or fish naked from outrigger.

Split Bill Ballyhoo

This extra step, added to a standard mono-rigged bait will turn skipping surface baits into head-down swimmers. Being head-down gives it a swimming plug-like action without extra weight. They are very effective.

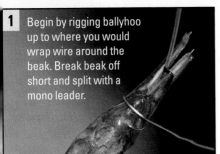

1 Begin by rigging ballyhoo up to where you would wrap wire around the beak. Break beak off short and split with a mono leader.

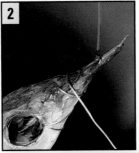

2 Continue wrapping the wire forward and lift the mono leader so you can wrap the wire in front of it.

3 Make a single wrap in front of the leader and finish wrapping back toward the bait's mouth until you are out of wire.

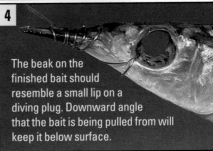

4 The beak on the finished bait should resemble a small lip on a diving plug. Downward angle that the bait is being pulled from will keep it below surface.

Double-Hook Ballyhoo

A double-hook ballyhoo rig really isn't very satisfactory for trolling because the added hook seriously hampers the bait's action. Moreover, the second hook isn't necessary for most offshore fish and, in fact, can be a disadvantage in billfishing. Not only does the double hook make it tougher to release a billfish, having one hook in a fish's mouth and the other through your mate's hand can be very serious.

You may, however, want to use a double hook when drift fishing—especially for king mackerel,

which have an uncanny knack for severing the ballyhoo just in back of the single hook. For drifting, it is optional to break the beak back.

The rig shown here is the easiest of all double-

hook rigs.

The second hook goes after the bait is completely rigged in the usual way. Do not add the other hook before you rig, or you will be unable to rig in regular fashion at all. Slip the eye of the second hook over the point of the first one, then press the point of the second hook upward into the bait. The flesh of a ballyhoo is soft, and the teeth of a kingfish sharp. He will get hooked even though the point of the hook is buried.

There are two main ways of attaching the second hook:

1. Pry open the eye of the second hook, then press the eye closed again with pliers after the hook is in place.

2. With pliers, bend down the barb of the first hook just enough to permit the eye of the second to slip over it. Then pry the barb back to its original position with the blade of a screwdriver (don't risk breaking your good knife).

Open-eye trolling hooks are also available, requiring only a sturdy plier to close the eye around the bend of another hook.

Note on Hook Sizes

Ballyhoo come in various sizes, from about six inches long to more than a foot. Because of this, you should keep at least three different hook sizes handy for your ballyhoo rigging.

The O'Shaughnessy is by far the best hook pattern for rigging ballyhoo, because the long shank allows the hook to be positioned farther aft in the bait. For tiny ballyhoo use a 5/0 or 6/0 hook; for average-size bait, a 7/0 or 8/0; for the largest ballyhoo, a 9/0 or 10/0.

When choosing the proper circle hook for offshore fishing, if you're using less than 30-pound tackle, a light wire hook in the 5/0 to 7/0 range with a slight offset is preferred. As the tackle gets beefier, the diameter gets wider. You'll need to do a little homework here, because a 6/0 hook designed for fishing grouper on 60-pound test is much heavier and stronger than a 6/0 hook designed to live bait sailfish.

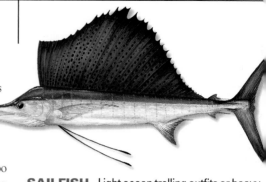

SAILFISH Light ocean trolling outfits or heavy spinning gear is used, with lines of 12- to 30-pound test. Live baiting, either by kite fishing or flatline-drifting, has become the most popular approach for sails, with blue runners, goggle-eyes, pilchards and pinfish being common baits. Trolling with rigged baits, especially ballyhoo, is still popular to cover ground and in places where live baits are not easily available.

Swimming or Leaded Ballyhoo

A dead ballyhoo can be made to "swim" just under the surface instead of skipping the top. This rig is valuable for days when the seas are so rough that skipping baits seem to stay airborne longer than they stay in the water. And even in good weather, the swimming ballyhoo gives your spread an additional enticement that may well get some strikes from fish that ignore the skippers.

Rigging the swimming ballyhoo is essentially the same as rigging the normal, skipping ballyhoo. The obvious difference is that a sinker must be incorporated into your rig at the time when you wrap, or crimp the hook to the leader. The sinker weighs from ¼ to ½ ounce, depending on the size of the ballyhoo and the sea conditions.

Heavier sinkers will NOT provide any substantially deeper running depth.

First, slide an egg sinker onto your leader, then run the wire or mono through the bottom of the hook eye, out the top. If you're using wire, start your haywire twist tight against the sinker. If you're fishing mono slide the crimp snug against the sinker and close the sleeve. Don't forget to insert the pin before closing the sleeve. The pin can now be pushed through the head, bottom to top, and the rig completed exactly as with the unleaded ballyhoo. Whereas feathers, and plastic chuggers are popular with ballyhoo trollers, swimming ballyhoo perform much better naked.

The Circle Hook Rig

There are many different variations of the circle hook ballyhoo rigs. One of the easiest is the "O-Ring" rig. You'll prepare the ballyhoo just like you would for a J-hook, but that's where the similarity ends.

You'll need to first twist an O-ring (No. 3 for a small to medium bally, No.4 for select and horses) to the end of a 14-inch piece of copper rigging wire. Then poke a tiny hole through the upper lip, and out through the bottom jaw of your ballyhoo. Pull the wire through until the O-ring rests snugly on the center of your ballyhoo's head. Then take a wrap behind each gill, and come through the eye sockets twice. Wrap once behind the O-ring, and several wraps ahead of the O-ring, 30 percent of the way out the bill. Cut off any extra wire and cut the bill off squarely.

The beauty of the O-ring rig is its ease to deploy. Rig a few dozen the night before, and lay them on a sheet of foil, or bait tray on top of your ice. Leave your circle hook, and leader on your rod. After a bait is used just take it off the hook, and thread your hook through the next O-ring.

1

Using a 1/4-inch dowel or a discarded arrow shaft makes removing the eyes of multiple ballyhoo a snap.

2

Snip back the bills evenly, leaving about 1/4 of the length of the bill.

3

Cut off any backwards pectoral fins. Baits will swim better.

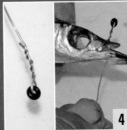

4

Wrap O-ring to wire. Thread it top to bottom through lips of bait.

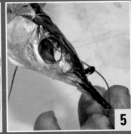

5

Pull O-ring snug. Wrap wire behind gill plates and twice thru sockets.

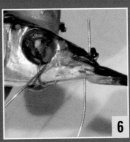

6

Push wire back up hole from step 4 and wrap remaining wire out bill.

7

Simply place your circle hook through the O-ring.

O-Ring Rig

There is no easier, more convenient way to rig multiple numbers of ballyhoo than the O-ring rig. By doing a few dozen baits the night before a trip, you make your fishing day so much easier and more efficient.

Being able to just pull an old bait off your leader and stick on a new one gets you back in the water immediately.

It is important, of course, to keep pre-made rigged baits properly cooled at all times prior to and during fishing. Bait trays are available to hold baits over coolers full of ice. It's best not to keep rigged baits directly on ice.

Circle Hook Ballyhoo Weighted

As circle hooks become more popular for both live baiting and trolling, many new tricks for rigging baits with them are being developed along the way. A popular technique for rigging ballyhoo for trolling involves preparing the baits without a leader attached. This method makes it much neater and keeps your bait cooler more organized.

Anglers wait for their rigged baits to be found by a hungry pelagic.

This approach is standard in Central America, where several dozen baits per day are required. It keeps the baitbox free of tangled leaders when the action gets hot. This rig is quick and easy and works like a champ for rigging a leaded "swimming ballyhoo."

As circle hooks become more popular, many new tricks for rigging them are being developed.

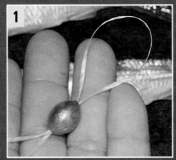

Begin by doubling 2 feet of waxed rigging line and passing looped end through small egg sinker.

Pull the looped end over the bait's head and slip it under the gill plates on both sides of the bait.

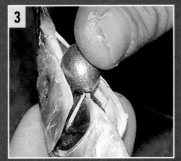

Slide the egg sinker down the rigged line so it fits between the gills forward of throat latch.

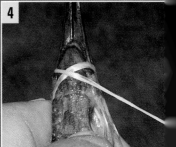

Bring the line's ends forward under the bait's lower jaw and wrap over top jaw. Keep line tight.

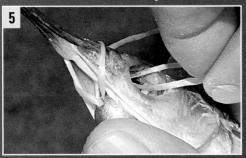

Pass both ends through eye sockets from opposite directions. Wrap gills over sinker and knot tight.

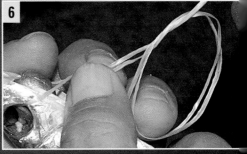

Tie another overhand knot in the two stands of line and pull it tight.

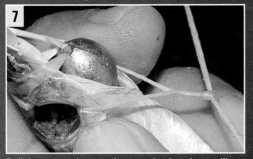

Pull the two ends away from each other; knot will slip down to egg sinker. Snug up and trim.

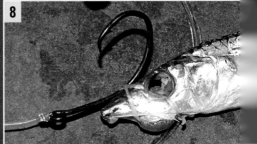

To complete, break the beak off short and insert circle hook under x-shaped loop of thread on top of head.

Saltwater Baits

Alternative Trolling Baits

Small Mullet

This is the rig to use with small mullet, or other small fish you may wish to troll.

Almost any type of small fish makes an acceptable trolling bait in an emergency, and if you get the chance to fish in foreign waters you might be faced with having to rig an unfamiliar species. Study the shape of the fish and the contour of its head, then decide whether to rig it in the fashion of the ballyhoo, or in the manner described here.

With this rig you do not use a "pin" of leader wire. In fact, you do not even attach your hook to the leader in advance.

A tail-walking sail tries to shake a hook during a fight offshore.

Lay your hook alongside the bait, with the eye of the hook even with the eye of the fish. This is how you measure the approximate place where the hook point will come out of the fish's belly. Take the point of a knife and make a small slit in the belly at that spot.

Now insert the eye of the hook through that slit, into the belly, then forward through the throat and into the mouth.

Run the leader through the bottom jaw, through the eye of the hook, through the top jaw and out the top of the head. Pull enough leader through for ease of rigging. CAREFUL—be sure your leader goes through the eye of the hook! You can test this by pulling gently on the hook to see if the leader moves.

Last, either wrap your leader wire close in front of the fish's lips, using the haywire twist, or slide the sleeve snugly against the bait's head before crimping it shut. If fishing with wire, make sure you break off the extra wire instead of cutting it. (See chap. 5 haywire twist.)

As you can see, the pull will be on the loop of leader through the bait's head. There should be no pull on the hook. If the bait tends to twist, enlarge the hook hole with a knife point. It also helps to flex the bait back and forth to break the spine in one or more places.

Large Mullet

Large mullet are rigged in essentially the same way as finger mullet. However, the backbone must be removed, and there is some sewing involved.

You'll need a de-boner (available in tackle stores) and a bait needle. Floss or any kind of small braided line may be used as "sewing thread."

Large mullet are mainly employed in marlin

Some fish just can't refuse a big mullet. Troll one near a wreck or reef holding big amberjack and hold on tight.

nd tuna fishing, but they take smaller species as well (to the distress of folks after big game). A large rigged mullet also makes a great bait for deep trolling in quest of amberjack and heavy grouper.

TO PREPARE THE BAIT Remove the entire backbone with the de-boner. If you haven't used one before, don't fret. It is much like coring an apple. The de-boner is a hollow tube with a sharp edge. Insert the edge under the gill, get it into position in front of the backbone, pointing toward the tail. With a slow, twisting motion, work the de-boner back for almost the full length of the fish. Bend the tail of the fish sideways and make a last gentle push with the de-boner to sever the spine close to the tail. Remove the de-boner and the entire backbone comes with it. A rod (supplied with the de-boner when you buy it) is used to expel the backbone.

Now make a slit in the belly, large enough so that you can remove all the mullet's entrails. Insert the eye of your hook in this slit and push it forward into position inside the mullet's mouth, directly under the eyes. Insert your leader through both jaws and through the eye of the hook,

A de-boner can provide fabulous bluewater baits when used on mullet or Spanish mackerel.

exactly as with the finger mullet. Make your leader is through the hook as before.

It is now necessary to tie the gills closed, so that trolling pressure will not tear the bait. You CAN simply tie a piece of string tightly around the head, in back of the eyes, to hold the gills down. To avoid all chance of slippage, however, run your string through the mullet's head, using your bait needle, and then tie the string off tightly under the head.

If the belly slit you made in removing the entrails is so large that it seems likely to catch water and tear while trolling, then use your needle to sew the belly slit closed.

Leaded Mullet on Wire

To make the mullet remain under the surface and "swim," you incorporate an egg sinker into the rigging.

The leaded mullet was the standard bait for giant bluefin tuna in the heyday of that Bahamas fishery. Many marlin anglers and potluck offshore trollers like to troll both leaded and unleaded mullet baits at the same time. In rough seas, where skipping baits might be in the air as much as in the water, the lead helps keep the baits where they belong.

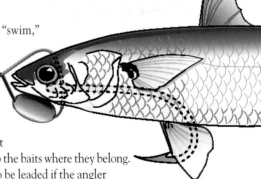

Obviously, finger mullet and cigar minnows can also be leaded if the angler desires, but with a smaller sinker, of course.

TO RIG THE LEAD Slide your egg sinker onto the leader wire before inserting the wire through the head of the fish and the hook. After the wire is inserted through the bait and in position for wrapping, slide the sinker down and hold it under the bait's "chin" while you make as tight a wrap as possible. Size of the egg sinker can vary, but is usually one or two ounces with large mullet; one-half to one ounce with finger mullet.

Prepping Cut Back Mullet

The "cut back" mullet is an easy way to rig mullet under 8 inches long, often deadly on medium bluewater gamesters such as sailfish and dolphin. Mullet are best rigged on the dock in advance. If you live in an area where there's a good run of silver mullet, you can catch your own, cut them fresh, brine them, and be ready when the bite starts.

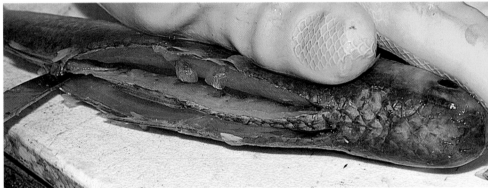

Scale the top of the head back to where the back bone begins. Insert small sharp bait knife immediately along backbone and cut to start of upper back fin. Turn mullet over and repeat process.

Using a pair of snips cut backbone at each end, and remove along with insides.

Using salt or better yet, a quality brine, pour liberally into body.

Rub sides together working brine into meat.

Rigging Cut Back Mullet

This is another option for rigging dead mullet, a very sturdy bait that will swim for hours behind the boat. With practice, it only requires a few minutes to rig before leaving the dock.

Using rigging needle or hook point poke hole through skull of mullet.

Place hook alongside head, checking to see where hook will protrude.

Using bait knife place small hole in mullet's belly where hook should protrude.

Place eye of hook into hole and push eye up into mouth of mullet.

Place egg sinker on mono, and feed leader up through bottom of the bait through the eye of the hook, and out through the top of his head.

Pull on the hook to make sure your leader is through the eye of the hook and either tie a loop knot, or crimp rig closed against the bait.

Rigging Mackerel, Barracuda

Mackerel, bonefish, small barracuda, and other rather slender species can be rigged with a hook inside, exactly the same way as for mullet. All make good trolling baits for larger species of gamefish, especially marlin. With mackerel and small barracuda it usually is not necessary to de-bone, as you can make the bait limber enough simply by flexing it and breaking the spine in several places. De-boning is not so necessary for baits intended to skip the surface, as it is for baits intended to "swim." Whether to de-bone or not, in a given situation and with a given bait, is largely your own decision.

In almost every case, however, it will be neces-

sary to sew or tie the gills closed. With mackerel, you should also sew the belly cavity around the hook, even if your original hookslit is not large. Mackerel flesh is very soft and tears easily.

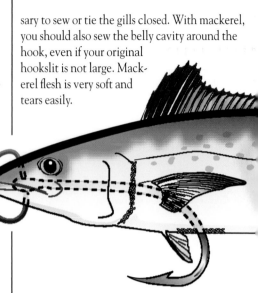

Marlin Rig, Hook Outside

With giant bait and an outside hook, the baitfish usually requires no preparation at all.

In marlin fishing, the larger baits such as mackerel, bonito, bonefish, jack, dolphin, etc. are frequently rigged with a circle hook outside the bait. This rig is especially desirable when seeking the biggest possible marlin on 80- and 130-pound-test line, and when using the biggest of circle hooks—12/0 to 15/0, or even 20/0. It is sometimes used with smaller baits, smaller hooks and light or medium tackle, but a rig with the J-hook inside is often chosen for those applications.

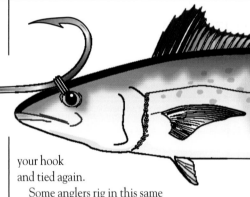

With giant bait and an outside hook, the baitfish normally requires no preparation at all. You use it as is, with no de-boning or cutting—although the gills and mouth should be sewed tight.

TO RIG THE OUTSIDE HOOK Take your bait needle, and thread a length of braided line through the eye sockets of the fish, remove the needle and tie the line tightly. Leave the ends of the sewing line long enough so they can be wrapped two or three times around the bend of

your hook and tied again.

Some anglers rig in this same way, although running the tying line through both lips of the fish, instead of through the eye sockets. Most, however, prefer the eye tie up.

A BETTER METHOD THAN EITHER is to use a metal figure-eight as an attachment between the hook and the eye tieup. This method is explained under the instructions for rigging live bonito. Refer to that section, as the rig is exactly the same whether the bait is alive or dead.

DOLPHIN Also known as mahi-mahi and dorado, the dolphin fish is one of the world's most popular offshore catches. Spinning, baitcasting, trolling and fly tackle are all popular for schoolie-size fish, but ones over 30 pounds can be a real challenge, even on trolling gear.

Trolling Squid

Trolling squid may be the most underutilized bait of all. Here's a rig to troll it on a wire leader. Before you start building the rig, see what size squid you'll have available.

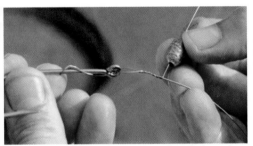

Using No. 8 stainless wire, run extra length through eye, around shank, through eye in other direction.

Make haywire twist with loose wraps for the length of the squid. Slide on ¼-ounce egg sinker.

Close rig with tight haywire twist.

Other end of leader through squid until sinker fills mantle. Piece of copper wire can wrap connection.

Place hook through head of squid until it protrudes outside the head.

Stretch leader so squid lays naturally. Add a Sea Witch or small Ilander, make haywire loop at end.

SWORDFISH Though swordfish grow to more than 1,000 pounds, commonly recreational anglers get fish in the 200- to 300-pound class. Among the best swordfish baits for day or night fishing is a rigged squid. Also good are bonito belly baits, or other rigged baitfish. Artificial squids, rigged, are also used as well. The fish are caught both by drifting and trolling, and in recent years, by daytime fishing for them in depths of up to 2,000 feet with heavy weights either rigged on a breakaway system or on a downrigger-style system with another rod. Tackle used is most often 80-wide, though some anglers opt for 130-wide reels in case a big fish strikes.

When drifting at night for swordfish with big squid and big hooks, this rig is entirely adequate.

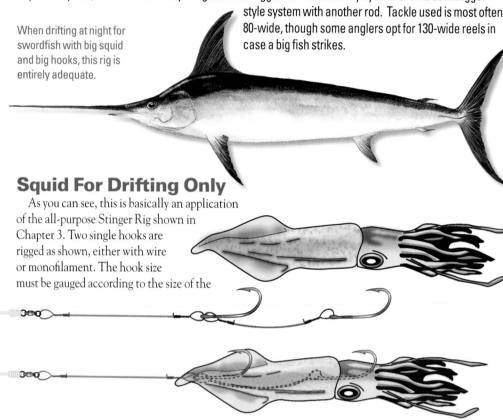

Squid For Drifting Only

As you can see, this is basically an application of the all-purpose Stinger Rig shown in Chapter 3. Two single hooks are rigged as shown, either with wire or monofilament. The hook size must be gauged according to the size of the squid, and so must the distance between the hooks.

Insert the point of the front hook into the end of the tail, and out as shown. The rear hook is simply pushed through the head of the bait from the underside.

Small squids drifted in this manner will take many kinds of fish. When drifting at night for swordfish with big squid and big hooks, this rig is entirely adequate, and holds up well because there is no heavy pressure on the bait. Still, most professional skippers who swordfish by drifting at night do rig their baits as carefully as for trolling.

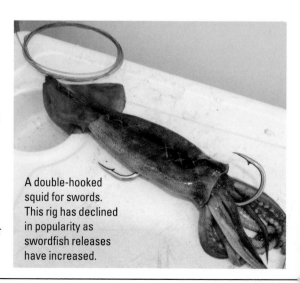

A double-hooked squid for swords. This rig has declined in popularity as swordfish releases have increased.

Swordfish Squid Rig

Here's an easy, single-hook swordfish rig that's made on heavy mono. It's quick, simple, and very effective. Build the leader by sliding the sleeve well up the line, so when crimped you have a 4- to 6-inch tag end protruding out the top of the sleeve.

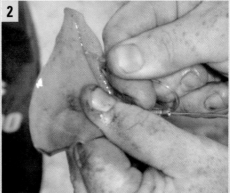

1 Start by threading either J- or circle hook into the body so crimp lays alongside squid at the bottom of the mantle.

2 Twist a piece of copper rigging wire around leader at bottom of sleeve.

3 Push heavy mono (250-pound test or up) tag from sleeve up through mantle. Mono should protrude out tip of mantle.

4 Wrap two pieces of mono together with copper wire to secure squid to leader, and take pressure off the hook.

5 Tug on mono to make sure pressure is on crimp and not hook.

6 Lay out squid, and make sure body lays straight to prevent twisting.

The Trolling Strip

A properly rigged strip is one of the best trolling baits. Private anglers seldom make use of it because it is more bother to rig than a ballyhoo, but many of the more successful charter captains insist on keeping a strip out at all times (in combination with other baits), and the strip frequently outfishes the rest.

As with ballyhoo, the strip rig requires a "pin" of leader wire. But note that in this case the pin points in the same direction as the hook, and you leave a much longer pin than for ballyhoo.

The most desirable strips are those cut from the white underparts of a bonito. Belly sections of mackerel, kings, dolphin, barracuda and other fish can be used. Mullet strips work well but are less durable.

The strip should be about 10 or 12 inches long and trimmed to teardrop shape—with a short taper at the hook end; a longer taper at the rear. Carefully trim off excess flesh so that the strip is no more than a quarter-inch thick, preferably less than that. The thinner the strip, the more action.

Prepping the Fillet for Strips

1 Start by cutting the bonito side down to 1/4 inch thick. Next, scrape the fillet down to flatten and produce an even thickness. For best results, always follow the grain of the meat.

2 Next, cut individual baits out of each side in the shape of a willow leaf. Baits can range in size from 4 to 8 inches. Plan your cuts carefully to get the most baits possible from each slab.

3 Fine-tune each bait to remove any ragged edges and bevel the edge of the meat, to improve action. Square off the forward part of the bait so it's pulled along with the grain.

But a thin layer of flesh must be maintained so the bait will hold shape.

TO RIG THE STRIP Insert the pin through the strip at the short-tapered front end. Note illustration on opposite page to see that the pin must now be bent forward and secured on the leader, ahead of the bait. To do this, take pliers and bend a tiny V-shaped or U-shaped catch at the end of the

pin, so that it can be fixed to the leader in much the same manner as a safety pin.

Now the strip must be bunched forward slightly while you insert the hook. After the hook is in place, the strip must lie perfectly flat. There must be no pressure from the hook on the strip. If there is, enlarge the hook hole with a knife point to relieve the pressure.

BLACKFIN TUNA Tackle used includes light classes of ocean tackle, plus spinning, baitcasting and also fly rod. For trolling, choose small offshore lures, feathers, spoons and plugs. Small rigged baits also work well, and live baiting for blackfin by chumming with small baitfish such as pilchards is also a successful technique.

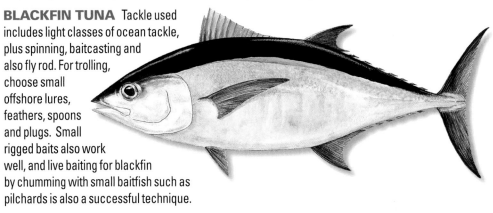

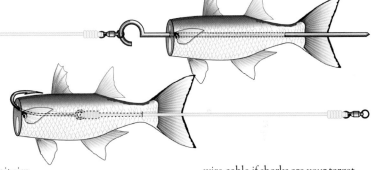

Gulf Coast Bottom Rig

This used to be the standard bait for tarpon fishing over much of the Gulf Coast. It also has taken many very big snook, and is one of the best deadbait rigs for sharks. It is fished directly on bottom, lying there until picked up. When a fish takes this bait, allow him to travel with it as you keep your reel in free-spool. After a few seconds, tighten your line gently, continue to increase pressure on a circle hook.

This rig should no longer be used for tarpon, for most tarpon caught this way are hooked deep, resulting in mortal wounds. Not many anglers want to kill tarpon these days. Check your particular state laws for legality if you are interested in keeping a tarpon.

For this rig, make up your leader in advance. Use a six-foot leader of 100 or 120-pound-test monofilament, or a six-foot leader of 90 or 135-pound-test

wire cable if sharks are your target.

If monofilament is used, tie a stout swivel to one end of the leader, a 10/0 hook to the other. The ties can be made with either the improved clinch knot or the two-wrap hangman's knot. In either case, use pliers and a lot of pressure to make sure the knots are drawn down tight.

If cable is used, attach the hook and swivel with sleeve and crimper.

TO RIG Cut the head off a mullet. Run a bait needle the full length of the mullet, alongside the backbone coming out at the tail. Hook the eye of the needle to your swivel and pull your complete leader through the bait, so the hook is positioned as shown.

Cut Fish

Cutbaits and unrigged whole dead baits are used for stillfishing, and occasionally for drifting. They differ, as a class, from rigged baits in that they are not calculated to give an appearance of live, swimming action. Nor is any special rigging necessary. You simply stick the bait on your hook and start fishing.

Mullet is commonly used for cutbait, because it is widely available and inexpensive. The same for menhaden. You can also cut baits from most any kind of fish you might catch with the cut mullet. Naturally, the fish you don't want to take home are the ones you're most inclined to cut up for bait—pinfish or sailor's choice, ladyfish, jack, small grunts, etc.

HOW TO CUT BAIT Always use a cutting board and a sharp knife. The fish may or may not be scaled, but scaling usually helps. Slice fillets from both sides of the fish, discard the rest (unless you wish to use the head for bait).

From each fillet you can cut squarish slabs of bait for bottom fishing, or rather narrow strips for drift-fishing.

Always use a cutting board and a sharp knife. The fish may or may not be scaled, but scaling usually helps to make cleaner, better cuts.

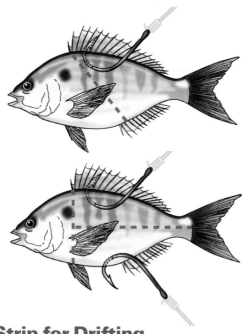

Strip for Drifting

If drift-fishing (speckled trout, etc.) take a rough-cut strip and hook it through one end, as shown in the illustration. There is no need to rig the strip, or taper it, as you would for trolling.

"Shiner Tail" Strips

Good baits for either drift fishing or bottom fishing can be cut from small fish such as pinfish. These are often called "shiner tails" and are widely used in fishing for seatrout. They produce a variety of other gamefish as well, and in many waters.

One illustration shows a single bait, cut diagonally from the dorsal. The other shows how you can halve the entire pinfish, then cut it again lengthwise to make two baits. With either method, you cut all the way through the fish (that is, you don't just slice off one fillet), and use the bait with bone in.

Such a bait is more durable than a strip of fillet, since it withstands the nibbles of "bait stealers" while waiting for a good strike.

HOOK POSITION If bottom-fishing, place the hook near the center of the bait as shown in the illustrations. If drifting, position the hook close to the "head" end of the bait.

Strip or Chunk for Bottom Fishing

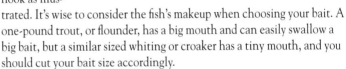

If bottom fishing, use either a rough strip or a chunk and run your hook through the bait twice (three or more times if using a bait large enough to permit it).

Dead Shrimp

Dead shrimp may be used whole, broken in half, or cut in small pieces.

If used whole, thread the shrimp on the hook as shown. Half a shrimp should be threaded in much the same way.

For panfish or baitfish, use tiny pieces of shrimp, with the skin peeled off, and cover the point of the hook as illus-

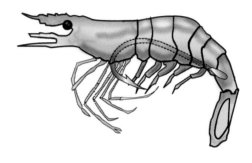

trated. It's wise to consider the fish's makeup when choosing your bait. A one-pound trout, or flounder, has a big mouth and can easily swallow a big bait, but a similar sized whiting or croaker has a tiny mouth, and you should cut your bait size accordingly.

Mullet Head

The head of a mullet or boston mackerel, hooked through both lips as shown, and fished patiently on bottom, is an excellent bait for snapper and grouper on the reefs, or for snook, tarpon, goliath grouper, etc., inshore. Snook do not hit a dead bait as readily as a live one, but some big snook are often caught on mullet heads. Obviously, you can use other kinds of fish heads too.

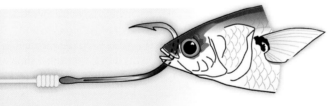

TARPON Anglers seek the big tarpon in channels, passes and deep bays and also along beaches. Reels and lines should test at least 30 and more like 50 pounds for the big fish. Spinning, baitcasting and fly gear are all used. Mullet, menhaden, pinfish and spot are popular live baits, as are crab and shrimp. Artificials at all depths work well, including plugs, jigs and swimbaits.

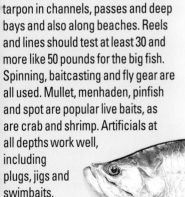

Cut Plug Bait for Mooching

Using downriggers lets you fish deep with light tackle suitable for kids.

To rig a herring or similar baitfish for "mooching" in the traditional style of salmon fishermen in the Northwest, first cut off the head, slanting the cut slightly rearward. Remove entrails. Now use our old friend, the stinger rig, shown in chapter 3. Again, hook size must be appropriate to the size of the bait. Insert the front hook in at the head and out the side. The rear hook goes in and out either side of the fish or the dorsal surface.

The mooching bait is drifted out and is worked by the current in an erratic, wobbling and spinning motion. It is also slow-trolled. In either case it can be rigged to a weightless leader when conditions permit, but more often is used with a downrigger, or else in combination with a trolling sinker to obtain the desired depth, as in the second illustration. The third drawing shows how a flasher or dodger can be incorporated into the leader ahead of the plug bait for additional attraction.

CHINOOK SALMON Also commonly known as king salmon, these fish have been on record caught with recreational gear weighing close to 100 pounds. Forty and 50-pound fish are not too uncommon. Spinning and baitcasting gear is commonly used for trolling with downriggers or heavy weights, and also for mooching with sinkers and natural bait. Fly tackle is mostly used in upstream waters. Deep-trolled lures take many king salmon, as do live and cutbaits, such as herring and candlefish. Bright dodgers rigged ahead of the lures add to the strikes. In the rivers, casters rely mostly on spoons and spinners.

Bait-Lure Combinations

Feather and Strip

An extremely popular combination for trolling offshore or on the reef is the feather-strip.

The trolling feather is threaded to your leader, after which you rig a strip for trolling as described earlier. In use, the feather slides down to the hook, covering the forward portion of the strip. Remember, strips are often deadliest when skittering on the surface. To try that hold the size of your feather down to 1/2-ounce or less.

Remember, strips often work best when skittering on the surface. To try that, keep your feathers either 1/2-ounce or less.

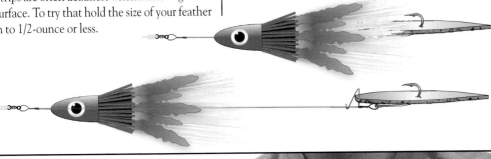

Dolphin are suckers for bait-and-lure combos. You can pull them faster than naked baits.

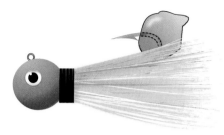

Jig With Shrimp

When you add a small "tip" of cut shrimp to an artificial jig you come up with one of the best casting lures for inshore waters.

You probably will catch more redfish and seatrout with a tipped jig than with a bare jig. You will also catch bottom feeders, such as sheepshead and drum, which rarely hit a plain jig. At the same time, the tip of shrimp does not hinder the action of the bait and so you catch just as many snook and other large predators that likely won't care if the bait smells or not.

But to make the jig work right, you have to use a SMALL piece of shrimp. Too large a tip causes the jig to twist on the retrieve.

You get more tips from a single shrimp if you cut them with a knife, rather than breaking them off with your fingers.

Jig With Strip

A small strip of cut fish or squid can be used in place of the shrimp. It does not work so well as the shrimp for a wide range of inshore species, but often pays off handsomely when you're fishing for schooling varieties, such as mackerel and bluefish.

Large Jig with Ballyhoo or Cigar Minnow

A heavy jig, weighing two to nine ounces, can be fitted with a second hook and rigged with a ballyhoo, cigar minnow, or some other kind of slender baitfish, as shown, to make a most productive bait for deep drift fishing.

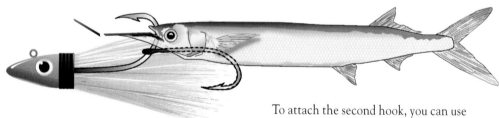

To attach the second hook, you can use either of two methods:

1. Pry open the eye of the second hook, slip the eye over the barb of the first hook, and press the eye closed. You can also press a swivel over the first hook and press the eye of the second hook closed on the swivel's other side, so that the trailer hook swings more freely on the shank of the front hook. To make it even easier, buy trailer hooks whose eyes are left open and can be easily closed when rigging.

2. With pliers, bend down the barb of the hook slightly—just enough to permit the eye of the second hook to slide over it. Then pry the barb back into position, using the blade of a screwdriver.

A lot of fishermen toss over this rig and let it go down deep—near bottom if depth permits, or at least 100 feet if fishing in deep blue water. They use the rig on a stout boat rod, and place the rod in a holder with the reel in gear and the drag set fairly light. Most any fish which takes the bait will hook itself. This rig has taken a great many big grouper, snapper, stripers, king mackerel and even quite a few sailfish.

Large Jig with Strip

A deep jig with a strip can be used in precisely the same way as described for a whole baitfish—on a drifting line down deep.

But it is more frequently used as a king mackerel rig when kings are schooling, and is one of the best. Use a nylon jig, weighing one or one-and-a-half ounces. Attach a second hook and hook on the strip as shown.

Cast it out, let it sink to or beyond the suspected level of the king school, then retrieve it with sweeps of the rod. Kings will hit it while it sinks, or during the retrieve.

This is also a good rig for bottom jigging. Let it sink all the way to bottom, then bounce it around a few times without retrieving any line. If a grouper or snapper is around, chances are that fish willl hit. If no strike occurs at bottom, retrieve all the way to the boat with sharp upward sweeps of the rod, cranking in line between sweeps. You can catch kings or other mid-depth species on the way in.

You're apt to find kings at any depth especially behind shrimp boats that just dumped bycatch.

Cast it out, let it sink either to or beyond the suspected level of the king school, then retrieve it with sweeps of the rod.

MUTTON SNAPPER

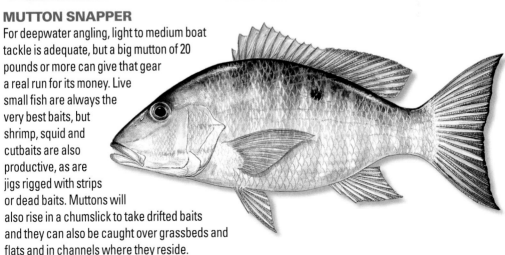

For deepwater angling, light to medium boat tackle is adequate, but a big mutton of 20 pounds or more can give that gear a real run for its money. Live small fish are always the very best baits, but shrimp, squid and cutbaits are also productive, as are jigs rigged with strips or dead baits. Muttons will also rise in a chumslick to take drifted baits and they can also be caught over grassbeds and flats and in channels where they reside.

CHAPTER 9

Artificial Lures

S altwater lures differ greatly in their applications from freshwater lures. Many saltwater lures are best used to make natural baits look better or to fish at different depths. Whereas a bass fisherman would have a stroke if you slipped a skirt over the hook holding his live shiner, it's standard for many kingfish fishermen to skirt their live menhaden.

Today's saltwater inshore fishermen have as many choices as freshwater fishermen. Many years ago it was unheard of to see a saltwater fisherman "walking the dog," or slowly rolling a spinnerbait over the top of a flooded grassflat. Many lures such as Zara Spooks have made the transition from fresh to salt water with only a change of the hooks.

Many years ago it was unheard of to see a saltwater fisherman "walking the dog," or slowly rolling a spinnerbait over the top of a flooded grassflat.

Flies, right, and lures, above, are made to perform specific actions in the water to attract fish.

Offshore Trolling Lures

Skirted Lures

Veteran bluewater fishermen in all waters of the world incorporate artificial lures into their arsenal, either pulling them exclusively, or fishing a combination of bait and lures in the same spread. The obvious advantages of fishing lures exclusively are the ease of preparation, and the ability to troll at least 20 percent faster, showing your spread to more fish.

Typically, the bigger trolling lures feature a hard plastic head and a plastic skirt. There are several basic head designs, each providing a different action and each generally requiring a different range of trolling speeds to bring out its best performance. Tapered or torpedo heads offer the least water resistance. They are straight runners and can be trolled at the fastest speeds. Flathead lures also run straight, but their blunt heads kick up more commotion.

Heavy resin or leadheads hold natural baits in the water at higher trolling speeds.

Color of lures is a matter of debate that resolves into personal preference.

Flatheads can be used at high speeds—up to 20 knots—although most anglers prefer to drag them at about 9 or 10 knots.

Lures with a slanted, concave head, have a wildly erratic, darting action, and for this reason are often used as teasers as well as actual lures. Because they aren't straight runners, they are usually pulled at the low end of the lure-speed range, eight knots or so, although somewhat faster speeds may be used.

Artificial lures in general eliminate the "dropback," which is standard procedure in attempting to hook a billfish that strikes a natural rigged bait. Marlin will often track an artificial, but just as often, the strike comes suddenly and savagely,

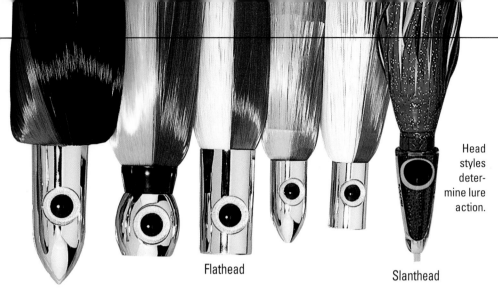

Head styles determine lure action.

Flathead

Slanthead

Bullethead

Fish are not so quick to drop softer trolling lures, and a modest amount of dropback can help.

and the fish is either on or off before the angler has much chance to influence the result. Note, though, that fish are not so quick to drop the softer trolling lures and a modest amount of dropback with those can be helpful.

Lures may be trolled directly off the rod, with the reel in strike-drag position, but most veteran anglers and captains much prefer to provide an elastic resistance to a striking fish. This they do by running a "tag" line off the outrigger line. At the end of the stinger line is a heavy-duty snap. A rubber band is half-hitched to the fishing line and then the other end of the band is placed in the snap on the tag line. When a big fish hits, both the outrigger lines and the rubber band provide shock absorption, and yet there is enough pressure to set the hook before the

line cuts through the rubber band and comes free.

After the fishing line comes tight to the fish, additional hook-setting tactics of a traditional nature are employed—gunning the engines briefly and striking with the rod.

The beauty of bluewater trolling lures is that they are ready to deploy at a moment's notice. Skirts, below.

Trolling Feathers

For want of a more widely used term, saltwater trolling lures that feature a weighted head in combination with some kind of soft trailer material are frequently called "feathers."

The principal difference between feathers and leadhead jigs is that the feathers are supplied without a built-in hook, whereas jigs have the hook molded into the head.

Often the trailer material is really of feathers, and at one time all such lures were made with feathers—hence the popular name, which has hung on. Nowadays, nylon is commonly used as trailer material. This type lure is also made with plastic streamers and, rarely, with hair.

Blackfin tuna, below, can be quick to go down when boats are near, so a popular technique is to troll small feathers far behind the boat to attract bites.

Feathers come in a wide assortment of sizes, and are used mostly for offshore trolling. You run your leader wire through the hollow head, and attach to it the hook of your choice.

The feather is often placed ahead of a rigged ballyhoo, mullet or strip of bait. All the angler need do is slide the feather onto his leader before rigging the natural bait.

Any ocean gamefish will at times hit the plain trolled feather; and for a lot of offshore species, the feather alone seems just about as productive as the feather-bait combination.

Williamson trolling feather

Dredges, Teasers & Daisy Chains

A dredge looks like a school of baitfish behind the boat to attract gamefish.

Teasers comprise a wide range of lures and lure arrays rigged without a hook and used merely as attention-getters, improving the visibility and/or action of a trolling spread.

In certain cases, such as light-tackle billfishing, a trolling spread may consist entirely of teaser arrays, aimed at encouraging a particular species to linger close to the boat as the angler readies himself to present (or "pitch") a bait, lure or fly on the chosen tackle. The crew may wish to avoid hooking a fish on any other tackle.

In other cases, a crew may deploy several large, bright teasers along with a mix of rigged baits and lures, with the hope of attracting the attention of gamefish away from a weedline, deep reef, bait ball or other feature.

Let's start with the basic "teaser." The first mass-produced teasers were nothing more than an oversized bluewater lure tied to a piece of stout cord pulled right off the transom. Whereas nothing smaller than a blue marlin, big shark, or perhaps a bluefin tuna could have eaten them, ordinary game fish like dolphin, sails, cobia, kings and amberjack were no doubt attracted by curiosity. Probably the most famous of all teasers is aptly named the "bowling pin." When pulled behind a boat, it dives, and jumps and no doubt looks like a fish chasing bait.

Dredges (a group of actual bait fish, or imitations, pulled below the surface on an umbrella rig) can be made with 50 fresh de-boned silver mullet, or with something as simple as Mylar strips with holographic fish emblazoned on them. Many anglers save leftover ballyhoo, or make a deal with their bait shop to get old ballyhoo bags that are no longer vacuum sealed, at a discounted rate to put on their dredge.

Many companies make lifelike rubber imitation ballyhoo and mullet. They are effective and greatly reduce the workload of readying for a day's fishing.

The trick with dredges is to pull them close to the boat where they can be seen while trolling. Catching the fish raised by the dredge is much easier if you can see the predators your bait ball attracts. Make sure you fish one of your hooked baits

Building natural bait dredges is a lot of labor, but produces results.

Bowling pin teasers

close to the dredge, and be ready to reposition it in front of any fish you spot following the dredge. The rig for attaching a ballyhoo or mullet to the dredge is simple but must be done correctly to work.

To attach the mullet or ballyhoo to the rig, you must build a pin rig out of the heaviest wire you can twist, or else one or more of the baits will get off center and spin. One bait spinning will ruin the entire presentation. That's also the reason you build the rig with oversized egg sinkers under the bait's chin (2 oz. for ballyhoo, 3 oz. for small mullet, up to 6 oz. for the biggest mullet you can find). Any small feather you pull on your hooked baits will work on your dredge baits and will help you see the dredge, as well as make the bait hold up longer.

Generally speaking, a 4- to 6-pound cigar shaped trolling weight will hold the arms of the dredge under water. That means most boats will be best served to pull them on sturdy downriggers or electric reels if they're pulling any faster than 3 knots.

Daisy chains are generally made from soft rubber squid between 6 and 10 inches long in several different colors. It's fun to experiment however, as everything from music CDs to soda cans have been rigged on a chain, and all of them have been known to raise fish. Chains are usually made from a single piece of 300-pound mono, with 6 to 8 squid secured a foot apart. To build your own, simply slide a small (1/2 oz.) egg sinker on the mono and secure a crimp to hold it in place, slide a squid down the line, and repeat

the process until all 6 to 8 squids are in line. Many captains insist on a ballyhoo or mullet rigged on a pin rig directly behind the last squid. That means you need to crimp a snapswivel after the last squid to clip on the pin rig. Daisy chains are designed to skitter across the water. Pulling them through the first eye on your outrigger is very effective. Bluewater billfish pros often insist on two dredges (one run off each outrigger) and a daisy chain over each dredge. That's a lot for a weekend crew to keep untangled.

Teeth marks on "birds" can show that wahoo aren't really very picky eaters.

BIRDS originally were large teasers designed with airplane-like wings that gave them a splashing, in-and-out-of-the-water action similar to flying fish. Birds now are available in many different models and sizes. They are frequently used as lures, or as a small teaser built right into the trolling rig (usually at the point where leader joins line). Like artificial squids, small birds can also be rigged in a daisy chain, then pulled as a multiple teaser.

Ocean Trolling Plugs

Some very large plugs are manufactured for saltwater trolling, and they can be deadly effective.

This bluewater lure, tied to a mono leader, indicates that sharp-toothed wahoo are likely not the target.

Any plug can be trolled as well as cast—even topwater models, which splash the surface and are very effective for aggressive species. Almost all plugs trolled inshore are simply casting plugs (crankbaits or floater-divers) that work equally well on the troll.

Some very large plugs, however, are manufactured specifically for saltwater trolling— they can be deadly for anything from tarpon to tuna. Big plugs with extra-strength hooks produce a lot of strikes from wahoo and king mackerel. And plugs which run deep are effective over the reef and deep rocks for striped bass, big bluefish, grouper, snapper and many other kinds of game fish, and in northwestern waters for salmon.

Basic Lure Rig

For rigging a standard (single-hook) lure for use on 50- to 80-pound tackle, you'll need leader (300-pound test is popular for this size tackle), crimping tool, chafing gear, colored tape (optional), spacer beads, hook and sleeves suited to the leader's diameter.

Start with a piece of 300-pound mono leader. Cut to your chosen length, 15 to 25 feet is standard although IGFA rules allow 30 feet in line classes heavier than 20 (with 10 feet of double line).

Match hook to lure size. A good rule of thumb for selecting a hook to fit the lure is choosing one just large enough to slip over the lure's head. The hook's gap should be about as wide as the head of the lure, or a bit wider. If you're rigging a double-hook rig, go with a trailer of the same size down to two sizes smaller.

Thread a sleeve over one end then slide on a piece of spring-type chafing gear or a thimble. Double the line, making a loop and slide into sleeve. Snug loop by pulling on double line and leave about an inch opening. While loop is snug, crimp one end of the sleeve leaving a flare shape on end to prevent line chafe. Finish by crimping other end of the sleeve and trimming tag end.

Thread lure onto leader. Add anti-chafing spring to prevent leader wear.

Position hook barely inside the bottom of the skirt. Add spacer beads to take up the slack.

Slide sleeve onto leader, add chafing gear and hook.

Snug tag end into sleeve and crimp. Hook point should be covered by skirt. Tape leader-to-hook connection to make stiff rig or leave alone for free-swinging hook.

1 Slide the tag end of your leader through the head of the lure and out the back of the lure, leaving at least four inches to work with.

2 Slide your crimping sleeve over the leader, followed by the chafing gear.

3 Pass the leader and chafing gear through the eye of the hook and back through the sleeve.

4 Crimp twice without getting too close to the end of the sleeve, giving it a flare.

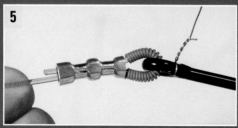

5 Haywire twist a length of copper rigging wire to the eye of the hook, to hold future ballyhoo.

6 Add crimp and chafing gear to the front of your rig to attach to main line.

Rigging the Trolling Lures

Offshore and marlin lures come both pre-rigged or unrigged.

Best leader materials for rigging trolling and marlin lures are heavy mono—80 to 600 pound—depending on lure and tackle size, and multi-strand cable. Mono is the hands-down favorite because many anglers believe that mono leaders draw more strikes. It is also easier to handle while wiring, gaffing, tagging or releasing gamefish. The lipped diver or "trembler type" lures are more likely to draw strikes from kingfish and wahoo and should be pulled on cable or single-strand wire.

Rigging lures can be done in many ways. Single, double, stiff-rigged and free-swinging hooks all see time in various trolling spreads. Marlin anglers, for instance, often prefer single-hook rigs while high-speed wahoo trollers like double 90-degree offset hooks. All hooks should be forged, big-game patterns with ring-eye hooks, sizes 9/0 to 14/0, for most applications.

For double-hook rigs, crimp the second hook onto first using a piece of multi-strand cable. Standard hook positions are either a 90- or 180-degree offset. To meet IGFA rules, the eyes of the two hooks must be at least a hook's length apart and the trailing hook cannot extend more than a hook's length beyond the lure skirt. Tape rigid with electrician's tape.

Blue marlin's aggressive feeding habits make it the perfect target for trolling lures.

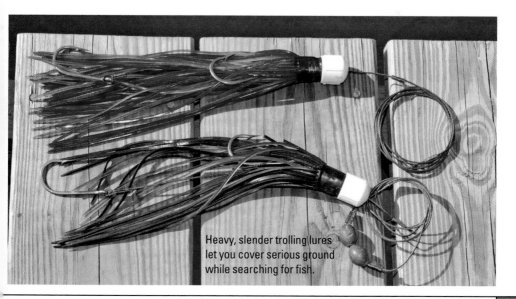

Heavy, slender trolling lures let you cover serious ground while searching for fish.

Trolling Spoons

Perhaps the most versatile of all trolling lures is the silver spoon. Many models, in many sizes, are made by a number of different manufacturers. For trolling in salt water, single-hook spoons are generally chosen.

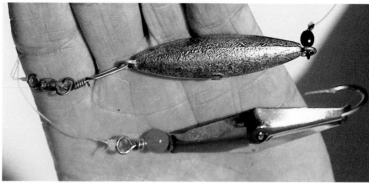

A trolling weight fished three feet ahead of a silver spoon will catch bluefish and Spanish mackerel all day long when those fish are present.

Size designation for saltwater trolling spoons is by number. Most-used sizes are between No. 1 (small) and No. 7 (large). Bigger spoons than No. 7 may be used for giant tarpon, or for offshore species. Unfortunately, those numbers denote relative size only in spoons of the same brand. One company's No. 2 may be another company's No. 5, so the angler must judge by sight.

Another way to gauge spoon size is by hook size. Most spoons do name the hook size on their packaging. Interestingly, spoons trolled for any of the offshore species all seem to troll better when pulled behind a trolling weight of appropriate size. Trolling a 3.5 size "Drone Spoon" on a 30-foot piece of 150-pound test behind a 16-ounce trolling weight is a time honored standard for catching kingfish, amberjack and wahoo.

A big trolling spoon may resemble a blue runner (shown) or other common prey species offshore.

1/0 - 3/0 **Inshore Trolling**, Mackerel, Bluefish

3/0 - 6/0 **Inshore Trolling**, Stripers, Snook, Reds

6/0 - 9/0 **Offshore & Tarpon**, Kingfish, Wahoo

Select a Spoon
of Appropriate Size

This table is a general guideline. Variations are common among different anglers.

Some spoons come with a built-on swivel. You should always use a swivel ahead of a spoon to help reduce line twist, so if your spoon has no swivel, be sure to use one between leader and line. If twist persists when using a barrel swivel—as well it might—switch to a ballbearing swivel, the most positive kind.

See the Wire-Wrapping section for a special rig that provides extra action when trolling a spoon. Remember, fishing spoons behind a trolling weight improves their catch ratio significantly.

CERO MACKEREL

Light trolling gear and casting and fly outfits will take this sharp-toothed mackerel, which has a range more closely limited to tropical waters and is often mistaken for a Spanish mackerel. Spoons are about the best trolling lures. Cero macks respond to chumlines and are taken on both live baits, including pilchards and shrimp, and also cutbaits on hooks and on jigs.

Plastic Squid and Other Molded Baits

Imitations of popular natural baits, molded of soft plastic, can be found on many tackleshop counters. For offshore fishing, they include ballyhoo, mullet, flying fish, squid, dolphin and even plain strips. Some are ready-rigged.

Among the most commercially successful of these molded baits are the squids, obtainable from several different manufacturers and in a variety of sizes and colors. Trolled plastic squids will take all the popular offshore gamefish. Though not widely used in this manner, artificial squid can also be drifted with effect, and even used for inshore casting. Quite a few sailfish, and even a number of swordfish, have been caught on drifted plastic squids. Squid are commonly the bait used in the making of daisy chains, described earlier in this chapter.

These Williamson trolling lures are lifelike imitations of the real thing.

Daisy chains of plastic squids with a natural bait wired to the end are standard on most bluewater boats.

High Speed Trolling

The rooster tail behind this boat means that they're probably pulling lures at high speeds.

Pulling offshore lures at 10 to 12 knots is apt to catch a variety of bluewater pelagics, but get a little 12- to 16-knot whitewater behind your boat, and you'll find almost all your strikes will come from wahoo.

To build a high speed outfit, you'll want at least a high quality 50-pound class leverdrag reel, preferably loaded on a bent butt rod, packed with 60- to 80-pound braided line. An extra heavy ballbearing snapswivel connects to a 3- to 5-pound cigar-shaped trolling weight. It is important to have 18 inches of heavy (No. 10 to 12) wire

A heavy trolling weight keeps the lure down in the water at a high speed.

on each end of your weight. Wahoo sometimes strike the lead, and without the wire their teeth would likely sever the line.

The most important part of the rig is the 30 feet of 200-pound mono between the trolling lead and the 300-pound cable holding your lure. It serves as a buffer, providing some stretch between the

wahoo's violent head shakes and the no-stretch braid. You'll need an extra-heavy ballbearing snapswivel on each end, and you'll want to double crimp it. Three feet or so of 300-pound cable leads to your choice of either a straight running metal-headed lure, or a giant swimming bait, such as a Cairns Swimmer or Trembler.

A couple tips you'll want to remember. First off, you can't set your drag until you're at trolling speed. Once you're comfortable with your speed, set the bait as far back as you want, and then slide the lever up, until the line is barely staying on the reel. Go over a wave, and the reel should give out a couple clicks. Hit some weed, and it should start paying out line. Get a strike, and you won't soon forget that sound.

Be very careful once you've got the lead to the boat. Assign someone the job of holding the lead overboard while you hand line the big fish (with gloves of course). That way if a green wahoo takes off, the man with the lead can simply drop it, and let him go. Never set the lead down where it can get snatched up, and hit someone, if a fish takes off.

"Wobblers" in bright colors are a great attractant to wahoo all over the world.

Dodgers, Flashers, Bells

A variety of shiny ornaments strung ahead of the trolled lure have proven effective for many different kinds of gamefish in far-flung areas. Although most often used with ball sinkers, downriggers and planers in deep trolling for trout and salmon on the Pacific, the Great Lakes and in other deep lakes, these flashy setups also have proved their mettle in salt water for bluefish and other species.

Flashers and dodgers differ slightly in action, but not much in effect. Flashers spin when trolled, while dodgers "swim" without fully rotating. Both provide not only flash and vibration, but also impart erratic action to the trolled lures.

Metal flashers and dodgers are built into the leader by means of swivels at each end of the device. The strings of spinners or wobblers called bells generally are purchased ready-made, although a few anglers do rig up their own.

Spoons and streamer flies, as well as many other lures, can be used as the trailing lures. Let preferences of the various fishing areas guide you on this. When depths are not too great, a sinker is used on the dropper line to keep the lures in the strike zone.

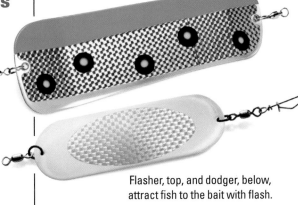

Flasher, top, and dodger, below, attract fish to the bait with flash.

COHO SALMON

Trolling for coho, also called silver salmon, is probably the most popular tactic. Drifting with live or cut baitfish is also popular. In the Great Lakes, cohos mainly eat alewives and smelt. Metallic lures and shiny streamer flies are also used.

Metal Jigs

Slender metal jigs can be cast when they weigh less, above, or dropped to the depths when they are heavy.

Metallic jigs are used by offshore fishermen in tandem with braided line, reels with superior drag and speed, and high-powered, high-action rods. The jigs are bar-shaped slabs of metal, often brightly colored, with extra-heavy-duty hooks that are free swinging on separate loops of heavy Dacron. Everything from sailfish, amberjack, tuna to grouper hit them, and they can be fished in extreme depths. A fast drop straight to a good piece of bottom structure, followed by a heavy jigging motion provides excellent deepwater results.

GREATER AMBERJACK Experienced anglers can battle these bruisers with spinning and baitcasting rigs, and even fly rods, but generally rods with backbone are required. They grow to more than 100 pounds, and it's not too uncommon for recreational anglers to catch them 50 pounds and more. Around reefs and wrecks, they take livebaits and bucktail jigs and also metallic jigs. These fish can be chummed to the surface where they will hit plugs, spoons and flies, too.

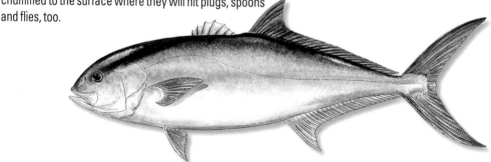

Artificial Casting Lures

Many models of artificial lures can be—and are—used in both fresh and salt water.

Bass fishing is where the most effective inshore saltwater casting lures earned their stripes.

The term "artificial lure" or simply "artificial," refers to any device made of synthetic material that is intended to fool a fish into thinking it is natural food.

All artificials require some sort of motion to make them work. Usually the motion is provided either by casting the lure and retrieving it, drifting or trolling. Some lures work well with no more motion than merely allowing them to sink or settle slowly in the water. Scented baits are sometimes allowed to just "deadstick" or lie still on the bottom. Others must be moved fast to draw strikes.

This section will cover artificial lures used mostly for casting, but often for trolling. Many models of artificial lures can be—and are—used in both fresh and salt water. With most of the others, the only difference between freshwater and saltwater versions is in size, and perhaps in hook strength.

Certain artificial lures designed strictly for saltwater trolling have been covered already.

Obviously, there are far too many different lures—thousands of them—to permit a comprehensive survey. Instead, this section will look at the major types of lures and discuss some of their applications. Any brand-name lures mentioned and/or illustrated are given only as examples of types. They are well-known models, but not necessarily recommended over similar ones from other makers.

Surface, Floating and Diving Plugs

Surface lures are the pets of many bass, pike and muskie fishermen, as well as a lot of saltwater anglers. They are designed to splash the top of the water and imitate a distressed fish. Some surface plugs make more noise than others, according to design. And some surface plugs float while at rest, but dive under and "swim" on a straight retrieve. These are called floating-diving plugs and can be used either as a surface lure or retrieved under water.

NORTHERN PIKE Topping a long list of productive lures are topwater plugs and spoons and spinners. For fly fishing, try very large streamers and poppers, usually in bright colors. Northerns respond well to speedily retrieved flies and also go after all kinds of small live fish.

THE SLIM-MINNOW TYPES These are slender, buoyant plugs with small plastic lips. Some, such as the original Rapalas, are made of balsa wood, and some—for instance the slender Rebels—are made of plastic.

The balsa wood models have a bit more action, and are preferred by many freshwater fishermen. Plastic ones are tougher and better suited for use in the sea. However, the plastic ones do work very well in fresh water, and many inland anglers prefer them if for no other reason than that they are easier to cast.

Several good retrieves are possible with this type plug. Try twitching them on the surface two or three times with pauses in between. Also try retrieving them VERY slowly, so that they "swim" but stay atop the water. You can also impart a fast, darting retrieve to them by sweeping your rod as you wind in. Or you can simply crank at medium-to-fast speed and treat them as crankbaits—swimming, underwater lures.

As surface lures, the slender minnows really shine when the water is very calm and a noisier surface plug might scare more fish than it attracts.

THE DARTING TYPES These are wooden or plastic plugs, designed so they will dig slightly into the water and dart when the rod is jerked. They are often referred to as "twitchbaits" because one common retrieve is to twitch them sharply, with only an instant's pause between twitches. These plugs are often "neutral buoyant" which means they will hang suspended in the water column and won't sink to the bottom.

In fresh water, these plugs normally are allowed to lie still for up to a minute (if one has the patience!), then twitched two or three times with pauses in between. On the retrieve, plugs of this type dive under the surface and swim seductively, becoming shallow crankbaits. Many strikes

The balsa wood models have a bit more action and are preferred by many freshwater fishermen.

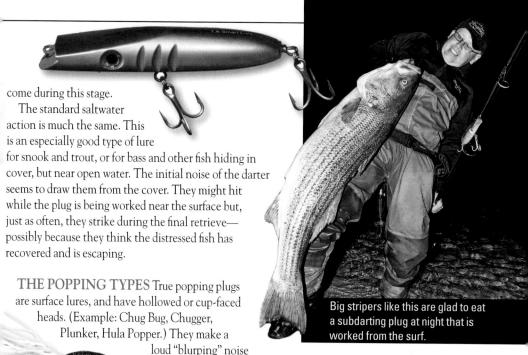

come during this stage.

The standard saltwater action is much the same. This is an especially good type of lure for snook and trout, or for bass and other fish hiding in cover, but near open water. The initial noise of the darter seems to draw them from the cover. They might hit while the plug is being worked near the surface but, just as often, they strike during the final retrieve—possibly because they think the distressed fish has recovered and is escaping.

Big stripers like this are glad to eat a subdarting plug at night that is worked from the surf.

THE POPPING TYPES True popping plugs are surface lures, and have hollowed or cup-faced heads. (Example: Chug Bug, Chugger, Plunker, Hula Popper.) They make a loud "blurping" noise when jerked hard with the rod, but the angler can control the amount of noise by how softly or sharply he twitches his rod to cause the pop.

In fresh water, a rather soft pop is usually preferred, with a long pause before the next one. Sometimes, however, a loud pop pays off better—especially if there is considerable chop on the water.

The pop-and-pause retrieve is good, too, for shallow-water fishing along the coast.

Large popping plugs are one of the very best, and most exciting, of lures for casting in deeper salt waters—such as over artificial reefs and around weedlines. Special large poppers with extra-strength hooks that are anchored to a center wire should get the call for this work. Various models are available in saltwater supply houses.

For such offshore casting, you have to use a stout rod, and then pop the lure as hard as you can and as fast as you can. The more fuss the better. A big popper in fairly deep water can take just about anything, including big bluefish, barracuda, jack, striped bass, amberjack, tuna, mackerel, kingfish, bonito, sailfish—and even big bottom fish such as grouper and snapper.

Some ocean lures (right, with rigged mackerel) as well as fly patterns (below, with sailfish) feature concave heads.

SURF POPPERS

These are slightly different popping lures, large and relatively heavy, used mostly for long-distance casting from the surf in quest of striped bass and bluefish. Most of them actually are sinkers, or are neutrally buoyant, but a steady retrieve with a long surf rod keeps them blurping across the surface with a seductive and noisy action.

Huge poppers can be cast to surface-feeding fish to catch their attention.

DANCING OR WALKING TYPES

These are torpedo-shaped plugs, weighted slightly at the tail so they sit on the surface at an angle. The Zara Spook, Rapala Skitterwalk, and MirrOlure Top Dog are widely known and venerable examples. Walking the dog is just one of many retrieves possible. However, bass anglers more often prefer a pop-and-pause retrieve with their Zaras and similar plugs, much the same as they use with other types of topwater baits. When the pop-and-pause technique is used with a dancing plug, it dives, then jumps high out of the water while remaining in almost the same spot.

Other good retrieves are possible, too. With steady cranking and a slower, rhythmic waving of the rodtip, these plugs swim on the surface in more leisurely fashion, much like an undisturbed mullet.

All these plugs are good at "walking the dog."

Walking the Dog

Anglers often use a retrieve called "walking the dog" in which the plug is made to zigzag across the surface by cranking combined with whipping of the rodtip. Actually, much of the whipping motion is produced naturally when you crank. This tactic simulates a fleeing baitfish and is deadly at times for freshwater bass and pike, and for most saltwater predators, including stripers, bluefish, snook, jack and seatrout.

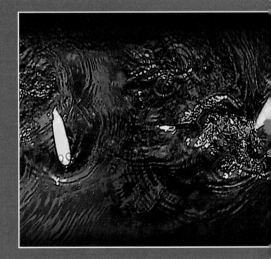

FLOATING-DIVING PLUGS

The slim minnow already has been mentioned as a floater-diver. But there is another type that has been popular in fresh water for many years. The two leading examples from the past are the Lucky 13 and Bass Oreno. They can be made to pop almost as loudly as a true popping plug, but dive below the surface and wiggle enticingly on a fast retrieve. Both those plugs have cupped and slanted heads that dig in and permit the diving and swimming.

Darters fit that description, even though they are primarily topwater lures. And many modern plugs feature a similar design. The models with longer lips—whether integral or attached—will run deeper on the retrieve and probably create less commotion when worked at the surface. And, of course, many plugs that float are seldom, if ever, used as topwater baits but instead are immediately cranked below the surface and retrieved as underwater swimmers. You guessed it: They comprise their own category, called crankbaits.

Jointed plugs imitate the swimming action of baitfish.

CRAWLING PLUGS Best-known examples of this type are the Crazy Crawler and the Jitterbug. Although they will draw strikes when fished in stop-and-go fashion, crawlers are most often worked with a straight, slow retrieve. They wobble or crawl across the surface with continuous noise and are often chosen for night fishing because bass, it seems, can zero in on them much better than on a lure which alternates noise and silence.

While the Jitterbug and similar types have long held a prominent spot in the tackle boxes of many freshwater fishermen, they have also gained some favor among saltwater anglers. In particular, they are doing sensational work for those who seek striking fish, such as redfish and snook, in very shallow water with a grassy bottom. Most ordinary surface plugs dive just deep enough to foul the grass, but the surface crawlers stay right on top. Moreover, their steady blurping gives fish the chance to track them down from considerable distances.

Shallow and Medium Crankbaits

Sub-surface plugs which require little action on the part of the angler other than winding the reel are called crankbaits. Most run at shallow or medium depth and they come in such a variety of shapes and configurations that they do not lend themselves to sub-classification so easily as did the surface lures. Therefore, such labels will not be used except in obvious instances.

Let's start with the plugs which sink by virtue of weight alone: that is, they have no lip or other planing device to help get them down.

Some of these plugs are slow-sinkers, the most famous of all perhaps—in salt water anyway—being the 52M series of MirrOlures. This is one of the most versatile saltwater plugs of all for shallow fishing, and takes anything from small seatrout to big tarpon. MirrOlures of other series numbers are similar in action, but vary in length and sink rate. Although these plugs are often fished in stop-and-go fashion as a jerkbait, they do qualify as crankbaits because even the plain-head models swim enticingly on a steady, moderately fast retrieve. Some models have metal diving lips.

In fresh water, one widely popular family of underwater plugs is the "shad-type." These have the general appearance of small shad minnows—flattened and thin, but relatively deep bodied. Some of the many examples include the Thin Fin, Rat-L-Trap and Spot. Some have molded-in lips that provide their swimming action. Others get their action from a slanted or vertically flattened head or a molded top fin. Anyway, all are shallow-running lures that take bass and a great variety of freshwater fish, and are excellent open-water lures. Most of them have counterpart models in their lines that are similar in size and action but run deeper.

Another prominent group, in much the same action category but vastly different appearance, are the "fat plugs" or "alphabet plugs"—so-called because they are, indeed, fat, and because the original models were named by single letters—such as "Big O" and "Big B." These are lipped plugs which generally float at rest, but which are not commonly employed as surface poppers, although they can produce fish as such. As a class they are shallow runners but, again, some models have larger lips for deeper diving.

This type plug is effective on a straight retrieve, although you should vary the speed to test for best results. There is nothing in particular to be gained by "jigging" your rod as you retrieve these lures; however, it often pays to impart a variable retrieve simply by cranking-and-stopping, cranking-and-stopping.

Let's move now to another group of shallow-to-medium plugs—those with rather short metal lips. Their action is about the same as the shad types and others with plastic lips. Some of them are old favorites in salt water as well as fresh, but usually in beefed-up models. Again, the best retrieve is a steady one with varying speeds.

Shallow-running plugs are excellent for trolling, as well as casting, whenever it isn't necessary to go down very deep. This holds for both salt and fresh water. By trying different motor speeds to determine what pace brings out the best action, the unlipped MirrOlures are also great trolling baits for salt water.

Countdown

Many slow-sinking plugs can be fished at great depth if you just take the time to let them sink before you retrieve. Try the "countdown" method: Count slowly as your plug sinks, and note the count on which it hits bottom. Next cast, shorten the count by one or two numbers, and you should be skimming close to the bottom.

DEEP-RUNNING CRANKBAITS

There are only three basic designs that can send a plug really deep—and keep it there. One features an extra-long lip of metal or plastic; another makes use of a sharply sloped head that itself acts as a planing "lip"; the third is a stamped metal plug with a weighted head that also acts as a planing surface. Many designs can gain added depth if they are weighted, but weight alone is not enough to keep a plug running really deep on a troll or a fast retrieve. You can prove this quickly with a heavy lead jig. Though one of the best lures of all for deep-casting with a slow re-trieve, even a jig weighing several ounces will rise far off the bottom when you crank it fast, or troll it.

Many lipped divers get deep enough to attract the attention of snapper, above, and grouper, as well as others.

Differently shaped lips will make each lure troll at different depths.

As already hinted, some shallow-running lures are offered in special deep models with much larger lips.

The great majority of deep-running plugs are used by anglers in deep lakes, particularly the Great Lakes and certain reservoirs, but deep-divers also work well in salt water, where they can be counted on to take striped bass, tarpon and snook in deep channels, grouper and snapper over reefs, and king mackerel, wahoo, tuna and other pelagic species offshore. It bears repeating that all ocean-going plugs should be beefed-up models with heavy hooks, preferably wired through the lure body, rather than simply screwed into it. Refer to previous comments under "Ocean Trolling Plugs."

Be aware that even the deepest-running plugs may not dig down as far as you wish to go without additional help from trolling sinkers, wire lines or, best of all, downriggers.

Even the deepest-running plugs may not dig down as far as you wish to go without additional help from trolling sinkers or other means.

RATTLING PLUGS

Plugs that rattle—usually by virtue of small weights inside a hollow chamber—have become accepted among both freshwater and saltwater anglers. "Rattlers" do not constitute a separate group of plugs; in fact, the majority of popular designs—shallow-running, deep-running and topwater—all can be found with rattlers these days. Most anglers think the addition of sound adds greatly to the appeal of a proven plug that is properly used. But sound alone is not likely to produce much, if any, action unless everything else is done right.

Let the water get a touch of color and many anglers will reach for a rattler to attract bites with sound effects.

Rattles, above, shake with the lure's action to produce noise that imitates fish feeding on bait to attract bites, right.

Soft Plastic Lures

Here's a subject which not only could fill a whole book of its own but should fill one. Baits molded of soft plastic come in countless shapes, every conceivable color, and any length from two inches up to a foot or longer.

The most familiar category of soft bait encompasses worms, eels, salamanders (usually called "lizards"), and crawdads, but just about

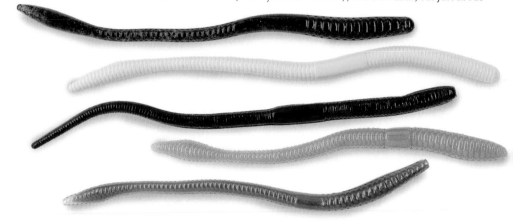

everything that creeps or swims has been by now modeled in soft plastic. Some excellent shrimp, squid and crab imitations join the mix for saltwater fishing.

Worms and eels, of course, are by far the most widely used. Although many worms can be purchased ready-rigged with one, two, or three hooks, most avid worm users prefer to rig their own.

Plastic worms long ago assumed a premier position in freshwater fishing and not long afterwards became almost as widely established on the saltwater scene. The use of soft-plastic worms and grubs in salt water has thus far been primarily in combination with leadhead jigs. (See the section on "Jigs" for more detail.) However, new uses are being discovered every day. For instance, the plain, unleaded worm has taken many tarpon, snook, grouper, snapper, striped bass and numerous other species. In certain situations it produces nearly as well as natural bait. What situations? The field is so wide open, all anglers should do their own experimenting.

Some of the enterprising uses of plastic worms are real eyebrow-raisers. Many fishermen use a grub or worm on a popping cork rig—

Modern plastics are molded and painted into incredibly lifelike imitations.

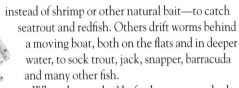

instead of shrimp or other natural bait—to catch seatrout and redfish. Others drift worms behind a moving boat, both on the flats and in deeper water, to sock trout, jack, snapper, barracuda and many other fish.

What about color? In fresh water, standard colors for a long time were black, blue and purple. However, many other hues become hot in their turn—green, various shades of red, spotted patterns, yellow, amber. Keep several colors on hand. Be guided by local advice, but don't be afraid to vary your colors if fishing is slow.

Plastic lures are designed to be retrieved much in the way the creatures they replicate move.

In salt water, the most popular hues seem to be yellow or chartreuse, white and pink—with orange a favorite for tarpon and snook. Also popular at sea is a clear worm, with a phosphorescent finish that glows in the dark. There isn't much light, you know, at depths of 100 feet or more, and the luminous worm does good work down there. Six inches has long been the most popular length of worm among bassers, although seven- to nine-inchers are about as widely used. Giant models of 10 and 12 inches have ups-and-downs in popularity.

Worms smaller than a half foot also get much play—and not just for panfish, but for bass. In clear water, or hard-fished areas, four-inch worms often get hits where larger models are ignored.

Scented Baits

It's hard to say where scented artificials started, but scented freshwater worms seem to have been around forever. Saltwater scented artificial shrimp, baitfish and crabs, squid, etc. are deadly anywhere you use artificials in salt water. They may lack the action of regular molded plastics, but there can no longer be a question as to whether or not fish are attracted to scent. Reds, flounder, sea bass, and grouper are foremost among the species you can often attract more often on scented artificials.

Rigging the Worm

Has any lure anywhere caught more fish than a plastic worm?

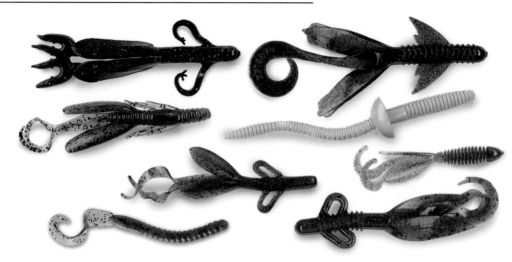

The following rigs work equally well with all elongated plastic baits—not just eels and worms but also lizards, crawfish and squid-like baits—so long as there is sufficient length and thickness in the forward portion of the lure to accommodate the chosen hook. Any plastic bait that is too short to rig with the hook hidden must, of course, be rigged with the hook exposed.

The original self-rigged worm consists of a single hook stuck into the worm at the head. This is still a good rig, particularly with six-inch worms and in open water. It can be used without a weight of any kind and allowed to settle slowly or allowed to drift with the current, adding a bit of rod action from time to time. If it must be sent deeper, you add a splitshot or a sliding worm lead in front of the hook. At least one shot is generally used in a lake or other still water, so that the worm can go to bottom and be retrieved slowly, with a stop-and-go technique.

If weeds are a problem, or if the bottom is snaggy, the same rig can be effected simply by substituting a weedless hook for the plain hook.

Worm rigs work equally well with all elongated plastic baits, not just eels and worms.

The Texas Rig

1 Insert hook point into top of bait and out again, just enough to hold the top part of hook in the bait.

2 Run the hook down the bait, just far enough to show the eye of the hook at the end of bait.

Weedless hooks, though, have largely lost out in angler appeal to specially designed worm hooks, which have an abrupt bend or angle in the shank, just behind the eye of the hook. They are rigged so that only the bent portion of the shank goes into the head of the worm. The rest of the hook stays outside, except for the point and barb, which are pushed upward into the worm and left buried.

The plastic worm, rigged weedless, has its hook point protected but not buried so deep to prevent it from catching a bass' mouth on the strike.

Weedless rigging can be accomplished in the same way even with hooks of traditional pattern, via the "Texas Rig." The Sproat pattern is most widely used. Aberdeen hooks work well with Texas rigs when light spinning gear is chosen, but are not sturdy enough to withstand the pressures of heavy baitcasting lines.

In the Texas rig, you insert the hook point into the head of the worm and bring it out only a quarter-inch or so below. Then the hook is spun completely around and pulled down so that the hook eye is buried in the head of the worm. Last, the hook point is inserted into the body of the worm. If there is no sharp bend on the shank to serve as an anchor, most anglers keep the worm from sliding down the hook by inserting a round wooden toothpick through the worm and the hook eye. The toothpick is then trimmed flush with the worm on either side of the eye. Toothpicks also can be used to lock the sinker in place, as we will see shortly.

Various specialty hooks are available for worm-rigging. In some, a U-bend takes the place of the standard hook eye. The short end of the "U" is pointed and barbed, and you simply insert it into the head of the worm, and then affix the hook to the

3

Spin the hook around and bury the point in the bait.

4

You now have a weedless rigged bait. Add weights to the line prior to tying your hook on, if desired.

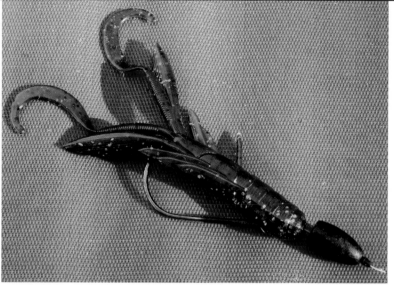

Creature bait gets a cone lead to slide through weeds better.

so—and thus leave a pronounced bend in the worm when the rig is finished. To help avoid line twist, a Carolina rig should incorporate a swivel, placed a foot or so above the worm, with a worm weight or egg sinker above the swivel.

Any worm rigged with the hook point buried should be used with quite a stiff rod. You have

body of the worm in regular fashion. A somewhat similar design does have a regular eye, but attached there, too, is a small barbed shaft which you insert into the head of the worm.

With the Texas rig, and most other worm rigs, care is taken to see that the worm lies as straight as possible on the hook to avoid twisting: however, the popular Carolina rig is deliberately designed so that the worm will twist on the retrieve. To rig a worm so it will twist, you simply position the hook point farther down the worm—an inch or

to take up all slack and give a mighty yank to make sure the point goes through the worm and into the fish. This is the reason why stiff-action freshwater rods, either baitcasting or spinning, are so often referred to as "worm rods."

The basic system for fishing a plastic worm, rigged or unrigged, is to let it sink to bottom and then wind it slowly back to you with short upward lifts of the rodtip, and pauses between lifts.

But, as with any other kind of fishing, the basic system is not enough by itself. Sometimes the worm

Worm Weights

A sliding sinker called a "worm lead" or "cone lead" is used in combination with the Texas rig and other weedless arrangements. The worm lead is threaded onto the line, where it slides freely; however, its pointed nose allows it to slither more easily than an egg sinker through weeds or among snags. It is common to "peg" the lead firmly to the line, flush with the head of the worm by shoving a tapered tooth-

pick into the channel of the sinker as far as possible, then breaking off the toothpick flush with the sinker's head—or by squeezing a small splitshot to the line in front of it. These weights, when made of tungsten, cost more, but serious anglers want their advantages—increased sensitivity to the bottom and to detect strikes; and a heavier sinker at about half the size of lead, so it will ease into holes and hard-to-reach places that lead may not get into (important sometimes when flippin' into tightly matted vegetation).

produces more strikes if wound steadily through the water at a slow speed. Other times, a medium or even fast retrieve is needed to attract fish. Not a few fishermen use worms just as they would a plug or other lure. They cast it to the shoreline or cover, retrieve it a few feet in stop-and-go fashion, then wind it in and cast again. These folks feel—and with considerable justification—that bass are will hit early in the retrieve or not at all.

The weedless-rigged worm is also a sensational lure for fishing in thick grass and lily pads. Toss it out in the jungle, wind slowly, and let it snake around reeds or over the top of lily pads. If it hits a small pocket of open water, let it sink a few seconds before starting it on its way again.

As a rule, some dropback, or slack line, should be given when a bass takes the worm. But not much. As soon as you sense pressure or any sort of steady pull—hit him!

There really is no standard procedure for timing your strike in worm fishing. When you gain some experience, your intuition probably will take over.

Drop Shot Worm

Many worm fishermen have been successful with what is called a drop shot rig. Drop shot, basically, describes a rig wherein the lure is affixed to the line or leader above the sinker. One popular and simple method of construction utilizes a Palomar knot tied to the eye of the hook, with the tag end left long and tied to the eye of a Dipsey or specialized drop-shot sinker. It is generally designed to fish a worm vertically straight below the boat while drifting across deeper structure.

With the drop shot worm rig, the worm will be suspended in the water above the weight.

Jerk Worms

This category is made up of lures that are molded of plastic that is soft, yet a bit harder than the usual formula for plastic worms. This, combined with additional thickness of the bait over the forward portion, allows the incorporation of an immensely valuable design feature—a long,

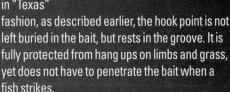

A jerkbait rigged weedless with the hook inserted in the bait's open groove, below. See how to rig the lure on page 69.

open groove in the top surface of the lure. Thus, when you rig in "Texas" fashion, as described earlier, the hook point is not left buried in the bait, but rests in the groove. It is fully protected from hang ups on limbs and grass, yet does not have to penetrate the bait when a fish strikes.

Jerkbaits by different manufacturers have different shapes. They can be worm-like, slug-like, shiner-like or simply cigar-shaped. But the hook-protecting groove categorizes them, as does the manner in which they are fished: They are generally retrieved slowly, with pauses and occasional jerks. Regardless of individual shape, all seem to simulate a creature in extreme distress, and they have proven to be among the most fish-catching of all lures for bass and coastal predators alike. Their phenomenal success is due in part to the fact that they are the most weedless of lures and can be thrown or retrieved virtually anywhere without hanging up.

Spoons

Spoons comprise one of the oldest and simplest types of artificial lure in existence, yet they remain perennially popular everywhere—in salt water and fresh water alike.

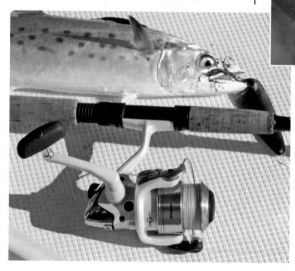

Though you'll find many variations in shape and great variation in color and finish, all spoons work in essentially the same way—their dished-out shape gives them a wobbling or darting motion, and their metallic finish provides flash.

Spoons painted on one side and shiny on the other are frequently used in fresh water, but seldom in coastal fishing. This is nothing but habit; painted spoons do attract saltwater fish.

Treble-hooked spoons are used mostly for casting—either in open fresh waters, particularly for schooling fish like black or white bass, or in open salt water for such fish as mackerel, bluefish and trout. However, any predatory fish will hit a spoon, and treble-hooked models are always a good choice whenever hang ups are not a particular problem.

The saltwater fisherman uses many more single-hook spoons than the inland angler, both for casting and trolling. However, a weedless spoon with

TIGER MUSKELLUNGE Stout baitcasting and spinning gear; some anglers try fly tackle. Lures for the tiger include splashy topwater plugs, spinners and spoons. Live suckers and other large baitfish top the list of natural baits.

a single hook is one of the ancient standbys in fresh water for fishing in thick grass, pads, or snaggy shallows, and this same design has also been adopted wholeheartedly by coastal casters for use on grassy flats or rocky edges, particularly for redfish.

Weedless spoons are the ticket for fishing in grassbeds.

In fresh water, the weedless spoon is almost always fitted with a trailer of some sort—a strip of pork rind, a pork-chunk frog, a plastic skirt or a plastic worm. Those embellishments are not nearly so universal in salt water, but are effective and often used.

About 90 percent of the time, a straight retrieve at slow-to-moderate speed gives any spoon its best payoff punch. Faster cranking pays off in salt water when the prey species are fast swimmers like mackerel. And in fresh water, it's a good idea to try holding your rodtip high, cranking fast, and making your spoon skitter along the top of the grass, when fishing in densely weeded water.

Believe it or not, bass and pike can shoulder their way through all kinds of submerged moss and weeds and nail a fast-moving spoon on top of the water. If they do miss, you at least see where they are and can cast to the same spot and try a slower return.

A straight retrieve at slow-to-moderate speed gives the spoon its best knockout punch.

Slab Spoons
Designed for "yo-yoing" or vertical retrieving in deep water, these are metallic lures that differ from other spoon designs in having flattened rather than dished-out surfaces. Larger lures of this type that are used in salt water are usually called metallic jigs (or butterfly jigs or speed jigs, rather than slab spoons). See the section on Jigs, which follows. One or more surfaces of the lure may be painted, or hammered for more reflection. A slab spoon flutters as it sinks and is usually worked by lifting the rod and allowing the spoon to settle back. The strike usually comes while the lure is falling.

A variety of slab spoons, both bright and reflective to catch the eye of fish.

Spinners & Spinnerbaits

The spinner is another ancient type of fishing lure and one that is found in many sizes, shapes and forms.

Spinners—again by tradition and not for practical reasons—are used more in fresh water, where one form or another of spinner has proven deadly for taking all types of freshwater fish, from small sunfish and mountain trout to huge largemouth bass, pike and muskies. Many fish in salt water will take spinners, but the lure never has caught on well in the sea.

When you hear the term "spinnerbait," it refers to just one branch of the spinner family—one that challenges plastic worms in the esteem of bass fishermen. In this type lure, a single or double spinner revolves above the dressed hook, in a V-wire configuration that is reminiscent of an open safety pin. Although not technically "weedless"—at least not in truly dense vegetation—the spinnerbait's very design makes it virtually snag-free in scattered grass, and the lure seldom hangs up on hard snags either. In fact, many experts

The term "spinnerbait" refers to just one branch of the spinner family.

like to knock their spinnerbaits against tree trunks and other woody structure whenever they can during the retrieve, feeling the noise generates impulsive strikes from lurking bass.

The basic retrieve for a spinnerbait is slow and steady, but stop-and-go tactics produce too, and a spinnerbait can sometimes be deadly when used much like a jig—with an up-and-down retrieve near bottom in deep water.

Very small spinnerbaits, weighing ⅛ ounce or less, are killers for crappie and other panfish. Many of these are simply miniature versions of the popular bass baits. Others feature marabou or other crappie jigs on the bottom leg of the "V." Still others—the Beetle Spins, for example—get their appeal from hooks dressed with molded plastic imitations of caterpillars and other insect baits.

Spinner blades come in a variety of shapes and skirts come in a variety of designs.

CHAIN PICKEREL Pickerel will hit the entire gamut of bass lures, but have special fondness for spinners and spoons. Likewise, they can be fished for with any sort of bass tackle. They strike hard, thrash and jump and take blistering runs.

Buzzbaits

These are simply spinnerbaits with large, modi-fied spinners that keep the lure splattering the surface, even on fairly slow retrieves. This concept in fishing has proven very effective in varied water conditions, from deep impoundments to brushy lakes and ponds. The buzzbaits are almost weed-less, due to the oversize spinner that "walks" over and around weed clumps.

In-Line Spinners

Spinners built on a straight piece of wire, rather than in the safety-pin configuration, are often called in-line spinners to distinguish them from spinnerbaits.

In-line spinners are very popular in smaller sizes. A few of the most popular lines are the Mepps, Rooster Tail and Panther Martin. The majority range from $1/16$ ounce to a half-ounce,

In-line spinners, often used in fresh water for panfish and bass.

but they are also offered in even lighter models, down to about $1/64$.

The best all-around sizes are $1/8$ and $1/4$ ounce, simply because little spinners of that size have no challengers in fresh water for constant action and sheer variety. Panfish love them, and they take a goodly share of bragging-size bass and other fish as well. There are a lot of better lures for large bass, but the lunkers do hit tiny spinners with surprising gusto at times. In addition to bass and sunfish, spinners regularly take pickerel, crappie (speckled perch), warmouth, yellow perch, white bass, freshwater trout, and of course, rough fish such as gars and mudfish. In short, anything that feeds on either minnows or insect life is apt to slug a little spinner. Even quite a few catfish are taken on them.

Similar but larger in-line spinners have histori-cally been standard lures for bass, pike, muskie

Spinnerbaits take plenty of saltwater fish, including flounder.

and other aggressive freshwater species, but the spinnerbaits have now largely stolen their thunder.

Hawaiian Wigglers, for example, were catching big bass for many years before the safety-pin spinnerbaits even came upon the scene—and they are by no means the most venerable of the classic in-line spinners. The Snagless Sally spinner is familiar to several generations of fishermen.

The Yellow Snagless Sally, below, is a classic spinner. Right, a Hildebrandt Hammer Time walleye spinner.

Walleye Spinners

Like most predatory gamefish, walleyes hit a variety of baits, lures and bait-lure combinations, but are so responsive to a specialized type of in-line spinner that it has come to be widely referred to as a "walleye lure." Its identifying features are that the spinner turns behind a leaded head (in most small spinner-lures, the blade rides in front of the head), and that it almost always wears a single hook instead of the trebles common on general-purpose spinners.

The walleye spinner will catch plenty of fish all by itself, but its single hook usually is dressed up with a live minnow, earthworm or leech. Dead specimens of the same baits are used too, as are plastic imitations.

In addition to manufactured spinner lures, the fisherman has a huge choice of plain spinners at his command (along with other necessary components) with which to create his own lures. Plain spinners are offered in several styles and many sizes, from small enough to use ahead of trout flies to large enough for custom-made bass and muskie lures.

Jigs

In most circles, the word "jig" refers to a single hook, molded into a leadhead and dressed with bucktail or other hairs, nylon filaments, feathers, Mylar strips, rubber skirts or any combination of those and similar materials.

Most fish seem to prefer jigs when they are retrieved quite slowly, near or on the bottom. Crank the reel a few times, then twitch the rod very gently to make the jig hop. Continue this pattern to boatside. But, as with all fishing rules, there are numerous exceptions. Fast retrieves

sometimes produce better, particularly when going after mackerel or offshore species. And even the kinds of fish which normally prefer a slow, hopping retrieve can often be enticed out of a stubborn streak by changing suddenly from a slow retrieve to a fast one.

And when fishing in open water, you obviously would not hop your jig near bottom when fish such as white or black bass are schooled and hitting at or near the surface.

How do you select the right jig? It really isn't too difficult a job, despite the hundreds of different jig designs and color variations.

The only consideration that might, of itself, spell success or failure is weight. Select weight according to your tackle and the depth you are trying to reach.

For freshwater fishing, and most inshore saltwater work—such as seatrout over flats, or for fishing along shorelines and around bars—the usual weight range is from ⅛ to ½ ounce. Freshwater bassers tend to stick almost entirely to jigs that wear multi-filament rubber skirts, often fitted with a pork chunk to make the lure called "jig-and-pig." Worms or other plastic trailers can be substituted for the pork.

Jigs of lighter weight will frequently prove useful for fish such as crappie, perch and bluegills, or in salt water for snapper blues, small jack and other panfish. Of course, very light weights cannot be used unless your tackle is light enough to toss them.

You'll need some jigs weighing ⅝ or one ounce, for deep-lake fishing, deep-hole coastal fishing, and for offshore and reef fishing in water up to say, 50 feet or so in depth. In water without current, a ⅝- or one-ounce jig can even be used at much greater depth.

Jigs weighing two ounces or more are used for deep-jigging, either for striped bass in impoundments or offshore in water of around 80 to 150 feet. Heavy jigs can be fished with baitcasting or medium spinning tackle but require extra-stout rods to make them move at such depths. Even larger jigs, weighing from eight ounces to more than a pound, are sometimes dropped on reefs and banks that lie 200 feet or more beneath the surface, but they obviously require heavy boat tackle.

Now for the matter of dressing. Animal hairs and plastic worms seem to give the most lifelike actions but feathers are not far behind. In fact, marabou feathers are the waggliest of all.

On the other hand, nylon is far more durable. A lot of fishermen use bucktail, feather or worm-jigs routinely, but keep nylon jigs handy for mackerel or other species which tear up jigs easily.

Note, however, that an awful lot of anglers use nylon jigs regularly for both light freshwater and saltwater fish, and get consistently good catches. You can see, therefore, that choosing the proper dressing material is not exactly a critical thing.

Only one item of choice remains—head style. Here, except for a couple of specialized purposes, the choice matters little. One such specialized head is the style known in saltwater circles as a "skimmer," and in freshwater areas as a "glider." These have heads which are flattened horizontally, and sometimes slightly dished out. When retrieved, they plane upward in the water, hence the name "skimmer." They are preferred by bonefishermen, and other saltwater folks who fish very shallow flats. Lake fishermen use much the same type of head for a different purpose. They allow it to sink slowly in deeper water. As it sinks it wobbles or "glides" with very enticing action—hence the other name, "glider."

For all-around use in shallow and medium depths, you'll find votes for bullet-shaped heads, round heads, lima-bean-shaped heads, and others. Every style has its staunch followers and there is no way to determine which is "best."

Bullet-shaped head

Round head

Skimmer head

How deep a jig sinks, and how fast, is determined by its weight and shape. Below, rigged with shrimp.

Baittails

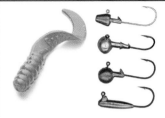

Consider the size of the tail and the shape of the head when selecting a jig.

Another jig "material" has been added to the list of dressings in more recent decades— soft plastic baits, such as worms, curly-tail worms, grubs, shrimp, crawfish and other creepy-crawlies.

Whether these are threaded onto the hook of a bare leadhead, or used as an added attraction for a bucktail or rubber-skirted jig, they do some pretty devastating work on a variety of fish, from inland waters to the deep sea.

Jigs wearing the molded plastic devices are often referred to as "baittails." They can be purchased in numerous ready-made forms, or fashioned in tailor-made style by the angler himself. The fisherman who makes his own can instantly create anything from a crappie or bonefish jig to an extra-heavy deep jig—just by threading a worm, or the tail piece of a worm, onto a leadhead of appropriate size.

These bucktail jigs can be fished naked, with a soft-plastic tail or with a natural bait. Below, a well stocked box of jigs and tails.

Of the many plastic tails used with jigheads, one of the best and most popular features a curled, flattened tail which has the most natural swimming motion imaginable. These are usually referred to as "grubs," or "twisters"—after the original Mr. Twister tail.

Regardless of whether your jigs are dressed with conventional materials, plastic grubs, or a combination of both, they are all fished in essentially the same style.

The term swimbait commonly refers to a ready-made baittail jig whose weighted core is completely covered by a soft-plastic outer body.

Alternately, some freshwater fishermen (trophy largemouth bass anglers, in particular) use swimbait to describe an articulated, fish-shaped lure of either soft or hard-plastic body composition.

Spoon-Like Lures

Designed to cast far and sink fast so that they can be retrieved fast (although they are also trolled, or cast in the surf), these lures wear the name "jigs" in certain coastal areas. Some types are called squids or diamond jigs. Hopkins and Bead Chain are among popular brands. Most metallic saltwater jigs are heavy, weighing from one ounce to several ounces,

Pork Rind Baits

Pork eels, for example, were predecessors of plastic eels as "revolutionary" bass baits.

Strips and chunks of pork rind have been used by fishermen far longer than have their plastic counterpart. Pork comes in almost as many variations, though their popularity and availability has, in recent years, been pushed back by plastic baits.

While pork baits are perhaps most widely employed as trailers tacked onto other lures, such as spoons, spinners and jigs, many are also excellent producers of fish when allowed to perform solo. Pork eels, for example, were predecessors of plastic eels as "revolutionary" bass baits. Stuck to a weedless hook and snaked slowly along bottom, or through pads, weeds and grass, the "eel bait" would frequently clobber bass when they could not be caught on the standard hard lures. They remain just as productive, of course, even though the plastic eels and worms that came along at the height of the "eel bait's" popularity stole away most of their thunder.

The advantage of plastic eels is that they do not have to be stored in brine when not being fished. On the other hand, plastic baits are many times less durable.

Pork frogs also can be killers when fished in and around pads on weedless hooks.

In salt water, large pork rind strips take many species of fish, from stripers and blues up to billfish—

Pork strips come in a variety of sizes, colors and patterns.

whether rigged to a pinned hook in the fashion of a saltwater fish strip, or used as a trailer with jigs and trolling feathers. There again, however, the ease of using plastic has eroded pork's popularity.

Pork strips come in all sizes, from an inch to 10 inches, and every one has great appeal to fish of appropriate size. Pork also comes in various shapes, of which the pork frog is probably the most familiar.

These spoon-like lures can be trolled or cast and retrieved.

and are best used with stout rods. Smaller versions of this type lure are used for inshore casting, and also used in fresh water, where they usually are referred to as "slab spoons."

In the sea, metallic jigs—or butterfly jigs as discussed previously in this chapter—draw plenty of strikes while sinking. After reaching bottom, they

are effective when simply raised a few feet with the rod and allowed to fall back. And, as icing on the cake, they swim with a wobbling motion and so get hits when retrieved steadily and with speed. These are also known as speed jigs.

A good imitation shrimp pattern will catch a variety of species, including pompano.

Flies & Flyrod Lures

It's hard to imagine, but there are many more variations in flies and flyrod lures than even in plugs or jigs or other kinds of artificials.

That's because for every one of the hundreds of different patterns and models offered by large suppliers, there are hundreds more variations made by small commercial tiers, or by individuals.

Many ponderous books have been written about fly patterns. We can only concern ourselves here with a look at the various categories of flies and flyrod lures, for familiarization.

Local advice is always of strong importance when selecting flies—particularly for freshwater trout fishing, but also for bass and panfishing, and saltwater fishing.

Dry Flies

Dry flies are tied to imitate insects in specific stages of development.

Dries are used in fresh water only, and can be identified by the very heavy hackle that allows them to float on the surface. Even so, they must be dressed to assure high floating qualities over extended periods. The dry fly user also false casts several times between actual casts to dry the fly. Dries are cast upcurrent, with the aim of letting them float over

Dry flies, tied to imitate land insects such as grasshoppers and others, are referred to as "terrestrials."

Wet flies ride in the current under the surface to attract fish.

a targeted spot or area. And they must be allowed to float for as long a distance as possible without line drag.

In trout fishing, it is often important to imitate—or at least strongly suggest—common insects of the particular locality when selecting dry fly patterns, especially if a "hatch" of insects is taking place. Dry flies tied to imitate land insects, such as grasshoppers, beetles or ants, are referred to categorically as "terrestrials."

Bluegills and other panfish take dry flies readily and often (but, unfortunately, not always) are not very selective as to pattern.

Wet Flies

Wet flies are flies that do not float, but which are allowed to drift under the surface, usually near the top. Like dry flies, they are tied to imitate or suggest certain natural flies. Wets generally are cast across the current, or slightly upstream, and allowed a long natural downstream drift. The fisherman may strip line or twitch the rodtip to provide extra action at the end of the drift.

Again, bluegills and other panfish take wet flies without nearly as much selectivity as is often displayed by wild trout.

Streamer

These are also fished "wet" but are made to imitate minnows instead of insects. Though they can often be drifted with good effect, they are usually stripped in with short jerks, either across the current or upcurrent. In calm water, such as lakes or bays, streamers are always stripped in to imitate the erratic darting action of a small fish. Most bass flies and saltwater flies are streamers of large size.

One of the most widely familiar streamers is the Muddler minnow, which represents a common baitfish called a sculpin and is tied in different sizes and many slight variations in color. Developed for stream trout, the muddler has also proven deadly on many types of freshwater predatory fish,

The Muddler minnow represents a baitfish, the sculpin.

including large panfish and bass.

Bass, incidentally, are great streamer-fly fish. Bass streamers are mostly tied on hooks of No. 4 to No. 2/0 in size. Trout streamers generally are No. 10, 8, 6, sometimes even much smaller.

In the South, fly fishermen who go after bass rely heavily on popping bugs. Many who use popping bugs exclusively would be pleasantly surprised to see how streamers pay off many times when poppers aren't inducing any strikes at all.

Developed for stream trout, the muddler has proven deadly on freshwater fish, too.

LAKE TROUT When lake trout roam the shallows, they can be fished with all sorts of tackle, even fly gear. Generally, however, they are sought by trolling very deep with heavy baitcasting or spinning tackle, using downriggers or wire line. Spoons, large spinners and big streamer flies all produce, along with a variety of casting plugs. Deep trollers rely heavily on spoons, diving plugs and live small fish.

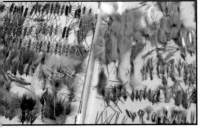

Nymphs

Nymphs are similar in usage to wet flies; however, they are tied to imitate the immature, or nymphal, stage of an insect rather than the adult, winged stage, and usually are fished deeper—often by tumbling them right along the bottom. Obviously, some weight may be needed to accomplish this presentation. The nymph itself may be a weighted tie, or a bit of lead can be added to the leader. Most nymphs are tied without wings though there are tiny wings on some. Generally, they are tied for body conformation, perhaps with material to suggest legs.

Although a major tool of trout fishermen, nymphs also take panfish well in rivers and creeks. For trout, local advice can be vital in nymph selection, but panfish, again, may not be choosy at all.

Nymphs in a box, top, and a nymph that, like many, is weighted to sink down and bounce along the bottom in the current.

> Although a major tool of trout anglers, nymphs also take panfish in rivers and creeks.

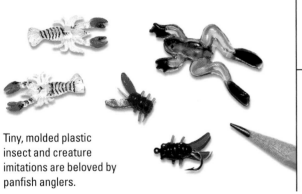

Tiny, molded plastic insect and creature imitations are beloved by panfish anglers.

Molded Flyrod Lures

These cover a wide range of actual molded plastic imitations of nymphs, grubs, caterpillars, hellgrammites, spiders, crickets, grasshoppers etc. A well-known example is the molded mayfly nymph, popular for bream and bass in Southern waters. Trout anglers generally shun the molded imitations, but they are dear to the hearts of panfishermen everywhere.

A spinner light enough to cast with a fly rod.

Flyrod "Hard" Lures

These include tiny plugs, spoons and spinners, made much like their larger spinning-lure counterparts. They are not overly popular among fly fishermen—except for some tiny spinners, which often are used in combination with wet flies, or with natural bait, such as worms.

Saltwater Flies

As mentioned, these are usually large streamers—tied with animal hair, long feathers or, ever increasingly, synthetic filaments of numerous variations. A very good addition to most saltwater streamers is a few strips of shiny Mylar. In addition to streamers, saltwater flies designed for bonefish and permit are tied to imitate shrimp or small crabs. Flies with epoxy heads have become popular on the flats because they dive to bottom quickly and can be worked much in the fashion of a jig.

Streamers for light saltwater use—small striped bass, mackerel, snook, seatrout, small tarpon, jack, ladyfish and other coastal varieties, should be up to about three inches in overall length, with a hook size of 1/0 to 3/0. Plain yellow, or plain white, in either hair or feather, are good producers. Mylar strips definitely help. There isn't a great deal of variation in pattern, but a wide choice in color combination. A streak of red, blue, or black helps in a white streamer. Red-and-yellow combinations are popular.

For all practical purposes, tarpon flies, offshore flies and other flies for big saltwater fish are mostly enlarged versions of the coastal flies. They may have an overall length of up to six inches, and a hook up to 5/0 or 6/0, occasionally larger.

Saltwater flies take every fish in the sea, from speckled trout to bluefin tuna.

The most popular tarpon fly is a breathing feather streamer in yellow, orange, yellow-orange combination, or grizzly.

Among the most common offshore patterns for billfish and big dolphin is a large, white fly tied with a dozen or more long hackles, interspersed with strips of Mylar.

As with freshwater fly fishing, it always pays to check for local preferences. Knowledgeable saltwater fly fishermen, guides and shop personnel are no longer hard to find, not even in many areas far removed from the saltwater grounds.

Popping Bugs

Poppers are the fly rodder's equivalent of surface plugs. They float atop the water and are made to pop by twitching the rod upward. Only occasionally are they used by trout fishermen, but are standards for panfish and for bass. They are often used in salt water too—in special ties, of course, with saltwater hooks.

Panfish poppers range from tiny things, as small as No. 10, to perhaps as large as No. 4. Bass poppers are usually found in the No. 4 to No. 2/0 size range, with Nos. 2, 1 and 1/0 being perhaps the most widely used. (Sizes refer to hook sizes.)

Popping bugs are made of cork, balsa, or hollow plastic, dressed with feather or hair "tails." A lot of them have rubber legs as well. They should be fished slowly—popped, then allowed to rest. Faster retrieves may pay off at times, especially in salt water. Really fast retrieves are best accomplished with bugs that have bullet-shaped rather than popping heads. These are called "sliders" because they skim across the top without digging in and, of course, make less noise. They should be tried if the loud poppers don't work, or when speedy retrieves seem to be required for fish such as mackerel and jacks.

There are also hair bugs, made entirely of tightly twisted or tied bucktail. These too ride the surface with little commotion and are deadly when fish seem spooky. Another very popular type of floating "bug" is the sponge rubber spider with rubber legs—one of the best-liked of all panfish lures.

Popping bugs may be tied with rubber legs or natural hair.

Big bluegill on a popping bug is good fun.

CHAPTER 10

Angling Accessories

Angling accessories see constant innovation. A wooden fish box with a block of ice in it has become a specialty-material fish bag that chills your catch to near freezing and keeps it there for days. A fish that "was at least 8 pounds" can now be shown to weigh 4.3 pounds while still on the water. There are now tackle storage systems that hold enough gear to turn your bream fishing trip into ice fishing for walleyes if a sudden blizzard freezes the lake while you're there. Advances in sun protection have benefitted our clothing. Polarized lenses not only help us see better, they actually cut down on the eye strain of looking into the sun all day. Accessories aren't usually the things that make us catch more fish. They are the things that make our fishing safer and a lot more fun.

Accessories are the things that make our fishing safer and a lot more fun.

Aluminum pliers, right, essential for removing stingy hooks. Top: Large net for magnum-size catches.

Ice Chests or Coolers

L ike tackle boxes, coolers come in a great variety of sizes, from six-pack to gigantic. Most are made of either fiberglass, hard plastic, or foam, but insulated soft-sided coolers are gaining popularity. Some of the soft-sided ones are even built to chill a large fish in a zipped up "coffin" with a modest amount of ice. Premium, roto-molded polyethylene coolers, both hard sided and soft, are capable of keeping just about any amount of ice for up to 5 days.

When selecting an ice chest, one good approach is to compromise on size and get the largest

High-quality coolers are built strong enough to double as seating and casting stands on boats.

capacity that you can lug by yourself from home or car to boat or fishing site. Certainly the most popular size range among fishermen is 40 to 50 quarts. Larger coolers are basically two-man loads, even when empty.

Medium or large coolers may well serve as repository for both catch and drinks, and some models have divided compartments to keep food or drink separated from fish or bait. These are the ticket for small, open boats but, if at all convenient, it's always better to use separate ice chests.

The insulation on high-quality coolers runs thick, left, and that makes the difference in keeping your catch chilled.

There is no better way to handle a fish you plan to eat than to deposit it directly on crushed ice. Livewells or stringers are fine, but only for as long as they truly keep the catch alive. Overall, you can't beat quick chilling for preserving freshness and taste.

You should keep the fish whole on ice until you clean them. After cleaning, they should

Use ample ice and don't try to fillet fish until they are very chilled, which makes the job much easier.

be placed in plastic bags or other water-tight containers before going back into the cooler. Dressed fish should not be allowed to come into contact with water.

Although most modern ice chests are very good, they do vary in cold-keeping ability as well as in ruggedness. While often costing several times the cost of regular plastic coolers, the effectiveness of high-quality, high-tech coolers is undeniable. Many boats are now factory equipped with high-tech coolers that double as comfortable seating.

Reusable containers of frozen artificial ice can be used in place of ice for convenience and economy to keep cooler contents chilled.

Whether high-tech or traditional plastic, rigid plastic chests are always preferred over inexpensive—often dirt cheap, in fact—foam coolers. The latter type, widely available in many sizes, are too fragile for general angling use but are very

efficient and can be valuable in a pinch, for such uses as transporting dressed or frozen fish for long distances in a car.

Keep in mind: use ample ice to keep fish cold, and don't try to fillet fish until they are very chilled, which firms up their flesh for cutting and makes the job much easier.

Insulated Bags

Fishermen needing special treatment for their catch, or those with fish box size restrictions on their boat, can turn to insulated fish bags to store their fish. First designed to keep large fish, like tuna and swordfish, chilled, the popularity of fish bags increased with their use on the kingfish tournament trail throughout the South and the Gulf. They open via a zipper along their long side and can be filled with ice to completely submerge the fish in a close-to-freezing hold.

Landing Nets

When a fish like a cobia, seen here, is of questionable legal size to keep, using a net to bring it aboard might save it for release.

Most present-day landing nets have aluminum handles and framing, with mesh of nylon, plastic or, in some cases, rubber. Many fisheries biologists endorse rubber nets, as they take less slime off a fish's body. All types of nets call for a good washing in fresh water after use.

Landing nets originally designed for salmon or muskies are finding their way into other fisheries. They often have extendable handles and collapsing hoops. They are not only easy to stow, but are invaluable when you need to verify the length of such species as cobia or grouper to see if they make legal limits.

Hoop diameter and handle length vary widely, and it's a good idea to use as large a net as you can comfortably handle and easily stow. A net with a three- to four-foot handle, and a hoop diameter of 18 to 24 inches will serve most inshore purposes.

With the ordinary landing net, you should scoop up your fish with a quick motion, but not a wild splashing one. If possible, put the net in the water, lead the fish close to it, and net him with a fast sweep, head first. If you touch a fish's tail with the net first, he'll often scoot right out of it.

Netting a cobia also leads to better table fare than ripping their flesh with a gaff.

Types of Nets

Nets are available in many sizes and configurations. Some catch-and-release anglers prefer certain mesh types, such as soft rubber or very fine mesh, to avoid scraping off fish slime.

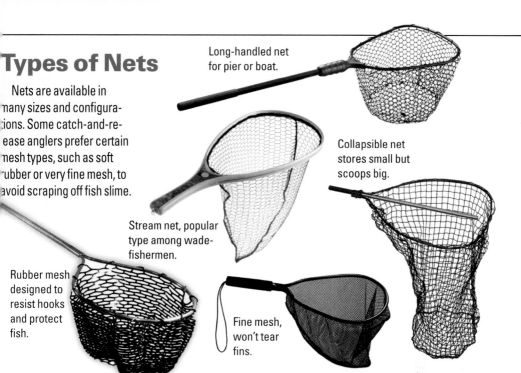

Long-handled net for pier or boat.

Stream net, popular type among wade-fishermen.

Collapsible net stores small but scoops big.

Rubber mesh designed to resist hooks and protect fish.

Fine mesh, won't tear fins.

Bridge Net

Special long-handled nets can be found if you fish, say, from docks or seawalls. But for fishing from structures higher than a few feet (many ocean piers and many bridges), the only practical landing net to use is a large hoop net lowered by a rope. These specialized nets are provided at many piers and some fishermen carry them to bridges, but they are not very portable.

Bridge nets save over-sized fish for release in good shape.

A snook caught on a bridge at night and brought up with a bridge net.

Fish Stringers

The safety pin-style stringer allows for fish to be strung and released alive if so desired.

The tags ID fish in the livewell and allow the fisherman to quickly determine whether new catches should be kept or released.

The two common types of fish stringers are the ordinary cord stringer, and the chain stringer with individual fish clips.

Made of cotton, nylon or twisted plastic, the cord stringer is fitted with a metal point at one end, a metal ring at the other. This type is used principally for panfish, but can be used for larger fish as well. You run the point under the fish's gill cover and out its mouth. Then you run the point through the metal ring. With all the fish after the first, you simply run the point in the gill and out the mouth, sliding the fish to the bottom of the string.

The chain stringer features a set of safety-pin-type clips of spring metal wire or nylon. Favored by bass fishermen who do not have access to a livewell, this type stringer is used by opening the "safety pin" and running the point through both lips of the fish. The pin is then snapped shut.

Tournament bass fishermen looking to maximize the aggregate weight of a bag limit often utilize culling tags. Basically, these are individual "stringers" consisting of a pin and a colorful float. The tags ID fish in the livewell, and allow the fisherman to quickly determine—through a balance scale—whether new catches should be retained or released. The vast majority of bass tournaments, of course, require live release of all catches, after weigh-in.

Cord stringers can be obtained in various lengths. The usual is six feet, for use when fishing from a skiff or from shore. Longer ones—sometimes much longer—may be needed by bridge or dock fishermen.

Most freshwater fish and some saltwater species will stay alive for hours if kept on a stringer in the water—that is, if they are not injured before stringing.

Stringers are widely used by wade fishermen to keep their catch in tow as they move.

Gaffs

This angler uses a hand gaff to pull in a dolphin via kayak.

Although a net serves most landing needs for the freshwater and inshore saltwater fisherman, anyone who fishes the reefs or offshore waters should definitely have a gaff aboard. Even inshore you're likely to need a gaff from time to time in order to handle a catch too large to get in your net. Should such a happy occasion arise, you'll be very glad indeed you have a gaff.

The best all-around gaff for light use is one with a stainless steel, two-inch hook—that is, the distance from point, straight across to shaft, is two inches. A three- or four-foot handle is long enough for most small boats. For boats with high transoms, a six- or eight-foot handle may be needed.

The two-inch hook is preferred for small-game fishing because it can be difficult to stick rather slender fish with a larger hook. At the same time, however, the two-incher will satisfactorily handle surprisingly hefty catches.

If you do a lot of offshore fishing, however, it would be wise to complement the two-inch gaff with another, larger one—say a four-incher.

Specialty gaffs are made for a variety of purposes, and can be highly useful, or downright essential, depending on your own fishing activities.

Boat gaffs come in different lengths and hook sizes to match the job at hand. At right, gaffing a dolphin.

Gaffing Fish

For surface fish it's better to extend the gaff over the fish (out of the water and behind the leader he's hooked to) and pull the point home. Or, for fish below the surface, lower the hook into the water under the fish, then tug smoothly upward. The fish should be hoisted up and into the boat with as little interruption of motion as you can manage, for many fish are adept at tearing loose from a gaff. All this, of course, presumes that you are attempting to land fish for food. It is also highly recommended you bring any fish about to be gaffed alongside the boat, with the boat moving forward. Keeping the boat in gear keeps constant pressure on the fish, and prevents slack line. Bringing him alongside keeps him in clear water, without boat turbulence. That gives you a much clearer view of your target.

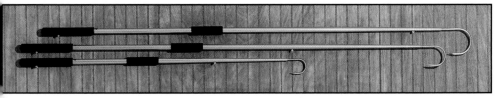

A bridge gaff is nothing more than a line and weighted gang hook spooled up.

Bridge Gaff

The bridge gaff is nothing more than a large gang-hook (usually a 10/0 size, or larger) that has a hefty chunk of lead molded around the hook shanks.

Since many bridges—and piers—are too high to permit use of a conventional gaff with a conventional handle, the bridge gaff is used because it works well and can be easily stowed in a bridge-fisherman's kit.

The bridge gaff is tied to a stout line—usually nylon cord. After a fish is whipped and lying on its side below, the fisherman snaps an ordinary shower-curtain ring around both his fishing line and the gaff cord. Then he lowers the gaff.

The shower-curtain ring serves as a guide to steer the gaff to the fish's head. And the ring is large enough so that it can slip over any swivel or other terminal tackle on the fishing line.

The angler may have to do a bit of jiggling with either or both lines to make sure the gaff slides all the way into position.

Once the gang-hook is at the fish's head, the angler jerks the cord until the hook takes hold, then handlines his fish up to the catwalk.

Bridge gaffs are also useful on high fishing piers where wave action can make the use of nets difficult.

CAUTION: Laws in some jurisdictions prohibit the snagging of gamefish, or certain species of gamefish Picky enforcement officers might stretch this rule to cover the bridge gaff—even though it is not used to catch the fish, but only to land it.

Release Gaff

A release gaff is nothing more than a small gaff hook with a very short handle—just large enough to hold in one hand. Some release gaffs have no handle at all—just a loop of rope that is slipped around the gaffer's wrist. The loop, of course, must be large enough so that you can slip out of it in a hurry.

The release gaff is used mainly on tarpon and other big fish that you want to release while doing the fish as little harm as possible. First, the fish must be played until thoroughly whipped. Sometimes, however, playing a fish to the point of exhaustion renders the fish unable to revive strength quickly enough to be able to evade predators in the area. For instance, exhausted tarpon make much easier prey for big hammerhead and bull sharks looking for the easiest meal.

Once beside the boat, slip the small gaff hook into its mouth and through the lower jaw. Now you can hold the fish while you remove the hook.

Release Gaff or "Pick"

The surf gaff is pretty much the same as a release gaff, except that it might have a larger hook, bent at a wider angle. It is worn at the belt by surf fishermen. When they hook and whip a large fish that they wish to keep, such as a channel bass or striped bass, they gaff him around the head or "shoulders," and use the short-handled gaff to drag him up the beach.

Fish Grippers and Other Landing Devices

Alternate types of landing devices are available for use in situations where nets or gaffs are either inefficient, unhandy, or more likely to injure fish that are to be set free. Perhaps the oldest example is the tailer, which grabs the fish just forward of the "tail," or caudal fin. This device can be described as a loop on the end of a handle, which is designed to keep the loop open until it is in position, and then to close it tightly and quickly. Many shorebound shark anglers use tailers to pull sharks onto the beach prior to release.

A much more recent and more widely useful device (made by Boga-Grip and others) resembles a small set of ice tongs at the end of a short handle. With the handle firmly in his grip (and further secured by a lanyard around his wrist), the angler uses his forefinger to pull back a spring-loaded trigger. This opens the tongs, which are then positioned on either side of the fish's lower "lip." Upon release of the trigger the tongs snap shut around the lip—and simply cannot be opened again until the trigger is pulled once more. Thus the fish is securely held until the hook can be removed, after which it can be instantly released by a simple movement of the forefinger.

Yet another type of gripper is a large padded glove with a metal, studded palm. The method for using this one is obvious: the glove grips a fish around the body just aft of the head, and the studs provide a non-slip hold. The shortcoming, of course, is that the fish must be slender enough to fit the hand. The glove is often used with pickerel and smaller northern pike.

Two grip-and-weigh devices. Jaws open with "trigger" action, and close securely when trigger is released.

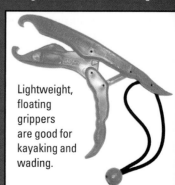

Lightweight, floating grippers are good for kayaking and wading.

Tags and Tagging Pole

agging equipment is standard gear these days on nearly all boats that specialize in going after billfish and other big-game species, such as tuna and sharks. Tagging of these fish is a joint project of The Billfish Foundation and the National Marine Fisheries Service. Kits containing tags and reporting forms are distributed directly by both groups, and also through selected tackle merchants. Tagging poles are not supplied and must either be fashioned by the angler or crew, or purchased from dealers who offer them. The poles are long shafts of tubular aluminum, fitted at the end with a stainless steel rod or applicator, and a stopper to keep the tag from being inserted too deeply in the fish. The photos show details of the business end, and also the desired area for tagging—in the thick muscle of the "shoulders."

Many freshwater and inshore anglers have the idea they should also tag their released fish to help science, and in the past certain non-government groups have provided or sold tagging materials. Most biologists and fishery departments, however, do not recommend private or random tagging and, indeed, some agencies prohibit the practice entirely.

These days most billfish caught by recreational anglers will get a tag, not a gaff.

Tagging equipment is standard these days on boats that specialize in billfishing.

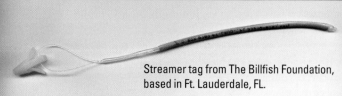

Streamer tag from The Billfish Foundation, based in Ft. Lauderdale, FL.

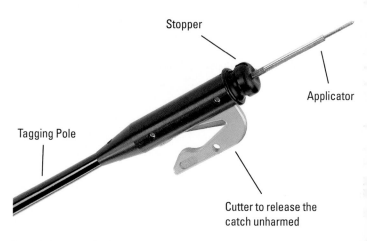

Stopper

Applicator

Tagging Pole

Cutter to release the catch unharmed

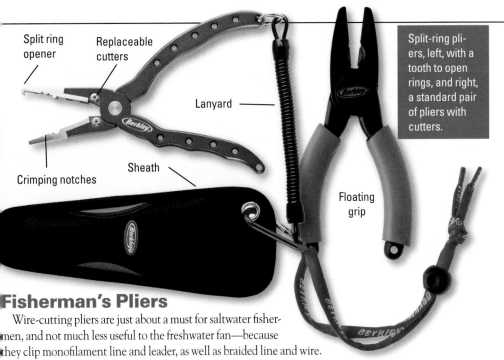

Split ring opener

Replaceable cutters

Lanyard

Split-ring pliers, left, with a tooth to open rings, and right, a standard pair of pliers with cutters.

Crimping notches

Sheath

Floating grip

Fisherman's Pliers

Wire-cutting pliers are just about a must for saltwater fishermen, and not much less useful to the freshwater fan—because they clip monofilament line and leader, as well as braided line and wire.

You have your choice of three basic styles. One is a saltwater standard—the blunt-nosed, square-jaw type with the cutters on the side. With this style, you can cut wire much more handily than with the other popular type—the long-nose, in which the cutter is at the bottom of the jaws. The long-nose, however, does clip wire or heavy monofilament well enough, and its extended jaws are often a big help in removing hooks from a fish's gullet. A third type of plier—the split ring plier—is essential for opening the rings that attach hooks to lures for replacing or changing those hooks. It has a tooth-like wedge on its jaw to be inserted into the ring to open it.

All basic styles can be found in a number of angling versions and in a wide range of prices.

Clippers and Scissors

A familiar pair of fingernail clippers is one of the handiest gadgets an angler can use. No tool is better for clipping monofilament line. Small tools incorporating this type clipper are offered especially for fishermen, and may feature additional accessories—such as a cord for looping to a buttonhole, and a blunted needle for clearing hook eyes or picking out tangles. However, the accessories aren't used nearly so often as the clippers themselves, and for all practical purposes ordinary fingernail clippers from the drug counter do just as well, though they will rust quickly in a saltwater environment.

Never attempt to clip wire of any kind with fingernail clippers. You'll only nick their edges and ruin them. Also note that clippers are nearly useless for cutting braided line. Those lines, in fact, also defy cutting by knives and fisherman's pliers, so if you fish with the thin braids often, you will have to carry either snips designed for the job, or a small pair of well machined scissors.

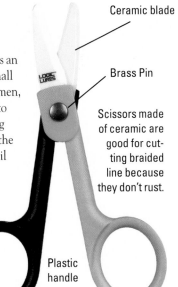

Ceramic blade

Brass Pin

Scissors made of ceramic are good for cutting braided line because they don't rust.

Plastic handle

Hook Removers

R emoving hooks from fish can be almost as difficult as sticking them there. It should be done routinely with a tool rather than with the bare hands, because it can be a dangerous procedure for the fishermen and a delicate one for the fish—especially a fish that you want to release uninjured. The job becomes even trickier, of course, when the hook is well inside the fish's mouth or gullet. Either a pair of toolbox pliers or any of the fishermen's pliers already discussed make pretty good removers—the long-nose styles more so than the snub-nosed types, and numerous dedicated hook removers can also be found on tackle counters.

The cheapest device is a plastic disgorger with a small, grooved head at one end and a larger grooved head at the other. Each head is also fitted with a slit for your line. You choose the large or small head—according to which one best accommodates the fish's mouth and the size of your hook—then place your line in the slit and let the disgorger follow your line down until one of its grooves comes to rest at the bend of the hook. A firm push should then dislodge it. Once free, the hook is protected by the groove so you can ease both line and disgorger out of the fish's mouth together.

Another and more elaborate device features a set of metal-toothed pincers at the end of a long and slender neck. The pincers, operated remotely by your grip, grab the hook firmly so that it can be worked free.

Very small hooks, like those on most freshwater flies, are best attacked with forceps or hemostats, similar or identical to those used by physicians. They are available in nearly all flyfishing supply houses and many general fishing shops.

Long handled removers work by clasping the handgrip to close the small, hook-removing pincers.

Two styles of baitfish hook removers help keep sabiki-caught baits in good shape.

Prepping a fish for cooking whole calls for complete scaling of the skin.

Fish Scalers

With many species of freshwater fish, scaling presents no problem at all. The scales are small, soft and can be flicked away with light pressure of a pocketknife, or even a table knife.

Most members of the sunfish family—bluegills and crappie—are easily scaled. One especially nifty scaling device for those and other soft-scaled varieties is simply a garden hose. Use a restricting nozzle, turn the pressure up full and direct the flow of water "against the grain" while you hold a fish in your hand. Saltwater fish are extremely variable in their willingness to give up their scales, which may be the chief reason why most of them are filleted and skinned. A few varieties, such as weakfish, are nearly as quickly scaled as most freshwater fish. Others, such as red drum, are very tough. In general, saltwater varieties require more scaling effort, and you should not use a knife, because there's a strong chance the blade will slip, or will catch and skid, and give you a nasty cut—scaling devices should be employed for the heavy work. In a pinch, with no scaler handy, use the edge of a tablespoon.

Again, you may wish to fillet and skin your fish rather than scale them. This is largely a matter of personal preference and experience with various species. Fish cooked "whole"—dressed and drawn rather than filleted—should be scaled and left in their skin. A few types, though, should be skinned because their skin imparts a "muddy" flavor. This is true, for instance, of largemouth bass and some other fish taken from still, murky waters. While panfish generally are at their sweetest when scaled, very large panfish taken from mud-bottomed lakes can definitely be improved by filleting and skinning.

The new generation of fish scalers make the job even easier to do.

Freshly caught fish, such as this snapper, taste great when scaled and grilled whole.

Knives

Long bladed fillet knife with flexible tip for cutting around and over bones.

I t would take a whole book just to list the different models of knives offered for sale to fishermen. We'll content ourselves here with a general discussion.

Though it wasn't always so, we have long been able to get numerous knives with stainless steel blades that take and hold a very keen edge. Only a few anglers still prefer carbon steel knives, which are less expensive and easier to sharpen, but which rust quickly, especially in a salty environment.

As an all-around fisherman's tool, a tapered fillet knife with a six-inch, stainless steel blade can hardly be surpassed. Many models of these come with sheaths, which protect the blade when stowed in a tackle box, and which can be worn at your belt while fishing.

Such a knife does a great job of filleting most fish, cutting bait, or making rigged baits, and the stainless steel blade has this additional advantage: It can be cleaned up spick and span in a jiffy, and

Electric Knives

Electric knives make quick work of filleting and skinning, and are invaluable when cleaning limit catches of panfish. They are so popular nowadays that many cleaning stations at fish camps offer plug-in sockets for them. Also available are 12-volt electric knives that can be powered by car or boat batteries.

When filleting a mess of medium or small fish, an electric knife can make the work much faster and easier.

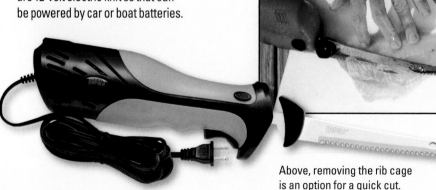

Above, removing the rib cage is an option for a quick cut.

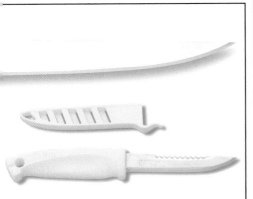

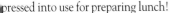

Fish to be eaten whole can be scaled "against the grain" of the scales with the edge of the knife blade. Left, short blade bait knife.

pressed into use for preparing lunch!

Some fishermen, particularly saltwater fans, may need a fillet knife with a blade longer than six inches—8 or 10 inches perhaps. On the other hand, many freshwater anglers might find a six-inch blade too unwieldy for convenient dressing of stream trout or a mess of panfish. Smaller models of the standard curved-blade fillet knives are available, but a sharp pocketknife works well too.

Charterboat mates and others who prepare lots of rigged baits also prefer a short-bladed configuration. Small bait knives with good, sharp blades are widely available at reasonable cost, so pass over cheapies that look similar but have soft plastic handles and dull blades to match.

Knife and Hook Sharpeners

Every angler's tackle box should contain a sharpening tool—both for his knife and for his hooks.

A small whetstone will do a pretty good job of both. But it isn't a bad idea to carry a larger stone for the knife (it's faster and easier), and either a small stone or a small file for putting a keen point on hooks.

Modern anglers have other choices, including battery-powered sharpeners that are portable enough to fit in a tackle box.

Truth be told, so many of today's hooks come out of the box sharper than anything our forefathers could have achieved with any sharpener. That certainly doesn't mean hook sharpeners will go away anytime soon. It's just become easier to tie on a new hook and trust that that it's going to be sharp when it comes out of the box. Saltwater fishermen in particular need to thoroughly examine hooks before they use them more than once. The sharper they start out, the quicker they dull when exposed to salt water. A good rule of thumb is, the thicker the hook, the more likely it is to need a few strokes with the sharpener.

File used to make triangular cutting point on a tarpon fly.

Precision-guided knife sharpener

Tackle Boxes

Hard plastic tackle box with slide-out trays and right, a case with see-through trays strapped in for quick access.

Tackle boxes come in an endless array of sizes, shapes and interior arrangements. Every angler must select his own to fill his particular needs and preferences.

In the past, hard boxes with folding trays inside were the dominant design. They are still far from dead, being offered in many configurations and sizes—some so large that it takes a pretty husky angler to lug them around, and a lot of boat space to completely open them. The space problem with big boxes is eased by certain models that are fitted with drawers instead of pop-out trays, but the weight problem with oversize hard boxes persists.

For anglers who need lots of terminal gear, especially if they fish for various species with different kinds of tackle in different watery environments, splitting their equipment into several smaller boxes makes more sense, and this has become a common approach.

Nowadays, small, inexpensive boxes made of clear plastic probably hold more lures, hooks and various angling gadgets than any other type of container. They come in various sizes, and many of them provide removable

dividers so that the user can arrange the compartments to his own needs and specifications. These small containers are useful in one way or another to just about everyone. They can separate small items inside a larger hard box, or serve as pocket boxes for a quick outing when only a few items are needed. Best of all, the availability of clear plastic boxes in a range of sizes has led to the development of a broad line of canvas shoulder bags, designed to pack a certain number of clear boxes of a particular size. The small boxes are inexpensive, so the angler

Soft-sided tackle bag for easy portability has plenty of zippered pockets.

can keep a stack of them on hand and custom-pack the appropriate boxes into his soft bag whenever his requirements change. In that way, one soft box can replace several large, hard boxes.

Many specialized containers are also available for lures that just can't be made to fit in compartments of normal size, such as big spinnerbaits and very large plugs. Sets of sealable plastic envelopes are also offered, and they handily store various sizes and colors of worms and other soft lures (spinnerbaits too). These sets are available packed in zippered cases and/or looseleaf binders.

Form-fitting foam insertions hold jars of bait, easily visible through the see-through lid.

Gloves

Gloves are obviously invaluable during cold weather for keeping the angler's hands functional, but they serve numerous protective uses as well.

In salt water, heavy-duty gloves are vital when fishing offshore. Always wear gloves when handling a leader as you lead a fish in for releasing or gaffing. This is especially good advice for wire leaders, but even if the leader is monofilament, gloves might save a burn.

Caution also dictates that you should wear gloves when gaffing a fish, whether you handle the leader or not. Although many experienced fishermen do the job barehanded, they will probably pay in blood or blisters sooner or later. The same goes for handling any fish with teeth, sharp gills or dorsal spines. Again many experienced folks don't take the trouble to put on gloves.

It's something like ignoring the seat belt in your car—999 times out of 1000 there's no harm done. But that thousandth time—oh boy!

A great many private boaters now seek sailfish, and they often get them. Gloves are essential for proper unhooking and releasing of a sail. You should not use a gaff, but should take the leader in gloved hands and carefully pull the sail close enough so you can get both gloved hands around his bill. Then you either remove the hook or, if that seems too harmful to the fish, cut the leader and let him go.

Cut-proof Kevlar gloves, worn while filleting fish, will also save a lot of wounds.

Casting gloves, same as golf gloves, are used by some anglers to protect their hands. These are fingerless. Various cold-weather gloves designed for fishing are available, some of which allow the fingers to be quickly exposed for casting.

Rod Belts

A sailfish thrashes and jumps in its fight, making a tough battle for most anglers.

In saltwater fishing you may be called upon to fight a fish for many minutes, an hour, maybe two hours or more. Unless you have a rod belt with a socket in which to rest the rod butt, you'll end up with a very sore tummy indeed. This goes for light, one-hand tackle as well as for a heavy ocean rod.

If you do not use rods with gimbal butts, you'll need only a rod belt with leather or plastic cup to hold the rod butt. For gimbal butts, you need a gimbal belt—that is, a deep socket fitted with a pin, and usually on a swiveling or semi-swiveling mount. The pin, of course, fits into the gimbal slot of your rod butt, and helps you keep the rod upright as you do battle.

Rod belts of special design are needed for standup fishing (see Chapter One). They feature sockets backed by wide, strong plates that prevent undue pressure on the angler's body. They also ride lower than conventional belts, generally over the crotch or upper thigh.

Rod Harnesses

Harnesses help considerably during long fights with ocean tackle, and are essential for big-game fishing—marlin, giant tuna, deep-fighting of big amberjack or grouper and shark fishing.

Without a harness, you must support the weight of the rod, and apply fighting pressure, with your arms alone. Nobody's arms can stand the strain of this, except with light classes of tackle and in relatively short fights.

With a harness, you can let your shoulders or back do the hard work, and can even drop your arms to your sides for brief rest periods.

One type of harness is the traditional shoulder harness. You put this on as you would a vest. Two straps in front of you are clipped to the harness rings of your ocean reel. The rod butt, of course, rests either in your gimbal belt, if

Fighting belts can be quickly strapped on to help anglers with a big or especially tough fish.

A good standup harness combines the best advantages of a shoulder harness and a fighting chair harness.

Standup harnesses and 360 degrees of movement on deck let anglers battle big fish on center console boats.

standing, or in the gimbal of your fishing chair, if seated. The other type of harness is the kidney, seat or back harness, which is used in conjunction with a fighting chair. There's a big difference between a "fishing chair," mentioned above, and a "fighting chair." The former can be any kind of light, usually swiveling, chair that's fitted with a gimbal. A fighting chair is a massive and complex piece of boat furniture that has an adjustable or removable backrest and a sturdy, adjustable footrest.

The ends of a seat belt are connected to the reel rings by means of heavy ropes or straps, and metal snaps. Often the harness is made with an integral padded seat, on which the angler sits, but a chair belt may be just a heavily padded belt that rides around the angler's lower back. The seat is a fine touch because it keeps the harness from "riding up" the angler's back while he's fighting his big-game fish.

Harnesses for standup fishing are similar to the old shoulder harnesses, but only superficially so. The best ones cradle the angler's entire back so

there are no weak points to torture his shoulders or other specific places in the anatomy. They also position the padded gimbal lower on the angler's body.

In essence, a good standup harness combines the best advantages of a shoulder harness and a fighting-chair harness.

A rod butt holder like the one above lessens the impact of the butt where it meets the hip or abdomen of the angler. These holders can be kept at the ready to put on the end of a gimbaled rod, and it's a good idea to carry one in case you go on a boat without fighting belts.

Castnets

Cast nets are the most efficient of all tools for catching live baitfish and, in certain waters, live shrimp. Proficiency with these nets can only be learned through practice, but if you haven't used a cast net before, here are some suggestions that will help make sure you get a net that is suited to your particular needs. As for learning, lessons are widely given at tackle outlets and sports shows, and instructive videos are also available.

Nets made of monofilament are best because they are lighter in weight and sink faster than nets made of braided nylon or cotton. The latter, however, will certainly do a decent job under ideal conditions if you are compelled to use them because of economy or legality. Monofilament nets come in about as many prices as sizes. The inexpensive ones generally are machine-made of lower quality components and often have less lead. Costlier, hand-tied nets will more than repay their price in the extra bait they will give you, due to their ease of handling, positive sinking and longevity.

Various net sizes are offered for sale, ranging from 3 or 4 feet in radius to 10 feet, sometimes even 12. If properly thrown, each size will, of course, cover a circle with a diameter twice as large as stated net size. A 5- or 6-foot net is a good compromise, being large enough to provide the bait needs of most private anglers yet not nearly as

> Contrary to popular belief, throwing a big castnet isn't about muscle, but rather about good technique.

difficult to throw as the huge 10- and 12-footers, which are best left to professional guides and crewmen, who often need to produce huge quantities of bait in little time.

The most common mesh sizes are ¼ inch, and ⅜ inch. The choice of course, will depend on the size of the bait you figure on catching—the ¼ inch mesh is built for smaller minnows, shiners, herrings, etc., down to around two inches long, or even less. The ⅜ inch will handle a wide range of bait sizes and is a good choice for most anglers, and especially those who often shoot for bigger baits of three inches and longer. Nets with even larger mesh sizes—up to 1-⅛ inch— are available, too. Those are for really big baitfish, such as full-grown mullet and large menhaden. While such baits could possibly be caught with smaller mesh, the wider mesh has the added advantage of a faster sink rate, due not only to the more open mesh but also to the fact that good quality nets generally are made with more lead as

> **Nets made of monofilament are best because they are lighter in weight and sink faster than nets of braided nylon or cotton.**

he mesh size increases.

Leery baitfish are very skillful at evading nets, ven after they are thrown, especially in deeper vater. That's why a professional charter crewman s pretty sure to prefer a large monofilament net of op quality, with large mesh and plenty of weight.

NOTE: Monofilament nets are prohibited in some areas. For that matter, all cast nets are prohibited in certain places or for certain species. Such prohibition is widespread in fresh water throughout the country and not rare in salt water, so be sure to check pertinent laws.

Bait Buckets

Flow-through bucket (left) is good in the water, but on transport you'll want to aerate bait, below.

The simplest bait buckets re merely containers that old water, and have lids to eep the bait from jumping ut. But to hold bait for any ength of time, or in any quanty, provisions must be made o replenish the available xygen supply in the water.

Buckets made of papiernache or plastic foam hold ne oxygen supply better and onger than metal or solid lastic buckets. To assure an oxygen supply in any ontainer, take one or more of the following steps:

Use O-Tabs, a commercial product which releases oxygen into the water.

Change water at frequent intervals.

Keep water cool and shaded. Adding chunks of ice can help.

Best of all, use a small pump or aerator. Some very good ones are available at low cost. They clip to the side of the bucket and run on flashlight batteries. For big bait containers, there are heavy-duty aerators that connect to the battery of a boat.

Two-piece buckets are popular. These have an nner, perforated container, in which the bait is ept. The inner container is removed and held in ne water on a heavy cord. To transport bait, you imply fill the outer bucket with water and place ne inner container into it.

There are one-piece buckets which do a similar b. These hold enough water in the bottom to ansport bait. But they have perforations at the p, so that when the bucket is lowered by cord om boat or bridge, water freely circulates and

keeps the bait frisky. Some live baits, of course, do not require water at all. Crickets and grasshoppers are kept in light cages of wire or plastic mesh. Some are bucket-shaped with a handle for carrying. Others are tube-shaped and can be worn at the belt.

Belt boxes also are available for carrying worms, grubs and other freshwater goodies.

Refer to the section on Live Shrimp in Chapter 8 for instructions on how to keep shrimp frisky.

A portable aerator can turn a cooler into a live well.

Chumming Aids

Chumming is the practice of "sweetening" the water to attract fish to your bait. In fresh water, the most common targets of chumming are catfish, panfish, carp and baitfish such as shiners and shad. The chum is usually cereal, cracked corn, bread balls, dough balls or commercially-made fish pellets, and it is most often either broadcast by hand or else placed in an onion sack or feed sack and hung in the water. More sophisticated chumming pots and devices are available, but they are generally used to feed fish in private waters than to chum them.

In salt water, the most common type of chum is ground fish—again, either cast freely into the water with a ladle, or else contained in a mesh bag that is hung over the side of a boat. Nylon chum bags are sold at most tackle stores. You can also find them among laundry supplies in the department store. Frozen chum blocks also are widely sold, but serious anglers often have their own chum recipes and freeze their own blocks.

Big chum bags, left, can hold multiple chum blocks. Below, a single-block bag in the water.

Various small perforated plastic cylinders or mesh cages are sold in tackle shops as chum dispensers.

Menhaden (mossbunker) and other very oily fish make the best ground chum. Plain menhaden oil can be mixed with other ground chum to increase its appeal. In the Southeast, menhaden oil alone is a strong attractor of king mackerel. Many boats slow-drip menhaden oil from plastic bladder-and-tub devices that resemble hospital IV apparatus—which, indeed, is basically what they are.

Many types of panfish and schooling baitfish can readily be chummed with canned cat food—the fishier the better—or with oatmeal, or with a combination of both.

Chum bucket in the water spreads the scent of chum, at top. Canned cat food serves as a convenient option for saltwater chum. It is also a good idea to throw chunks of the same bait that you'll use on your hook either into the chum, or by hand into the chum slick, but be certain not to overfeed the fish you attract.

Marker Floats

The choppier the surface and the faster the drift, the larger your marker must be to be seen.

A workable marker buoy can be home-made in short order.

wrap enough line around the jug to reach bottom in your selected fishing area—with an ample amount of extra line, or "scope," allowed. A large snap at the end of the line will allow you to affix a heavy sinker, or a piece of scrap metal of suitable weight. When you want to mark a spot, just toss over the jug. The sinking weight will spin the jug and unwrap the line automatically. When stowage space is a problem, and visibility not so bad, you might use a one-quart plastic bottle instead of the jug.

All boating anglers can benefit from keeping a pre-rigged marker float—or perhaps several of them—at hand for quick use. A float is extremely valuable for marking a particular productive spot you might locate, or for orientation in drift fishing. You may drift for long periods with little or no luck, then suddenly start hitting some fish. Throw over the marker, and you will then be able to circle updrift of it and go back over the productive area repeatedly. It can be surprisingly difficult to retrace your same drifting course without such a marker, because a boat seldom drifts directly downwind, as it might seem. In smooth, shallow water, your marker need be nothing more than a large fishing float with light line and light sinker.

Lake fishermen can make excellent use of a series of small floats—either manufactured offerings, plastic bottles or fishing bobbers—for marking contours on the lake bottom, such as the course of an old stream bed, or a submerged point or long edge.

The choppier the surface and the faster the drift, the larger your marker must be for visibility. A good choice for coastal fishing is a gallon or half-gallon plastic jug, preferably of a glaring color for good visibility at a distance. Tie some nylon cord or discarded fishing line to the jug's grip, and

Manufactured floats are available for deepwater use too. These are equipped with conveniences such as reels for the line and flags to make them more visible in a heavy chop.

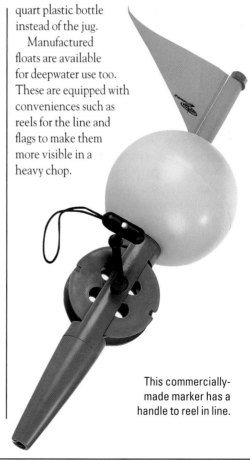

This commercially-made marker has a handle to reel in line.

Some repellents use natural agents, some processed chemicals.

Insect Repellents

An item often overlooked by an angler—and sometimes to his great pain and suffering—is insect repellent.

If you can't spare the space in your tackle box for a spray can, you can at least carry a small bottle of repellent lotion, or a stick.

Don't run the risk of being caught without protection from insect bites just because you "don't think" bugs will be a problem in a particular place or a particular season. They can be a serious problem virtually everywhere.

The most effective repellents are those containing "DEET"—a civilized way of saying "N-N-Diethyl-M-Toluamide"—and the more the better. Concentrations as high as 100 percent are available, most in lotion form. Aerosol sprays typically contain from about 15 percent to about 40 percent, but some are all DEET. The lighter concentrations are, basically, more pleasant to use if the insect problem is moderate. But you won't complain about the stronger solutions when the bugs attack in clouds. Since many insects can bite through clothing, the sprays are the most effective form of repellent, but sticks and small bottles are, of course, handier and can be easily kept in a tackle box to prevent getting caught short. In addition, they are better for exposed skin because of higher DEET concentrations.

Other packs available include roll-ons and treated wipes.

If you are going to be fishing in one location for the entire trip, setting up a device called a Therma-Cell is highly recommended. It is a simple little device that heats up a small cloth bathed in repellant. You won't come in contact with the repellent, or even smell it for that matter, but the bugs will be long gone.

Hungry mosquitoes plague fishermen in every corner of the country.

DEET, unfortunately, also can damage certain finishes, including fishing line, so be sure to wipe the palms of your hands as clean as possible after applying the repellent. And avoid spilling it on plastics and varnish finishes.

Some repellents are citronella-based; others even cosmetic-based! These do help, and may be preferred for children, or for adults who react adversely to DEET.

Lubricants

Always carry light lubricant with you when fishing. A spray can is more versatile, but it's a good idea to carry a small applicator of machine oil as well—just in case the spray can gets forgotten or misplaced.

The levelwind mechanism of a revolving-spool casting reel should be oiled once or twice during a fishing day for peak performance. And a bit of oil frequently will come in handy to smooth a sticky

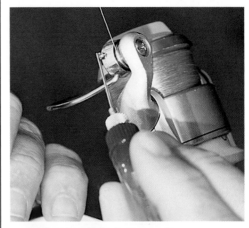

spinning reel bail or to remove the squeak from a crank handle. Heavier grease can be left at home, since it is used only internally—and not very often at that.

Don't hesitate to spray anything you wish to protect from corrosion—not only your rods and reels but also reel seats, tackle box hinges, zippers on cloth tackle boxes or clothing, boat hardware, battery terminals, outboard motors. The sprays replace water and improve electrical contacts, in addition to fighting corrosion. If you take the time to spray your lures after changing them, it will help prevent rusty hooks.

Light machine oil keeps line roller and reel handle turning smoothly. Below: Silicone spray is a good option for protecting engine components.

The sprays replace water and improve electrical contacts, in addition to fighting corrosion.

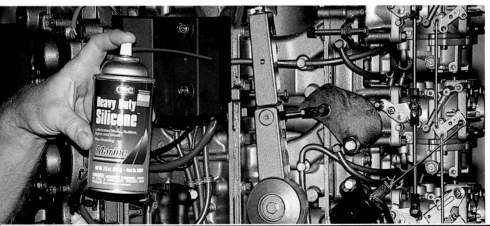

Polarizing Sunglasses

A well-garbed angler, with a bonefish, wears sun-protective gear including glasses, visor, long sleeve shirt and face mask.

Any good pair of sunglasses contributes to your comfort while fishing, but only those with polarizing lenses cut out enough glare to allow you to see fish under the surface of the water.

Without polarizing glasses, the shallow-water sight-fisherman will have a tough time finding targets. Even if you don't fish the flats, you would do well to wear polarizing glasses as a matter of routine. In any kind of water, fresh or salt, they'll improve your vision in regard to such things as picking out underwater snags, distinguishing the wakes of fish from wind ripples, or studying the bottom conditions in reasonably shallow or clear water. You also might see a lot of fish in deep water that you might miss if not wearing the glasses.

Generally speaking, most inshore fishermen prefer amber or green lenses as they can actually illuminate the desired target, while offshore bluewater fishermen prefer the darker lenses which tend to make fish stand out better against an indigo background.

Face Masks

Face masks can be used in place of sunscreen if they are worn constantly in the sun, or else in combination with sunscreen. They are lightweight and breathable and it is even easy to forget that you have them on.

Rainwear

High-quality rain gear is breathable and comfortable to wear.

Early in anyone's fishing career, he discovers two things—first, that he is going to get attacked regularly by rain, spray or fog; second, that ordinary raincoats afford little protection—next to none in really heavy weather.

Three types of rainwear are the most frequently chosen by active outdoorsmen for the best possible protection from the elements.

The short parka is excellent for use in combination with waders. It extends below the waist, over the top of the waders, and the drawstring can be tightened against chilly updrafts. The most complete protection is the full storm suit, especially when worn atop rubber boots. An excellent compromise is the parka, which gives overall protection when worn with hip boots. Even without the boots it is adequate for warm-weather use, keeping most of your body dry, although you get wet below the knees.

All three styles are obtainable either in inexpensive vinyl, more expensive PVC or quite expensive waterproofed fabrics. Though welcome in a pinch, the vinyl ones tear easily and are much hotter to wear. Higher-priced raingear is worth its price.

Waterproof gloves save your hands from cold and provide a better grip on gear in the rain.

Waterproof pants might be lined for warmth or unlined for warmer days.

Rubber boots with non-slip soles keep your feet dry—and provide traction on a wet deck.

Wade Fishing

A good wading belt can carry all that an angler needs away from his boat or away from the shore.

Stealthy wade fishers have an advantage over anglers in boats—the fish are much less apt to notice them. Whether the wade fisher takes off from shore, or jumps out of a boat or a kayak or some other vessel to approach fishy waters, the approach on foot offers a lower, quieter profile than motored vessels.

One of the keys to successful wade fishing is to have only the gear that you need, which means having the right gear for the day's fishing. What you can carry will be held by pockets in waders, if they have any, a wading belt, and on lanyards around your neck, if you so choose to wear one.

For most anglers, the essentials include waders, boots if they're not on the waders, a spool of leader, a net, a small box of tackle, stringer and a pair of pliers. Any gear not sealed in watertight containers is likely to get wet, so consider that when you pack. For long trips solo, it's also a good idea to pack your cellphone in a watertight case and then put that in a sealed bag.

Waterproof backpacks are a great way to store tackle boxes, pliers, and other essentials needed to wade fish.

Depending on the terrain and temperature, a variety of footwear might be worn—but wear some.

On cold mornings after the warmth of the sun lifts the early fog, the bite turns on, such as the case for this wade fisherman wearing a warm pair of neoprene waders with a stowed pair of floatable pliers, and holding up a nice speckled trout, above, and a good size flounder, below.

Stealthy wade fishers have an advantage over anglers in boats—the fish are much less apt to notice them.

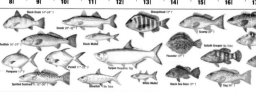

Sportsman's Best: Book & DVD Series

Each book in the series has over 300 color photographs and illustrations, techniques, tackle options and tips from experts. Average book size is 240 pages. **$19.95-$21.95 (DVD only, $14.95)**

I N S H O R E

O F F S H O R E

O T H E R B O O K S

NEW for 2015

Sport Fish Book Series
by Vic Dunaway

- **Sport Fish of Florida**
- **Sport Fish of the Gulf of Mexico**
- **Sport Fish of the Pacific**
- **Sport Fish of the Atlantic**
- **Sport Fish of Fresh Water**

Beautifully color-illustrated fish identification books. Food values, distinguishing features, average and record sizes, angling methods and more.
$16.95

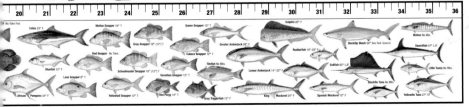

Many items also available at tackle and book stores.

BAITS, RIGS & TACKLE DVD

The *Sportsman's Best: Baits, Rigs & Tackle* DVD brings the pages of the accompanying book to life. Join author Rick Ryals as he covers some of the most important tackle, rigs, concepts and techniques you'll need to know to be successful as an angler.

DVD CHAPTERS:

- ▶ RODS & REELS
- ▶ POLES & SPECIALTY GEAR
- ▶ FISHING LINES & TERMINAL TACKLE
- ▶ ANGLING KNOTS
- ▶ WIRE MATTERS
- ▶ LEADERS & RIGS
- ▶ FRESHWATER BAITS
- ▶ SALTWATER BAITS
- ▶ ARTIFICIAL LURES
- ▶ ANGLING ACCESSORIES

"Fishing isn't always about catching fish, say some, probably the same folks who say how you play the game is more important than winning or losing. My personal feeling is that when you play a game, you want to win and when you fish, you want to catch fish. There's nothing wrong with spending time with family and friends as you go for a boat ride, or sit on the side of a river bank, with a rod in your hand, but if you're catching fish it's way better. If you want to catch fish more than going for boat rides, watch this DVD."

—*Blair Wickstrom, Publisher,*
Florida Sportsman

DVD Executive Producers: Chris Collins & Scott Sanders